Jonathan Berry

The Roman Empire Revived

Jonathan Berry

The Roman Empire Revived

ISBN/EAN: 9783337245139

Printed in Europe, USA, Canada, Australia, Japan

Cover: Foto ©ninafisch / pixelio.de

More available books at **www.hansebooks.com**

THE

ROMAN EMPIRE REVIVED.

AN OUTLINE OF COMING EVENTS,

AND

AN HARMONIOUS ELUCIDATION OF THE PROPHECIES HAVING
REFERENCE THERETO:

ALSO

THE RAPTURE OF THE TRUE CHURCH,

WITH

AND SATISFACTORY EXPLANATION OF THE
SYMBOLIC NUMBER 666.

M.

CONTENTS.

CHAPTER I.

PRELIMINARY REMARKS.

The lessons of time.—The use of history.—Law of sequence.—The question of the day.—Prophecy.—Map of the future.—Class of new theorists.—Statement of three propositions.—Theory of proof.—The same as in the physical sciences 9

CHAPTER II.

TIMES OF THE GENTILES.

Syncronizes with four universal monarchies.—Has no numerical limitation.—Metallic image.—Dominion over the earth conferred upon the Gentiles.—The ways of Divine Providence.—The hidden hand.—God's throne in heaven.—State craft 16

CHAPTER III.

PROPHETIC NUMBERS AND SYMBOLS.

Prophetic numbers chiefly found in Daniel and the Apocalypse.—Understood as literal time.—Seven times.—The import of prophetic symbols.—How determined.—*Usus loquendi.*—A uniform meaning must be assigned to symbols.......... 25

CHAPTER IV.

IMPENDING CRISIS.

Prop. 1.—Not in itself improbable.—The King of Rome.—Tendence of European diplomacy.—Survey of the nations.—Secret societies.—Revolutionary literature.—Disparity of condition.—Emigration.—Modern science.—The Christian religion.—Unfavorable outlook.—The remedy 33

CHAPTER V.

EVIDENCE FROM PROPHECY.

Our position on the prophetic chart.—The nations sprung from the disintegrated Roman Empire.—The identity of the symbols described in Dan. 7th and Rev. 13th.—This identity conclusive of Prop. 1.—Additional and independent specifications.. 54

CHAPTER VI.

FURTHER EVIDENCE FROM PROPHECY.

A *beast* the symbol of an universal, secular monarchy.—Can not symbolize the Roman Hierarchy.—The Roman Empire revived pointed out.—Additional reason for.—The great red dragon.—The woman clothed with the sun......... 66

CHAPTER VII.

FURTHER EVIDENCE FROM PROPHECY.

Having seven heads.—Five forms passed.—Tacitus.—Imperial form.—Triumvirs.—Summary of the duration of each form.—Six forms identified.—Ten horns and ten crowns upon his head.—Seven mountains.—The site of the city Rome.—Wounded head.—Charlemagne.—Image worship.—Pliny 76

CHAPTER VIII.

INCIDENTS AND ATTRIBUTES.

The sand of the sea.—Like unto a leopard.—Feet like a bear.
—Lion's mouth.—Name of blasphemy.—Symbolic number 666.—Forty and two months.—Prophecy points out cardinal events only.—Seventy weeks.—Messiah, the Prince, cut off.—Blindness of Israel.—The Prince that shall come.—Not Titus.—But he is a Roman.—Covenant.
—Three and a half years.—David Brown, D. D.—Restoration of the Jews.—Flight of the woman.—Heroic devotion of the Jews.—Time of trial.—Duration limited......... 99

CHAPTER IX.

Summary.. 137

CHAPTER X.

THE RAPTURE OF THE CHURCH.

Not the second advent.—But preparatory.—Special favor to believers.—Symbolized by the catching up of the manchild.—Resurrection of the saints special.—No resurrection at the second advent.—Relation of believers to Christ.—The first fruits.—The saints will come with the Lord when he comes to reign................................ 141

CHAPTER XI.

JUDGMENT OF THE NATIONS.

There will be no general judgment of both the quick and the dead.—But all the Gentile nations will be judged.......... 180

CHAPTER XII.

RECAPITULATION AND SPECIFIC TERMS.

The two comings of the Lord are indicated, each by a specific word in the original.. 189

CHAPTER XIII.

POPULATION AND TERRITORIAL LIMITS.

Brief review.—Prophetic symbols of uniform import.—The Roman Hierarchy.—The anti-Christ.—The Roman laws.—Peculiarities.—Extent.—In Europe.—In Asia.—Homogeneity of race.—Centers of civilization.—The Latin race.—Limits designated by the one-third part............... 201

CHAPTER XIV.

THE INCEPTION—IS IT THE GERMAN EMPIRE?

The boast of this age.—The vicegerent of the god of this world.—The contrast.—Holy Roman Empire of the German nations.—Was this the seventh?—Ten kingdoms.—Prussia.—Rise and present position.—Germans the modern Romans.—Their institutions and army.—Comparison...... 219

CHAPTER XV.

HISTORICAL CAREER AND END.

A real subject.—Atheism.—Evil the primary principle.—Woe trumpets.—General insurrection.—Effects.—Great Western Apostate.—Migrations of the Jews to Palestine.—Eastern Apostate, or anti-Christ.—First invasion from the orient.—Image worship.—Tests.—Fall of Babylon.—Apostates.—Great tribulation.—Limit.—Two witnesses.—Ancient of days.—Everlasting gospel........................ 233

PREFACE.

To the following pages must be entrusted the vindication of the things treated therein, both as to the merits of the matters presented, and the manner of presentation.

Were it not that a discussion of the topics here presented for consideration, is not to be found in any treatise of general circulation,—unless in isolated paragraphs, in certain rare books not accessible to the general public,—and, therefore, that much uncertainty, and even contradiction of opinion prevails in reference to *coming events*, on account of conflicting and unsatisfactory *theories*,—the responsibility of issuing the following treatise would not have been incurred.

Manifestly a theory, respecting the developments of the future, not so much the result of a patient and careful induction from the teachings of Divine Revelation, as the suggestions of an ardent aspiration, native to the human mind, for a higher state of civilization and moral development, has very much influenced the conclusions of expositors of the prophecies in modern times. A preconceived theory, is tantamount to an assumption, in advance, of the results sought to be established by a process of inquiry, if so fettered.

In the following pages, conclusions have been drawn from the analogies furnished by the past, and from a careful examination and comparison of the prophecies having reference to the future, and the results stated, and the reasons generally given, but not always.

Symbolic prophecy, which has been the fruitful source of so much that is vague and indefinite in the writings of those who have ventured upon an elucidation of this department of sacred learning, has, in the following pages, been interpreted upon an uniform system, giving to each symbol its previously ascertained import. As the hieroglyphics upon the monuments of antiquity have been induced to yield up their secrets to the talismanic touch of the Rosetta Stone, so has the patient researches of other Champollions furnished a guide for deciphering the apocalyptic hieroglyphics.

The unsettled state of the public mind in respect to coming events, seems to demand some such work as is here attempted, as may be inferred from the following extract, which is one of many similar:

Says a writer in a leading daily paper: "It is impossible to watch the Signs of the Times, *Religious, Social, Civil* and *Military*, without being impressed with the conviction that we are approaching one of the most pre-eminently important chapters in the whole history of the human race."

Such passages are significant. They indicate that much anxiety and uncertainty, as to what the future may develop, disturb the minds of the reflecting. Is not, therefore, a true and comprehensive statement, of what is yet in reserve for the nations, demanded? This we have aimed to give. With what success, let the inquiring and unbiased reader judge.

THE
ROMAN EMPIRE REVIVED.

CHAPTER I.

PRELIMINARY REMARKS.

"'Blessed is he that readeth." * * *
"For the time is at hand."

The lessons taught by time in his flight, have been slightly heeded by the millions of the past, and the multitudes of the present generation have profited little by their example. It appears to be inherent in human nature, that men should for the most part strive to walk in the foot-steps of their ancestry.

The wisdom and folly of the past, the successes and mistakes of the present, have little influence upon the judgments which are formed respecting coming events. Tomorrow shall be as this day and much more abundant, is the congenial sentiment of the hour.

History like a mirror, casts the reflections gathered from more than three thousand years of experience upon the dark shadows of the future. While a correct estimate of what the future may disclose, though of the highest moment to a wise use of the present, is the most difficult lesson to master. For men embark in enterprises of the greatest consequence to themselves, without hesitation, often recklessly, which may require years, even decades for their accomplishment.

Capitalists invest their means in securities, which may look forward ten, twenty or even forty years before maturity. All acting and presuming upon an invariable law of past experience, namely, that all things will continue to flow on in the same channels in the future, which they have followed in the past. But there is a settled conviction gaining strength daily, that the smooth onward flow of the current of human events, must sooner or later encounter interruptions. Even the experience of the past should render this highly probable.

Inquiries, therefore, even as to the probabilities of the future, are of the highest moment to the present, and should not, among the multiplicity of topics engaging the attention of the present generation, be entirely passed over as too uncertain in their nature, or too contingent in their relations to deserve serious attention.

What the near future may have in store is the great question of the day. It forces itself upon the attention of the present generation by considerations the most imperative.

The millions have long and patiently waited for the promised *"better time coming."* But they can discern, as yet, no traces of the outlines, in bright shadows, spanning the heavens of the bow of promise.

But dark clouds continue to hang, like the pall of death upon the horizon of the future, while deep toned thunders, though faint sounds, as yet in the distance, utter their ominous voices.

Nothing in human affairs can be deemed in a state of absolute repose. The ever restless activity of mind, seeks to explore some new avenue, which may lead on to something better.

PRELIMINARY REMARKS.

Human nature yearns for a state of amelioration. By the highest authority we are instructed, that the whole creation groaneth.

This conscious discontent, with the present state of things, goaded on by a thousand incentives, real or imaginary, can not long permit the affairs of the world to remain in *statue quo.*

The present order of things had a beginning, they must likewise have an end. And events follow each other, according to an invariable law of antecedents and consequents.

It is only necessary, therefore, to consider certain well defined laws of human conduct and the dominant incentives to action operating, to determine what men at any time, under a given state of things, will attempt, and therefore with reasonable certainty to infer from the present what may be in the future.

But we are not under the necessity of depending on the dim light of reason and experience, we have an unerring guide, in the prospective visions of divine revelation.

The great land-marks of the future are distinctly mapped out in the prophecies, and events follow each other in chronological order. If we can with certainty, therefore, identify any part of a prophetic vision, the remainder can be filled out with almost unerring precision.

Whoever will candidly consider the present state of things must come to the conclusion that we are passing through critical times, and are rapidly approaching an epoch of untried experiences. What these may prove to be, we can with a high degree of probability determine, if we can only fix our present position on the prophetic chart of time.

A survey of the conditions of the nations of the continent of Europe, lead to the following inferences:

That the signs of the times clearly indicate that the present order of things is very much distracted. That there is great trouble of the nations and distress among the people. Many alarming symtoms of decay are making their appearance, and a spirit of innovation is rife. And further, that present discontents demand radical remedies for existing evils. No mere change of policy or administration will satisfy the prevalent demand for reform. Nothing short of a sweeping repudiation of past and present institutions, and a plunge into the untried and unknown will satisfy the new class of theorists, who have suddenly come to the front. The sciences of ethics and political economy have passed under a new revision at their hands. It would seem as though the science of government itself, was about to be put on trial and condemned, as a failure by them; as though all its known forms tested under the most favorable circumstances had failed to alleviate the condition of the masses; that oppression and want, and consequent discontent continue to affect, and distract the millions, and therefore relief can be found only in revolution. Such is the growing conviction, not only among those most immediately interested in the propagation of the new ideas of social reform, but by the candid observers of passing events also.

Says one, "a great upheaval of the masses, it seems to be generally felt, is sure and imminent."

A member of the British House of Lords in a speech before that body quite recently held the following language, which is more significant at this time, than when spoken, he said, "the foundations of political faith are broken up. Notions which even a few months ago, would have been inconceivable, are now made the subject of debate. There is nothing so steadfast, and nothing so sure in the constitution that is not already a matter of question. This is a very dangerous temper. It is a temper which before now, has been the precursor of revolutions, and those who mark the signs of the times may well look with anxiety at the dark and unknown country into which we are invited to enter." When men who belong to an order in the state which would be most immediately and sorely affected by revolution, openly avow such opinions, it must be regarded as significant. The present foundations are giving way. Society must be organized on some other than existing platforms.

Governments, especially in Europe, are letting loose from their ancient moorings; all will soon be adrift upon the unknown ocean of the future. What next?

With the map of the future drawn by the pen of inspiration as a guide, we may be fully apprised as to what lies immediately before us. Though at variance with received theories, we expect to establish by proofs satisfactory and convincing to all believers in divine revelation, the *following propositions* as an outline of *coming events:*

Prop. I. *The great political event imminent in the near future will be the revival of the old Roman Empire, under a new and last form of organization,* ATHEISTIC *in principle and composed of a confederacy of ten kingdoms, with an imperial head, within the geographical limits, or nearly so, of Ancient Imperial Rome.*

Prop. II. In close connection with the foregoing and before the calamitous times, shall set in, which are about to come upon all the world, the church of the Lord Jesus Christ, will be suddenly taken up from the earth to heaven. This is usually called the *rapture of the church.*

Prop. III. As a factor in the readjustment of the map of the world, the Jews as a separate people will be compelled by the spirit of persecution that shall characterize the coming great revolution, to take refuge in Palestine. They will there be organized into a distinct commonwealth.

The first and second of the above propositions, will only be fully considered in this volume. The third indirectly.

The prophecies point to these three cardinal events, as in the near future. Many other important, but subordinate events, closely connected with and contingent upon the foregoing, will occur simultaneously with them.

We do not expect to be held to a more rigid method of proof in the establishment of these *propositions* than is required by the nature of the subject discussed, or is demanded in analogous cases. Surely not more rigid than is demanded in the physical sciences.

We hold divine revelation to be ultimate authority in such matters—to be truth—the most exact and the most comprehensive in its scope that the human mind can take cognizance of, and that it rests for its vindication in the capacity of the mind to discern and decide upon the fitness of things, upon the ultimate and incontrovertable conclusions of consciousness and conviction.

If upon an examination of the prophecies having reference to the future, it be found that many manifestly point directly to and receive an easy and natural interpretation upon the supposition of the truth of the above propositions, such fact should have a decided influence upon the mind of the sincere and unbiased inquirer after truth.

But should we find upon a further and more careful examination of all unfulfilled prophecies, both of the Old and New Testament, that upon a fair and liberal construction, they will completely harmonize upon the assumption that the above propositions are taught in the holy scriptures; then upon all fair principles of reasoning, these must be regarded as embodying the true import of the predictions having reference to *coming events*.

PRELIMINARY REMARKS. 15

If on the contrary, it shall be found that of the theories that have been advanced in reference to the prophecies yet unfulfilled, but in conflict with these propositions, none are satisfactory—either so general as to be without specific application, or so vague as to be without significance—in some instances contradictory of the plainest passages, in others depriving the passages cited of their natural and obvious import—doing violence to the revealed Word itself—and thus introducing obscurity and confusion into matters which are perfectly free from complexity, upon the explanations offered in the above three propositions, then we may with reason demand that the above statements, if found true in the sequel, shall be received as conclusive.

It is so in the physical sciences. The theory that will fully explain all the phenomena, if germane to the subject and consistent in itself, is taken as the true explanation of the hidden cause or principle in nature, which may be the subject of discussion. What is called the law of universal gravitation is an illustration. Namely that all bodies are drawn toward each other with a force, which acts directly as the quantity of matter and inversely as the squares of the distances. All questions in reference to the weight of bodies either at rest or in motion can be satisfactorily explained upon this theory.

So also the theory of Copernicus, that all the planets of the solar system move around the sun as a common center. Before this theory was advanced, all things connected with planetary motions were in complete confusion. On the supposition of the truth of this theory, all the phenomena of the solar system in reference to the positions, phases and motions of the planets, are easily explained. Eclipses calculated to the minute of the time of beginning or ending, even 100 years in advance. No one at this day calls in question the truth of this theory.

CHAPTER II.

TIMES OF THE GENTILES.

It is deemed expedient at this place to introduce some preliminary observations respecting the period designated in the scripture as the *times of the gentiles*.

This is necessary to an enlightened understanding of the ways of divine Providence in the government of the world. The *times of the gentiles* syncronize with the four universal monarchies, symbolized by the great metallic image described in Daniel, second chapter.

They commenced with the Babylonian Empire, under Nebuchadnezzar and will continue until the God of Heaven shall set up a kingdom which shall never be destroyed.

The attempt of the learned Faber and others to determine, numerically, the duration of this period, has proved futile, as all such attempts must. It proceeds upon the groundless assumption, that the "*seven times*" (Daniel, fourth chapter and twenty-fifth verse,) must contain a mysterious symbolic number, the full elucidation of which requires the wonderful amplification of the *seven times* into 2,520 years, as the entire period of the times of the gentiles. Whereas the very language limits this period to Nebuchadnezzar himself, "until *seven times pass over thee*," and points to the duration of his insanity, and consequently of his disqualification to rule.

Times and seasons are in the power of the Father, and he will make them known at maturity.

Into such mysteries man has no warrant to push his inquiries.

All interpreters of prophecy, ancient and modern, as well as those of all the different sects of Christians, are agreed that the great metallic image which Nebuchadnezzar saw in his dream, described in Daniel, second chapter, symbolizes the *times of the gentiles.*

Beginning with Nebuchadnezzar, as the head of the first universal empire of the gentiles, "*Thou art this head of gold.*"

Following the Babylonian, rose the Medo-Persian Empire founded by Cyrus the Great. After this came the third or Macedonian under Alexander the Great, and his successors. And lastly the Roman Empire.

All these have passed into history, except the fragments of the last.

The fourth or Roman Empire, characterized in the vision of the prophet, as in appearance "*dreadful and terrible and strong exceedingly,*" is the most remarkable of all. This power growing up from a small beginning, gradually acquired strength and importance, and finally attained to universal empire—then began to decline, was divided into the eastern and western empires, symbolized by the lower extremities of the metallic image, and finally disintegrated and divided up, its elements blending in a manner with the invading hordes from the north, forming out of the fragments, several nominally independent powers, from which have sprung the present nations of modern Europe, symbolized by the toes of the metallic image. These nations are not composed of homogeneous elements, but antagonistic, and therefore contain the germs of revolution, for "*they shall not cleave one to another, even as iron is not mixed with clay.*" And they are furthermore, the last of the *times of the gentiles,* for in the days of these kings, the God of heaven shall set up a kingdom. We find therefore our stand point, as located upon the great chart of prophecy. Under whatever form of administration the kingdom of the God of heaven shall exist, it will be set up in the latter times, in the last days of the times of the gentiles. It will supplant all existing earthly kingdoms and be a ruling power on earth and its sway universal. " For the stone that smote the image became a great mountain and filled the *whole earth.*"

The symbols of the four beasts of Daniel, seventh chapter, and verses 1 to 8 inclusive, run parallel with the different parts of the metallic image and point out the same four universal monarchies.

"In the first year of Belshazzar king of Babylon, Daniel had a dream and visions of his head upon his bed: then he wrote the dream, *and* told the sum of the matters.

2 "Daniel spake and said, I saw in my vision by night, and behold, the four winds of the heavens strove upon the great sea.

3 "And four great beasts came up from the sea, diverse one from another.

4 "The first *was* like a lion, and had eagle's wings; I beheld till the wings thereof were plucked, and it was lifted up from the earth, and made stand upon the feet as a man, and a man's heart was given to it.

5 "And behold another beast, a second, like unto a bear, and it raised up itself on one side, and *it had* three ribs in the mouth of it between the teeth of it: and they said thus unto it, Arise, devour much flesh.

6 " After this I beheld, and lo, another, like a leopard, which had upon the back of it four wings of a fowl; the beast had also four heads; and dominion was given to it.

7 "After this I saw in the night visions, and beheld a

fourth beast, dreadful and terrible, and strong exceedingly; and it had great iron teeth: it devoured and brake in pieces, and stamped the residue with the feet of it: and it *was* diverse from all the beasts that *were* before it; and it had ten horns.

8 "I considered the horns, and behold, there came up among them another little horn, before whom there were three of the first horns plucked up by the roots: and behold, in this horn *were* eyes like the eyes of man, and a mouth speaking great things."

What filled the prophet with most astonishment was the appearance of the fourth beast,—strong exceeding, its great iron teeth and its destructive and domineering conduct. It stamped the residue under its feet. This beast had also ten horns, and among them there arose another little horn, manifesting great intelligence. It had eyes like man.

A horn is the symbol of a kingdom, as is explained further along in this same chapter.

The ten kingdoms symbolized by the ten horns of this fourth beast, belong to the same period and are identical with the ten kingdoms pointed out by the ten toes of the great metallic image. They belong to the last age of *the times of the gentiles.* The little horn points to the revival of Imperial Rome before the end.

The *times of the gentiles* therefore which commenced with the Babylonian monarchy will continue until the God of heaven shall set up a kingdom on earth. The restitution of all things, the gathering in of the out-casts of Jacob—the restoration of Jerusalem—the rebuilding of Mount Zion, the joy of the whole earth. " *For Jerusalem shall be trodden down of the gentiles until the times of the gentiles be fulfilled.*"

God's relation to the world during the times of the gentiles is that of an abdicated sovereign. He abdicated the throne of the world in favor of Nebuchadnezzar king of Babylon, and his successors, and removed his throne from earth to heaven. The visions of the dying Stephen, and of John the revelator, on the Isle of Patmos, show us that the throne of God is in heaven. He is no longer styled the God of the earth, but the God of heaven. In Abraham's time, He was styled the God of all the earth. He has abdicated that title until the time of the gentiles shall be fulfilled.

The prophet says of Nebuchadnezzar, "Thou, O king art a king of kings : for the *God of heaven* hath given thee a kingdom, power, and strength, and glory. And wheresoever the children of men dwell, the beasts of the field and the fowls of the heaven hath he given into thine hand and hath made thee ruler over them all." Dan. 2 : 37, 38.

God in His supreme sovereignty, as the creator of all things declares that He has a right to dispose of them according to His own good pleasure; and therefore, He says, "I have given all into the hands of Nebuchadnezzar, king of Babylon, my servant."

"I have made the earth, the man and the beasts that are upon the ground, by my great power and by my outstretched arm, and have given it unto whom it seemed meet unto me.

6 "And now have I given all these lands into the hands of Nebuchadnezzar the king of Babylon, my servant: and the beasts of the field have I given him also to serve him.

7 " And all nations shall serve him, and his son, and his son's son, until the very time of his land come: and then many nations and great kings shall serve themselves of him,

8 "And it shall come to pass, that the nation and kingdom which will not serve the same Nebuchadnezzar the king of Babylon, and that will not put their neck under the yoke of the king of Babylon, that nation will I punish, saith the Lord, with the sword, and with the famine, and with the pestilence, until I have consumed them by his hand." Jeremiah 27 : 5, 8.

The supreme authority on earth having thus been conferred upon Nebuchadnezzar king of Babylon, the head of the first universal gentile monarchy, the *times of the gentile domination commenced*. . The sovereignty of the world having been transferred to the gentiles, God removed his throne from Jerusalem to heaven. For the Jewish form of government, at first, was a theocracy, and Jehovah was king. The prophet Ezekiel gives the reasons why God removed from the midst of His ancient people—their idolatry.

The Shekinah, the emblem of the divine glory, and the evidence of the divine presence in the Holy of Holies, which graced and sanctified the first temple, built by king Solomon, never appeared in the second temple, which was built under the auspices of the gentiles.

Ezekiel assigns the reason why the glory of the God of Israel forsook Jerusalem, "that I should go far away from my sanctuary," Ez., 8 : 6. The whole city was filled with the abomination of idolatry. Ez. 8 : 9, 10, 11, 12, 16.

The prophet describes his vision of the departure of the divine glory; he represents it lingering first upon the threshold of the holy house, as if loath to depart. The glory of the Lord then departed from the threshold of the house, and stood over the cherubim, and the cherubim lifted up their wings and mounted up from the earth. And they went up from the midst of the city, and stood upon the mountain which is on the east side of the city—upon the Mount of Olives, from which our Lord ascended and unto which he will return. "This same Jesus which is taken up from you into heaven, shall so come in like manner, as ye have seen Him go into heaven."

The Jews, as the chosen people of Jehovah, had been put on trial under the most favorable auspices and found wanting.

By a visible token, God manifested his presence among them; but such was the irresistible inclination so common to human nature, to adopt the customs of the surrounding nations, that it led them to attempt to maintain a divided allegiance,—to conform to the ritual of Moses externally, and publically, while in a more private way, they participated in the idolatrous practices of their neighbors; and this, notwithstanding the monotheism established by Moses was perfectly exclusive.

"*Thou shalt have no other gods before me,*" is the commandment given in a voice of thunder from Mount Sinai.

The Jews having proved recreant to the trust reposed in them, to maintain the exclusive worship and institutions established by Jehovah, are cast down from the honored pre-eminence accorded them, and the responsibility for the government and good conduct of the world is cast upon the gentiles. How they have succeeded in executing the trust, profane history amply attests.

God's throne is in heaven. The earth is given over to Satan, who is the god of this world; nevertheless, God has not entirely forsaken the workmanship of his own hands; under His inscrutable Providence, all things are ordered according to the good pleasure of His will, and not a sparrow falleth to the ground, without the permission and cognizance of the Father.

The cherubim is the symbol of divine government. The prophet Ezekiel saw in vision the form of a man's hand concealed under the wings of the cherubim. In the wonders of Providence the hand that moves the world is hidden behind the scene. Nevertheless made bare and outstretched whenever transgression becomes ripe for excision. In the midst of the revelry at Belshazzar's feast, this hand appeared when "*they brought the golden vessels that were taken out of the temple of the house of God, which was at Jerusalem; and the king and his princes, his wives and his concubines drank in them. They drank wine, and praised the gods of gold, and of silver, of brass, of iron, of wood, and of stone. In the same hour came forth fingers of a man's hand, and wrote over against the candlestick upon the plaster of the wall of the king's palace: and the king saw the part of the hand that wrote.*" Dan. 5 : 3, 4, 5. The sublimity of the language is only excelled by the awfully solemn grandeur of the event itself. This same hand though concealed behind the scenery of universal nature, still, nevertheless, moves and directs every agency.

The bounds and limitations of all things are determined by the sovereign will of Deity. Beyond these, it is fatal to attempt to pass.

Human madness and satanic malice are alike restrained within the limits fixed by omnipotence. Nay, further, they are the *agencies employed for the accomplishment of the good pleasure of his will;* if man, however, in the pursuit of a selfish purpose, accomplishes the will of God, he is nevertheless responsible for his selfish acts. Such is God's relation to the affairs of the world during the *times of the gentiles*.

All operations of direct divine agency in conducting the governments of the world must be excluded, they are in the hands of the gentiles—the servants of the god of this world. Human councils are not allowed to produce their logical effects. If it were so, all peace and tranquillity on earth would be at an end.

For the very fundamental principle of state-craft is supreme selfishness. It discards all ideas of abstract equity or direct responsibility to God. It limits its inquiries to what may be expedient for the hour, as a means to an end. But for ulterior and gracious purposes, God causes the wrath of man to praise Him, and the residue He restrains and renders subservient to the accomplishment of what he has proposed in His own councils, having supreme regard to the ingathering of his people, as preparatory to the resumption of His right over the earth as the supreme Lord of Lords and King of Kings.

CHAPTER III.

PROPHETIC NUMBERS AND SYMBOLS.

Prophetic numbers have proved a fruitful source of mistake to interpreters. And nothing has so much contributed to bring the study of the prophecies into discredit as miscalculations, based upon *these numbers*. All the great prophetic periods, so called, founded on them have run out and the events have proved the fallacy of the principles upon which they were predicated.

These numbers are chiefly found in Daniel and the Apocalypse. They are the following:

1. "The seven times" of Daniel, fourth chapter. This number according to the learned Father constitutes the *sacred calendar of prophecy* and spans the entire period of the *times of the gentiles*. The fallacy of this assumption, has been alluded to elsewhere.

2. "The seventy weeks" of Daniel, ninth chapter. This number, when rightly understood, furnishes a key to the elucidation and correct application of almost all the numbers that occur in Daniel and the Apocalypse, and may be regarded as the very *rosetta stone* in deciphering *prophetic numbers*.

3. "The 2,300 days" of Daniel, eighth chapter, has long since been accomplished, as will be presently shown.

4. The same period of three and a half years duration, is variously expressed in Daniel and the Apocalypse, as 1,260 days; as forty-two months; as a time, times, and a dividing of time; or as a time, times and a half time, each making just three and a half years. Allowing twelve

months to the year, and thirty days to the month, 1,260 days will just make three and a half years, or forty-two months. These must be taken as literal indications of time. Each of these numbers identify the same event.

5. There also occur in Daniel, the numbers 1.290 days and 1,335 days. These have close relation to the foregoing and must be understood as so many literal days.

6. There also occur the numbers five months, ten days, three and a half days, and also a day, a month and a year in the Revelations. Each must be regarded as literal time.

The fatal mistake in regard to the true import of all these numbers has arisen from the unfounded assumption, that a day in prophecy means a year. Whereas this is never the case, except when so explained in the context. As in Numbers 14 : 34; and in Ezekiel 4 : 4, 6.

In each of these passages, it is expressly stated that a day shall represent, in the fulfillment of the events predicted a year. To infer from the language in Numbers : "After the number of the day in which ye searched the land, even forty days. Each day for a year, shall ye bear your iniquities,"—a general principle that a day must be understood as a year in prophetic language, would indicate a sad lack of precision. It is illogical to infer a general principle from a particular example.

The *seven times* in Daniel, fourth chapter, refer to the period of Nebuchadnezzar's insanity, and consequently, the period of his disqualification for discharging the duties of the kingly office; "*until seven times shall pass over him,*" and again "*until seven times shall pass over thee,*" it is expressed.

These seven times are seven literal years and had their accomplishment. For at the *end of the days*, he says—meaning the period of seven years of his insanity—

"*I, Nebuchadnezzar lifted up mine eyes unto heaven and my understanding returned unto me.*" If the period therefore indicated by the *seven times* was accomplished as the phrase *end of the days* indicates, how can it have any further application? Notwithstanding this phrase had a specific reference, and the period indicated has long since been accomplished, nevertheless, upon this *seven times* expanded into 2,520 years, has been constructed the grand system of prophetic periods, so called, all of which have run out, and the affairs of the world still continue to move on in their accustomed channels. These prophetic periods have been the fruitful source of presumption and fanaticism.

Many have, therefore, concluded that the import of the prophecies is so hidden and enigmatical, that all pains bestowed upon this study would only be time lost.

These mistakes among students of prophecy have arisen from the too common predilection to infer the existence of a mystery where there is none.

An illustration, that a day must be understood in a literal and not a symbolic sense, is afforded by the accomplishment of the period indicated by the 2,300 days of the eighth chapter of Daniel, "*until 2,300 days, then shall the sanctuary be cleansed.*" This illustration alone should suffice to establish the principle of interpretation, unless the contrary should become apparent from the context. 2,300 days are equal to six years, four months and twenty days, allowing twelve months of thirty days each to the year.

It is stated in the First Maccabees, first chapter, that Antiochus Epiphanes, first visited Jerusalem, B. C. 170. He desecrated the sanctuary and despoiled the temple of much of its valuable furniture. Three years after he sent a chief officer of his treasury, to collect his revenues; this officer, *acting under orders no doubt*, profaned the holy house, stripped it of many remaining valuables, took away the altar of incense, set up the statue of Jupiter Capitolinus, within the precincts of the temple, and offered swine's flesh upon the altar of sacrifice. Thus the profanation of the sanctuary was completely accomplished, which had commenced with the first visit of Antiochus, B. C. 170.

On the twenty-fifth day of the Jewish month Chisleu, B. C. 164, Judas Maccabæus at the head of his victorious countrymen entered Jerusalem and found the city in a state of desolation. He proceeded without delay to *cleanse the sanctuary*, and restore the sacrifices and temple services, according to the law of Moses. So the times from the desecration of the temple, at the first visit of Antiochus Epiphanes, B. C. 170, until the cleansing of the sanctuary B. C. 164, was six years. But as the month Chisleu corresponds to the ninth month in our calendar, the twenty-fifth day thereof would fall late in the year 164, B. C., and therefore afford ample ground for the additional four months and twenty days, which are necessary to make up the 2,300 days. Greater precision could not be expected in such matters, the month and day of the original desecration of the sanctuary by Antiochus is not given. It is true Josephus says: "So on the twenty-fifth day of the month Chisleu, after three years to the day the temple and the services thereof were dedicated anew." But according to Josephus' own account, Antiochus first visited Jerusalem, six years before, that is B. C. 170, and according to First Maccabees first chapter, he despoiled and desecrated the temple at that visit. There is a variance between Josephus and Maccabees First, as to the second visit of Antiochus, according to the latter, he sent his chief officer of revenue, but did not visit the city himself, what he did this second visit, three years before the cleansing of the sanctuary, is not known.

It is of the first importance to a right understanding of the prophecies, to bear in mind continually, that they were given to the Jews, and that therefore their fulfillment must concern this people. The sanctuary was the more sacred precinct of the Jewish temple, therefore without an express warranty in the prophecy, it would be a fatal error to refer it to something else.

A few words on *prophetic symbols* seems expedient in this place. These will be more fully explained, and the principles applicable to them as they occur.

The import of prophetic symbols must be sought for chiefly in the Holy Scriptures. The Bible contains the means of its own elucidation; the book may be regarded as a treatise upon the science of sacred things—of revealed truths. And as every treatise on any particular branch of science should and does contain—if written by a competent author, a full explanation of its mysteries, so the means necessary to an understanding of the prophecies, as well as other parts of divine revelation, must be sought for in the book itself, by a careful scrutiny of what has been written. *God is His own interpreter.*

Symbolic language however, in which the prophecies abound is not peculiar to the sacred writings.

Symbols are used as a vehicle for thought by all classes. By the rude and unlettered, as well as by the cultivated and refined. By the former as a necessity for making known his desires or wants. By the latter as the means of giving expression to the highest conceptions of the fancy or the imagination, as *expressed* in poetry or metaphysics. The oratory of the aborigines of our own country afford a most striking illustration of the use of symbolic language.

Symbolic language resembles in some respects a system of hieroglyphics, as it affords the means of communicating thoughts by signs. But a word may have a two-fold meaning. It may be used in its ordinary acceptation only, or to denote the idea or thought symbolized by it. That a word is used in a symbolic sense, it does not follow that it is always so used. An earthquake may be used symbolically to denote convulsions and revolution among the masses of the people; and is so used in the prophecies, but not always. It is sometimes used in its primary sense to mean a shaking and upheaval of the earth's crust.

The sun, the source of light and heat to our world, and that which affords the germinal principle of vegetable life, may be regarded as the emblem of power and majesty; and therefore according to many expositors should be looked upon, as the symbol of the king of the realm or state. And the moon, as reflecting his majesty and as peculiarly lovely, as the queen.

From this we dissent. Light is the symbol of truth. Truth is light, light makes manifest. The sun is the source of light to our system, and therefore it must be understood as symbolizing the source of divine truth, or sometimes truth in the abstract. *"Shall the sun of righteousness arise with healing in his wings."* Mal. 4: 2.

After fully examining the prophecies, I am convinced that the sun symbolizes the embodiment of divine revelation. The logos, the Revelator, more especially revealed truth, as a system in opposition to other systems. The sun shall be darkened when divine revelation shall be set aside to give place to the revelations of science and philosophy, so called—and what follows? The moon shall be turned into blood. The moon symbolizes the state of society, modeled upon the truth, as reflecting its supreme excellency.

The manners, customs and moral principles, which adorn and beautify every community or society, where the authority of the scriptures is received, as containing the rule of life and moral conduct; the harmony and loveliness of domestic economy, which pervades every Christian community.

When the sun shall be darkened, these institutions will be literally drenched in blood. So it is predicted. So it has, and will happen again.

A system, for the interpretation of the prophetic symbols can not be established upon general principles, which govern figurative language. Much depends in the use of figurative language upon the subject discussed.

To attempt therefore to establish upon general principles of reasoning, from the nature of things, or to infer from the *usus loquendi*, a system of rules, for the interpretation of the prophetic symbols, would be as irrational, as to attempt to explain the symbols of a mathematical formula, by oriental hieroglyphics. But there are in all sciences technical terms, so called. It is the duty of every author to define such terms, and to indicate in his treatise, the precise sense in which each term shall be understood throughout. Such terms must therefore, be understood in the sense so attached, unless the contrary shall appear from the context; so also, whenever it shall clearly appear by any suggestion, intimation, or allusion, or even by an apparently unimportant word or phrase, that a specific import is to be attached to a symbol or word, it must be invariably used in such sense, unless there shall be satisfactory reasons to the contrary. But then there must be sufficient reason to identify a word as symbolic. (The symbols of any treatise on algebra may illustrate.) The word day is not a symbolic word. There must appear reason therefore in the context, before it can be so considered. To infer from Numbers 14, 32,—that a day is to be understood generally as the symbol of a year, would lead to the sacrifice of all precision in language; whereas the language of divine revelation is the most exact, when rightly understood.

When the signification of a symbol has been once determined, that signification must be maintained throughout; unless the context clearly shows that a symbolic sense is not intended.

As an example, *a beast* is the symbol of a secular monarchy or an empire, so explained in Daniel seventh. A beast therefore, must be understood to symbolize an *empire* whenever it occurs as a prophetic figure.

NOTE.—This whole subject may be fitly illustrated by the *mathematical symbols.* These by common consent have an invariable import. By their use, the most abstruse principles in the physical sciences or mechanics, may be demonstrated to positive certainty, and formulated intelligibly. Whereas, without the aid of such symbols, neither would be practicable. Of similar use are the prophetic symbols. In both, primarily, the import of the symbol is defined, the method only is different.

CHAPTER IV.

THE IMPENDING CRISIS.

Prop. I. *The impending political crisis of the world, now in the not distant future, will prove to be the revival of the old Roman Empire, under a new and last form of organization—consisting of a confederation of ten kingdoms under one central Imperial Head.*

It will be ATHEISTIC in principle and will occupy the same geographical limits, or nearly so, of the old Roman Empire.

Efforts at improvements, though always prospective in their aim, do not strive to lay under contribution the new and untried. Such efforts are not unfrequently retrospective in the selection of means to ends, aiming to utilize, or to impart a new phase to something of the past. The wise Solomon says, *"there is nothing new under the sun."*

That the old Roman Empire should be again *revived*, not only in name, but also with all its essential features, as an imperial despotism, is not a thing in itself improbable. The Roman name has been revived more than once. At the coronation of Charlemagne, by Pope Leo, as Emperor of Rome, A. D. 800. In the organization of the Holy Roman Empire, of the German nations subsequently. The great Napoleon placed the iron crown of Italy on his own head, and as soon as born, bearing in his arms his only son, he showed him to his marshals and proclaimed him—*The King of Rome.*

These illustrations show, at least, that there is a lingering potency attached to the Roman Name.

The governments of modern Europe are indebted for their organic elements, chiefly to the political maxims wrought out during the existence of the old empire.

This is evident from the general resemblance they bear each other. There is in all these governments a wonderful sameness in the essential elements of their constitutions. A senate or deliberative body, for the enactment or sanction of laws, more or less limited in their functions. An executive authority vested somewhere, usually in a king or emperor, and a co-ordinate department of justice for the interpretation and administration of the laws, are essential elements in all modern governments. All these may be traced back to the old Roman Commonwealth, and appear to have been distinctly recognized and practically adopted, as inseparable concomitants of government.

Profound and difficult as the problem of government has proved to be, necessity, the mother of inventions, has always appeared to be the presiding genius at every emergency. The same necessity which has laid under contribution the brightest talents, for the service of the state in the past, will prove equally potent to evoke expedients, adequate, when calamitous times shall come.

The signs of enervation and decay among the governments of Europe are too apparent. The light shed on this subject by passing events, renders the evidence of the past, cumulative.

What strikes every careful observer most forcibly, is the obvious want of cohesiveness among the elements, which constitute those nations. And the tendencies of the times rather favor alienation. In place of attempting to remove the causes of internal discontent, the European cabinets are intent upon watching their external relations. The prevalent political expedient of erecting each people or nationality into an autonomy, with the expectation of allaying discontents and promoting tranquillity and harmony, will be found in the end not to subserve the intended purpose. It must result in widening existing differences and in keeping alive national peculiarities, and in nursing hereditary distinctions and prejudices. The practice of the ancients was just the reverse, they aimed to promote homogeneity among their populations by the blending and transformation of nationalities.

The anomaly, therefore, is presented to the world by the nations of modern Europe, of attempting externally, to draw more closely together in their diplomatic relations, while internally, their elements are driven, by one cause or another, more widely asunder.

This is a manifest sign of conscious weakness. It looks like a move in the direction of entering into a mutual agreement, for common assistance, should the necessity arise. For mutual aid in suppressing insurrections, whenever they should prove too formidable for the local authorities. We have an example, in the armed intervention of Russia to assist Austria in suppressing the Hungarian revolt under Kossuth. And intervention has frequently occurred. A confederation of the strong powers, will in the progress of events become a necessity. Tendencies once set in motion never retrograde, revolutions never move backwards. Such a confederacy would require a head. Such head, from the necessity of the case, must needs be an emperor; the result must be the formation of a centralized imperial confederacy. In order to secure efficiency, the central imperial head of the confederation must needs be invested with supreme power. Such a power, which present indications point to as imminent, time being the only question, would most likely, following the analogy of the past, assume the name Roman. "*The Roman Empire of the European nations.* A glance at the condition of the several nations of Europe will serve to convince any one that they can not long maintain their present status. Great Britain, the most prominent, as well as the most powerful in resources, in appearance at least, can not claim immunity from threatened disasters or assurance of permanent stability. March the 28th, 1879; "Lord Beaconsfield, the prime minister, acknowledged before the house of Lords, that the depression of the agricultural interests was unprecedented. It was estimated he said, that the public wealth had diminished $400,000,000 and that the area of land under cultivation had diminished 1,000,000 acres. April 2d, 1879, David McIver, a member of Parliament and one of the proprietors of the Cunard line of steamships, writes, "that he does not know of any nation, whose trade prospects are so gloomy as Great Britain's."

Add the failure of harvests and of some of the oldest and wealthiest banking institutions, derangements and distress in the great industrial centers, with the long list of bankruptcies and failures in business, with the panic and derangement resulting from a loss of confidence, and it must be acknowledged by the most hopeful and sanguine, that the prospect for the future of Great Britain is gloomy.

When the affairs of a nation, as those of an individual are such, that every condition must be favorable in order to success and any failure must prove a disaster, its condition is desperate. In this state of things, one or two reverses of her armies in the field, and she is never quite free from war; one or two failures of her harvests at home would so intensify internal distress and discontent, that revolution would follow as an inevitable result. How could a revolution at home, if general, be suppressed, her armies being far away in India, in Africa, Australia and North America? Foreign assistance to put down the revolution might become a necessity—but Great Britain from her insular situation and extensive foreign colonies, is far more favorably situated than the balance of the European family of nations.

Whoever has carefully watched the progress of events in France, if not an enthusiast for the impossible, must have come to the conclusion, if the past of this nation teaches any lesson, that she is moving on step by step to anarchy, and what next?

The German Empire is but recent, but it is manifest can not exist long without essential modifications in its organization. An internal struggle is now going on. The novelty of its sudden formation and the eclat achieved by its armies at Sadowa, at Sedan and on other victorious battle fields, has doubtless served the temporary purpose of keeping alive among its not entirely homogeneous elements, a national sentiment, but old customs and prejudices will assert their energy and constitute a more powerful influence than mere sentiment. The former will form a constant force, the latter an evanescent. Causes now at work will compel this power to assume the form of a consolidated military despotism, as the means of self-preservation. This, or disruption, there is no alternative.

The Austrain Empire is liable at any time to disintegration. It is most probably a question of circumstances and time only. The new kingdom of Italy is on trial. The Papacy distinctly announces, that it lays claim to the temporalities of St. Peter, as the estates of the church were formally styled, to have relinquished none of its pretended claims to secular power, but on the contrary of its intention to prosecute them.

Spain under her young king is slowly convalescent. This, with her disordered constitution is most likely to prove temporary.

While the Rhenish States and the Scandinavian kingdoms present a tempting prey to their powerful and ambitious German neighbor.

Besides these nations are weighed down with burdens, which must prove insupportable—standing armies and taxation.

To maintain security at home, and to provide against external violence: The four principal nations of Europe, namely, Great Britain, France, Germany and Austria, are induced to support standing armies which, even in time of peace, aggregate nearly 2,000,000 of men under arms. All these withdrawn from the active pursuits of productive industry, remain consumers, and become a public charge. When placed on a war footing—for which the men are more or less liable to be withdrawn from their civil avocations, for the purpose of training and instruction in the art of war, in the time of peace,—the armies of these four powers will amount to about 5,000,000 of men, while the entire population of these nations does not exceed 140,000,000 of Europeans. Making allowance for those exempt from military duty, by reason of age, as well as those exempt for other causes, and also for the women and children, and of those remaining, about one man out of every four is subject to military duty, and liable to be called to arms any day. In an emergency every man would be liable. These enormous armies must be supported, and their support must come from the producing classes. These standing armies and the wars which have occurred, have entailed enormous national debts upon these nations.

The aggregate national debt of three of these powers, namely, Great Britain, France and Austria, amounts to about $10,000,000,000. A sum far exceeding comprehension, and represents an indebtedness of about $100 to every man, woman and child in these three empires.

This enormous debt has been accumulating for centuries, and the increase has more than kept pace with the increase of population and wealth, and is still steadily growing in magnitude.

The annual revenues of these three powerful nations drawn chiefly from taxation, directly and indirectly, amount to about $1,000,000,000, and still the yearly exhibits of the financial condition of each, shows, as a general thing, a deficit. The balances, from year to year, must be added to the aggregate indebtedness, increasing at compound interest, or their liquidation be provided for, by an increase of taxation. The latter is no longer practicable. For every expedient, that the most ingenius and daring financier could devise, for increasing the revenue, has been called into requisition, and every resource laid under contribution. Prosperity may enable them to maintain their present position for awhile, but adversity must end in irreparable disaster.

The treaty of Paris and the still more recent conference and treaty at Berlin, present the great powers, as they are called, in a new attitude before the world. Taking counsel in reference to matters, which but remotely and incidently, if at all, affect many of them. But the fact is significant. It shows that there is a sense of a common interest among these powers, and indicates a disposition to act in concert, when occasion may demand. The eastern question offered such an occasion, but this is trivial compared with other questions slumbering nearer home.

Mental activity has been quickened in more recent times by the general diffusion of knowledge. And men deliberate upon their rights. They begin to see, that under the present conditions, their prospects are most hopeless and forlorn. Minds enlightened and emancipated from the thraldom of ignorance, will not passively endure oppression, but will seek out ways and means for attaining to a better condition. Hence, the formation of societies to promote concert of action, the joining, hand to hand, in an endeavor for mutual relief.

The promotion of these societies, whether socialistic or communistic, bodes no good to the present established order of things. It is a feature of the times, in which we live, and is going on throughout the civilized world. Attempts at repression on the part of the Government, would be regarded as acts of tyranny.

A recent writer says: "These arrests," referring to what Bismarck is doing to save society, "will end in no results advantageous to the despotisms; though for a time, no doubt, it will seem to do so. Revolution in Europe is growing stronger and stronger every day. The millions are gradually brought to such a state of slavery and starvation that it is impossible to endure the sad condition!"

There is no reasonable prospect of any change for the better. Governments are powerless to make the reforms demanded. And the malady in the masses is incurable. A deep seated discontent aggravate by intolerable surroundings. Its complaints are uttered in prose and verse. This is shown by the following revolutionary ballad:

> "The curse of God sweeps o'er the land,
> We die, and feel no helping hand,
> Famine and horror, plague and blight,
> Enwrap us, as in triple night,

The great are throned on seats of Gold,
　The starving Poor are bought and sold,
The swollen Rich oppress and slay,
　While Millions curse the light of Day.
The Mothers weep in want and woe,
　The new-born Babe brings joy no more.
Disease, Starvation, Crime and Fraud,
　Bear on their wings Thy curse, Oh, God,
Lord, Lord, have mercy!"

The sad condition of the masses, is doubtless owing in a great measure, to the increase of population, beyond the means of comfortable subsistence. The heavy drains upon their scant earnings in the form of taxation, caused by enormous public expenditures,—aggravated by the smarting of wounds inflicted by reiterated wrongs.

Many evils are inseparable to any state of society, and nations have gone on increasing in population, wealth and civilization, with much poverty and distress among the people. But there is a culminating point in the career of a people beyond which their evils can not be borne, at which there is a pause in their onward progress, and from which they begin to decline. All history proves this.

The accumulation of wealth in a few hands, usually goes hand in hand with the impoverishment of the masses, and this tends to the centralization of power; wealth usually engenders luxury, pride, and extravagance, with indolence and a want of modesty and integrity. Such was the state of society at Rome in the days of Cataline. Evil examples in high places corrupt the masses. They tend to inflame the passions and render those in straightened circumstances discontented with their own lot. In no period in the history of the world has there been so great an inequality in the distribution of wealth, as at the present time in Europe.

Never was the limit between the enormously wealthy, and extremely poor man, so wide.

This has led to the formation of classes between which there is no compatibility, no sympathy, but hostility irreconcilable. It has effaced all love of country from the poor and down trodden. It has embittered their recollections of the scenes of their childhood, and millions have sought refuge in foreign and strange lands, from evils intolerable at home. How else can the constant flow of emigration, that has been going on for the past one hundred years, to all newly discovered countries and especially to America, be accounted for?

Had not their condition become in a measure intolerable at home, the people would never have voluntarily sundered the ties that bind the heart to home and their native land, and embarked for a strange and foreign land. Very few of the wealthy emigrate. The limit of production has doubtless, long since been practically reached in those countries, from which the tide of emigration has chiefly flowed.

There has been no emigration among the gentry and nobility, who own the landed estates and wealthy endowments. This shows that it is destitution and want, that have forced the peasantry to this course. The love of country and home, dies out with this class, last of all. But the peasantry of Europe have their recollections of home embittered by sorrow, oppression and privations. For the worst form of tyranny is the despotism of a system sanctioned by customs and laws.

The evidence of a healthy and prosperous government are found in a high tone of public sentiment, the whole body of the people being animated by some common object of pursuit, or stimulated by some grand national enterprise. What common ground is there for the extremes to unite on, in Europe? The wealthy and powerful roll in luxury at home, the poor seek for a subsistence and to better their condition by emigrating to foreign lands. But this outward tide of emigration must soon cease to flow. The available lands in America are all or nearly so, appropriated. The same with other accessible foreign countries. What then?—An accumulation of population at home, with an increase of destitution and corresponding discontent. Toward this, the present tendencies point,—a state of things, in the no distant future, which must give rise to riots and revolutions, is clearly foreshadowed by passing events.

But many persons blinded by false theories, imagine that certain reliefs will be provided, as the exigencies of the times may demand. Why are not such reliefs forthcoming now? Are there not alarming symptoms of discontent, even desperation among the populations of England, Germany, and Russia? Why is not the sovereign balm forthcoming, which is to heal and sooth every wound? The old remedy coercion, and torture is at hand! No means is yet forthcoming of closing the gulf, which separates poverty and wretchedness on the one extreme, from luxury and affluence on the other.

It may be answered, that in scientifically digested constitutions and skillfully conducted administration of the affairs of government, the present excels those of former times. It may be truthfully said in reply, your constitutions are enervated by attempts at excessive refinements, your administration and laws are befouled by corruption, from which good men turn away in sorrow and disgust. There is not a government in Christendom, which does not contain the elements of corruption, and therefore, symptoms of weakness and instability. If there had been any marvelous improvement in the art of government, there must have been somewhere after so long a time, an approximation to a perfect model. Whereas, on the contrary, the complexity and obscurity of written laws are perfectly appalling, while their volume has swelled beyond all precedent. The consequence is, that they have become inoperative, and remain a dead letter in many places upon the statute book. Such is the tendency of modern governments. These things indicate weakness and not strength. Strength is consonant with simplicity. A few well digested laws rigidly enforced. Complexity of laws argues weakness in the State, an attempt to accomplish by law that which should result spontaneously. And further, whoever will take the pains to examine into these matters, will see, that there exists the same anxiety, that always has existed, on the part of rulers. Distrust of the subject, and dread of the neighbor; that the one may rebel, that the other might declare war. If not so, why are the immense standing armies maintained in times of profound peace, by these European nations? It is too manifest, that they all rely for national existence, and the maintenance of social order, upon physical force.

But those who can see nothing but hopeful indications in the future, lay great stress upon the wonderful progress made in the arts and sciences, and the aid to be derived from them. It is admitted that there have been great improvements made, and wonderful discoveries in the arts and sciences. But the light of science seems unhappily to have been too intense, and like the effects of the full glare of the sun upon the eyes, it has tended rather to dazzle and impair, than to improve the natural vision. Surely this is too true, in reference to moral vision. It has become too much the fashion, to magnify the hasty deductions of science above the long acquiest in teachings of Divine Revelations. The aid of science has been invoked therefore to cast discredit upon the only true knowledge. Further than this, there is a tendency in the times to which science, so called, is contributing its aid, to unsettle all belief and introduce universal distrust. Theoretical reasoning has become so attenuated and so refined in its analysis, as to be beyond the comprehension of ordinary minds. This must be destruction to mental activity, and lead to indifference and distrust, for men will not interest themselves in that they do not comprehend.

The pretensions of the learned savor very much of personal vanity and self-glorification. A principle in nature, established perhaps upon a hasty and insufficient induction, is often magnified into such importance as to practically exclude the God of Nature. Such is the tendency of modern science. The painful fact can not be disputed.

Most assuredly alarming consequences are to be apprehended from this source. The devotees of modern science are too free to lend their aid for the establishment of modern atheism. What must be the fruits of a system of philosophy which ignores the existence of God? And such is the tendency of the teachings of the ablest scientists of modern times. That, therefore, which has a tendency to flatter vanity and undermine belief in Divine Revelation can not but have a most pernicious and deleterious effect upon morals, and hence tend to the dissolution of society, by removing its safeguards and restraints.

But the Christian religion is lending its benignant and sanctifying influence, says one, and this must prove the safeguard of modern institutions.

This expectation is based, not only upon a false assumption

as to the end proposed to be accomplished by the author of Christianity, but it is also at variance with the most obvious facts. It is true, if men were good Christians, they would be good citizens also, and a State composed of such would contain the elements of stability and domestic happiness. But where is such a State to be found? "Ye are not of this world," says the Lord to his disciples. Nominal Christian States there are, but a false Christianity is worse than paganism. Its influence on society is worse.

This age has incontestably some superiority over former times in freedom from superstition and from the influence of legendary lore. But while mind has been emancipated from under the influence of the marvelous, it has gone to the opposite extreme.

It has fallen under the influence of practical atheism. While organized Christianity, chiefly represented by the Roman hierarchy, remains an incubus upon soul and body. This institution must be considered not only for the most part a corruption of the true religion of Jesus, but as affording also, in a great measure, the pattern after which other organizations, professing to be Christian, have been modeled. There must be kept in mind constantly the distinction between true Christianity and Christianity as represented by organized bodies calling themselves Christians. The one is a living principle in the heart of the individual; the other, a body without a soul. Every candid person will admit that there has been a great departure from the simplicity of the true faith. That the spirit of the Reformation, which was a grand and glorious effort in favor of a purer Christianity, has been neutralized by the introduction of forms and customs derived from Rome. Into these it is impossible to infuse life, and men fall into formal religion, and remain only Christians in name. Besides, these organizations waste much of the little power remaining among them for good, in dissensions and opposition among themselves. The body of Christ is one; but where, if these bodies are to be regarded as Christian, do you find oneness? Divided into numerous sects, each sect chiefly intent upon maintaining its own peculiarities and defending and enforcing its peculiar tenets, the body is rent asunder. But the vesture of the Lord was left entire, and so will the true body remain. Organized Christianity is a body divided against itself, but the true is the one body.

Organized Christianity thrusts itself before the attention of the world, and claims to be recognized as the true. This organized body is a house divided against itself, and therefore can not stand. Its doom is authoritatively pronounced. Vital Christianity may animate some of the members, but the body is dead. True religion is not in harmony with the maxims of the world; its spirit is antagonistic. And therefore the stress laid upon culture, meaning the cultivation of secular literature and science, has not had a happy effect upon true godliness. It has, in too many cases, greatly impaired, if not entirely supplanted, the true religion.

Indeed Christianity has but little restraining influence over the world. Christian nations, nominally so, go to war, conquer and distress each other. Wars have been as frequent in modern as in ancient times, and carried on in the same barbarous manner. There may be some slight mitigations in favor of the modern practice of warfare, but it is essentially barbarous still.

For many reasons, moral restraints over the individual are losing their power, and crime stalks forth in all its shocking deformity. Robberies, homicides, suicides, murders, and adulteries are of daily occurrence. Human life is esteemed of little moment. The prospect of death inspires no terror; future retribution, no fear.

Why is this so? True religion is the salt of the earth. Its exhibition has always inspired the world with respect—even awe. It exerts a restraining and conservative influence over the morals and conduct of even ungodly men.

Has Christianity lost its power? The true Christianity has not, but the organized bodies calling themselves Christian, but invoking the aid of auxiliaries hostile to the spirit of the true religion, have corrupted or supplanted vital Christianity.

Christianity is, in itself, a Divine Science, ample and complete for the accomplishment of its mission in the world, which will most assuredly be accomplished. But, convinced that these institutions assuming the name Christian are sailing under false colors—that they are used to subserve human ambition and selfish ends—men will turn away from all religious thought and drop into indifference or atheism. This process is going on. Worldly Christianity will, therefore, prove an important factor in hastening the great catastrophy which looms up in the no very *distant future.*

The state of religion in Europe, at this time, is such that the true vital faith in the Lord Jesus is to be found only among the groups and assemblies of believers, who have no visible recognition before the world.

A brief review of the nations of Europe has shown that their affairs are critical.

That there is a great depression in trade, and wide spread distrust and alarm; that taxation is a grievous burden; that great discontents and symptoms of revolution exist among the people; that the diffusion of knowledge among the masses tends to increase this discontent; that pantheistic philosophy, infidelity, and atheism are spreading to an alarming extent, exerting a deleterious influence upon the moral sentiments of the people; that there is a growing dislike for all that has the sanction of past traditions as sacred, or that hitherto has been deemed venerable or holy in religion; that men, having thrown off the restraining influence of traditional maxims and of Christian ethics, are left free to follow the instincts of passion and the dictates of revenge,—to make war on a system of abuses which has so long held them under a thralldom, hopeless of relief.

For this state of affairs there is no apparent remedy, except in revolution. Prosperous seasons, good harvests, the resolution and industrious habits of the people, and a hopeful disposition, looking for better times to come, may buoy up the masses for a time, and enable those governments to maintain their present status. But not one of them is in a condition to sustain any serious disasters, whether of famine or war, without internal commotion. Instance the commune in France. And whence could a remedy be applied? From increased productiveness? This would be the only sure remedy, under the present state of things, but this is wholly out of the question. From disarmament and other government reforms? Disarmament is an impossibility. The armies are necessary to hold in check the discontented and revolutionary populations, and to maintain the balance of power, as it is called. Government reforms are, therefore, out of the question. It is impossible to reduce taxation. There are already annual deficits in the revenues amounting to many millions. How then reform? How remove the burden from the people? The case is purely hopeless. The tide of outward emigration must shortly be stayed, for want of suitable places to emigrate, and population must increase, and with it an increase of misery. The history of the race shows that there is no recuperative energy in men to rise as a mass above their surroundings, but that conditions are omnipotent in shaping human destiny.

The crisis is, therefore, inevitable, and not very remote. The nations have already taken steps somewhat resembling a confederation for certain purposes.

An extraordinary character at the head of a leading power in Europe will be the immediate instrumentality in organizing the coming Roman Empire; but extraordinary occasions always bring out such.

The great Napoleon, and the Imperial Confederation which he organized, afford an illustration. But the head of the Revived Roman Empire will be, in many respects, a more extraordinary character than the great Napoleon. The coming character will be an unscrupulous, impious, daring person, endowed with satanic intelligence and skill, and wielding a species of superhuman power over the minds of men. He is styled by the inspired Apostle, "*that man of sin*, the son of perdition, who opposeth and exalteth himself above all that is called God, or that is worshiped."

The most sweeping reforms will be inaugurated by him, and carried through by the sword. He will assume the title of the *irresistible*, and claim to represent Omnipotent Power among men. He will put his heel upon every form of religious faith, and claim, after the manner of the old Roman Emperors, divine honors,—showing himself that he is a god. These things we expect to prove to the satisfaction of every believer in the Scriptures.

Nor is there any thing improbable in itself, prior to proof, in the proposition, that the Roman Empire should be revived again, among the people inhabiting the geographical limits of the old empire. These nations contain a large Latin element. There are certain things connected with the existence of this Latin race that are wonderful and significant.

The old Roman Empire was the most wonderful, as well as the most powerful government that has existed on earth. From the founding of Rome by Romulus, 753 years before the commencement of the Christian Era, until the final subversion of the Eastern Empire, A. D. 1453, there was a period of 2,206 years, extending through more than two-thirds of the historic age.

The Roman Empire has exerted more influence on the nations of the world than all the nations of antiquity, and modern nations, largely composed of the Latin race, have many of them adopted the Roman laws, and are all more or less indebted to Rome for their institutions and improved system of jurisprudence. There are two wonders of providence, significant in respect to coming events; the one, the preservation of the distinct nationality of the Jews, and the other, the preservation of the Latin language.

The Latin language and literature, and that implies the laws and institutions of the Romans, are studied everywhere, and deemed indispensable to thorough scholarship. The civil law, which is the old Roman law with slight modifications, is the law of most civilized nations, and enters largely into the jurisprudence of the remaining nations where the common law prevails. Says an eminent English judge: "Inasmuch as the laws of all nations are raised out of the civil law, as all governments are sprung from the ruins of the Roman Empire, it must be owned that the principles of our laws are borrowed from the civil law."

When, therefore, fear shall fall upon the nations,—when

perilous times shall come,—when the present nations shall prove inadequate for the emergency, and fail to secure the ends of government, the tranquillity of the State, and the security of domestic institutions,—and when, amid dissension and convulsion, a consolidated imperial confederation shall, for the purpose of the preservation of society, be formed under the auspices of an extraordinary leader, what name will such a power be most likely to take, if not that of the Roman Empire? The old empire will furnish every implement of despotism that may be wanted, ready formed, and adapted to any emergency.

The *Revived Roman Empire will be an atheistic and idolatrous power.* Atheistic in the true sense, but idolatrous in practice. True religion will not be tolerated, but homage to the imperial image will be enforced by law as a test of loyalty.

The Christian religion in Europe exerts very little power over the conscience, at this time. Its practice consists, for the most part, in the observance of certain external forms and ceremonies, but, nevertheless, expensive. This is true of most of the forms of worship patronized by the people and encouraged by the State.

The cost of supporting the swarms of ecclesiasts, consisting of various grades and orders; the maintenance of the numerous religious houses and convents; the preservation of Church property and repairs of Church edifices and other expenses necessarily borne by the devotees of the religion of the times, is an oppressive drain upon their resources.

It would be quite probable, therefore, that in times of great excitement and social convulsions religious institutions should suffer. This was the case in the French revolution. The commune of Paris made war on the clergy recently. The recent appropriation of Church property for the use of the State in Italy shows the temper of the times, that governments in a strait will regard the endowments of the Church liable to seizure and confiscation. Besides, the wide spread of rationalistic and atheistic principles is hostile to religion, and as men grow irreligious they become more and more embittered against all religion and its advocates. The populace have not failed to show their hostility to religion and its teachers whenever occasion has presented.

The State encourages religion for its real or supposed influence over the people as a conservator of morals and of the peace. If religion loses its power over men the State has no further use for it, and will, consequently, repudiate it as soon as it is apparent that it can exert no further control over the masses. Habits, and veneration for long established institutions, may have their influence in extending to the religious establishments a period of probation. It is, therefore, rendered morally certain that when the time comes for the introduction of radical changes—when the existing governments, more or less complicated with the institutions of Christianity, shall be abandoned as having failed to subserve the ends of government, that war will be declared against all religious institutions. The "man of sin" will aim to change times and laws, and to introduce a new era, a new order of things. He will aim to regenerate society by the introduction of a new code of political and ethical philosophy. Like Nebuchadnezzar, who sought to establish homogeneity throughout his vast empire by setting up an image on the plains of Drura, which all were commanded to fall down and worship; so the Roman Emperor will seek, by prohibiting, on pain of death, all forms of religious worship, and by substituting therefor homage to be paid to his own person and image—showing himself that he is a god—to introduce uniformity in religious worship, so far as tolerated.

CHAPTER V.

EVIDENCE FROM PROPHECY.

The attention of the reader is now invited to the direct evidence furnished by Prophecy. It will be seen that the probabilities suggested by present tendencies,—political, social, and moral,—as well as the conclusions stated in the preceding chapter, adduced from facts,—statistical, military, and financial,—are not only fully verified, but clearly, and with cumulative evidence, foretold in the writings of the Ancient Prophets. Theories of prophetic interpretation, advanced by others, must be passed for the present. Of these, we shall speak as the subject shall advance.

All interpreters of the prophecies are essentially agreed that the nations now dwelling within the geographical limits of the old Roman Empire, and even spreading beyond those limits, which are formed out of, or permeated by, the disintegrated elements of this disrupted power, embracing, indeed, most of the nations of modern Europe and of western Asia, are symbolized by the ten horns of the fourth beast (Daniel, 7: 5) and ten toes of the *great metalic* image which Nebuchadnezzar saw in a dream, described in Daniel, second chapter.* There has been much readjustment, it is true, and reblending of the parts in the transition, while the little better than chaotic elements have been transformed from a state of discord into more symmetrical organizations. But there now exists, essentially, the ten

---

*Note.—" We must, therefore, look," says Bishop Newton, "for the ten kings or kingdoms where only they can be found, amid the broken pieces of the Roman Empire." Vol. I, p. 254.

kingdoms, of which it is said: "*And in the days of these kings (kingdoms) the God of heaven shall set up a kingdom, which shall never be destroyed.*"

Our position on the prophetic chart is in the last days of the *times of the gentiles*. As this period has no numerical limitation we can only judge of our place by passing events and present tendencies. "When the transgressors shall come to the full a king of fierce countenance shall arise."

The ten toes of the metalic image, and the ten horns of the fourth beast, described in Daniel, 7th chapter, are identical in their symbolic signification, and both point to the same ten nationalities. The little horn which sprang up among the ten, described in Daniel, 7th chapter, 8th verse, and elsewhere, is an additional and independent symbol— though belonging to the principal—and points to the coming Roman Empire, or, more particularly, to its last state and extraordinary head, with whom the existence of the Empire, so far as referred to in the prophecies, is identified. It will rise to supreme control with him, and fall with him, as did the Empire of Alexander the Great, or that of Napoleon. This Empire will rise out of the people composing the ten kingdoms, now existing within the territorial limits of the old Roman Empire, or nearly so. This will fully appear in the sequel.

A brief review of this remarkable vision of the prophet will serve to place the subject in a more satisfactory light.

The four beasts, which Daniel saw in a night vision, chapter 7, symbolize the four universal kingdoms or monarchies which are allotted by Divine Providence to the *times of the gentiles*—the fourth and last being the Roman Empire*

---

* "The fourth kingdom can be none other than the Roman Empire," says Bp. Newton. St. Jerome, who wrote in the fourth century of the Christian era, says of the fourth beast of Daniel, 7th

—and, therefore, a beast, or wild beast, as the word in the original Hebrew signifies, is the symbol for an Empire, or universal monarchy. This fully appears, from the explanation given to Daniel—chap. 7 : verses 16, 17, 18.

But it was the fourth beast that specially interested him. After having received the general explanation of the vision from the angelic interpreter, he says: "Then I would know the truth of the fourth beast, which was diverse from the others, exceeding dreadful, whose teeth were of iron, and his nails of brass; which devoured, broke in pieces, and stamped the residue with his feet." Verse 19.*

chapter: "Regnum autem quartum, quod perspicue pertinet ad Romanos, ferrum est quod comminuit et domat omnia: sed pedes ejus et digiti ex parte ferrei, et ex parte sunt fictiles, quod hoc tempore manifestissime comprobatur." Vol. 3, p. 1032, Edit. Benedict.

The fourth kingdom manifestly pertains to the Romans. The signs of decay of this power in the time of St. Jerome clearly indicated the clay in the lower extremities. Says Bishop Newton: "All ancient writers, both Jewish and Christian, agree with St. Jerome in explaining the fourth kingdom to be the Roman."

St. Cyril of Jerusalem, who wrote about the middle of the fourth century, says of the prophecies of Daniel : " Even as he, Gabriel the archangel interpreted, saying thus: *The fourth beast shall be the fourth kingdom on the earth, which shall excel all the kingdoms;* but that this is the Empire of the Romans."

*NOTE.—St. Jerome says of this fourth beast: "Satisque minor quod quum super leænam et ursum, et pardum in tribus regnis posuerit, Romanum regnum nulli bestiæ compararet: nisi forte ut formidolosam faceret bestiam, vacabulum tacuit; ut quicquid ferocious cogitaverimus in bastiis, hoc Romanos' intelligamus." Vol. 3, p. 1103, Edit. Benedict.

Upon this passage Bishop Newton remarks:

" The fourth beast was so great and horrible that it was not easy to find an adequate name for it; and the Roman Empire was described as dreadful and terrible and strong exceedingly beyond any former kingdom." Vol. 1, p. 251.

EVIDENCE FROM PROPHECY. 57

"And of the ten horns that were in his head, and of the other horn, which came up, and before whom three fell: even of that horn that had eyes, and a mouth that spake very great things, whose look was more stout than his fellows."* v. 20.

"Then he said," i. e. the angel or celestial person who gave the explanation, "the fourth beast shall be the fourth kingdom upon earth, which shall be diverse from all kingdoms, and shall devour the whole earth, and shall tread it down, and break it in pieces. And the ten horns out of this kingdom are ten kings, that shall arise,"—a king implies a kingdom. "And another shall arise after them: and he shall be diverse from the first, and he shall subdue three kings," i. e. kingdoms or sovereign powers, v. 23, 24.

All that is signified in these symbols of the fourth beast has passed into history, except the ten horns, and the notorious LITTLE *horn*, that shall arise after them. The ten horns have their antitypes, fulfilled, most probably, in ten existing kingdoms; that of the *little horn* has not yet appeared above the horizon, or if so, has arrested the attention only of the thoughtful student of prophecy.

It is deemed more conducive to a full and clear elucidation of our subject to arrange the prophecies cited some-

*NOTE.—The little horn of Daniel, 7th chapter, must not be confounded with the little horn of Daniel, 8th chapter. The latter symbolizes quite a different character from the former; a character who had his place among events which have long since passed into history. St. Jerome says of the little horn, Dan. 7: "Ergo dicamus quod omnes scriptores ecclesiastici tradidurunt: in consummatione mundi quando regnum destruendum est Romanorum, decem futuros reges, qui orbem Romanum inter se dividant; et undecimaum surrecturum esse *regem parvulum*, qui tres reges de decem regibus superaturus set. Quibus interfactis, etiam septem alii reges victori colla submittent." Vol. 3, p. 1101. Edit. Benedict.

what in an inverse order, chronologically, as the last become more fully significant in the light shed by those going before. Indeed the symbol presented in the beast ($\theta\eta\rho\iota o\nu$, Rev. 13), when interpreted by the light furnished by the prophecies of Daniel and other scriptures, giving to each part its due symbolic signification, amounts to a full and satisfactory demonstration of the first proposition above stated.

"And I stood upon the sand of the sea, and saw a beast rise up out of the sea, having seven heads and ten horns, and upon his horns ten crowns, and upon his heads the name of blasphemy.

"2 And the beast which I saw was like unto a leopard, and his feet were as *the feet* of a bear, and his mouth as the mouth of a lion: and the dragon gave him his power, and his seat, and great authority.

"3 And I saw one of his heads as it were wounded to death; and his deadly wound was healed: and all the world wondered after the beast.

"4 And they worshiped the dragon which gave power unto the beast; and they worshiped the beast, saying, 'who *is* like unto the beast? who is able to make war with him?'

"5 And there was given unto him a mouth speaking great things and blasphemies; and power was given unto him to continue forty *and* two months.

"6 And he opened his mouth in blasphemy against God, to blaspheme his name, and his tabernacle, and them that dwell in heaven.

"7 And it was given unto him to make war with the saints, and to overcome them; and power was given him over all kindreds, and tongues, and nations.

"8 And all that dwell upon the earth shall worship him, whose names are not written in the book of life of the Lamb slain from the foundation of the world.

"9 If any man have an ear, let him hear." Revelations, 13 : 1—9.

For the purpose of placing the subject more distinctly before the mind of the reader, and to set forth more clearly the train of reasoning adopted, a few preliminary words of explanation seems to be advisable, though anticipatory of what may, more fully, appear hereafter.

It is held that the "*beast with the seven heads and ten horns*," above described, symbolizes the *Roman Empire hereafter to be revived*, showing its symbolic identity with that of the little horn, Dan. 7. The several parts of the symbol serve, either more fully to identify the Roman power, or are descriptive of new features in the organization, which this power shall take, in its new and last form. It will appear under a different form, as an organized political power, from that of old. It will be differently constituted, and the administration of the government will be more assimilated to the usages of modern times. The political organization will be that of a consolidated confederation of kingdoms, under one despotic or imperial head.

The counsels of this ruling head will be greatly influenced by another character who will arise about this same time, and out of the East, most probably, as will appear. This personage is symbolized by the second beast, having two horns like a lamb. v. 11.

With this brief statement we will proceed with the general discussion of the subject.

Let it be borne in mind that the fourth beast (Daniel, 7th chapter) is, by common consent, allowed to symbolize the Roman Empire; indeed, the explanation given Daniel by the angel admits of no other. It shall be *the fourth kingdom on earth, and shall devour the whole earth and tread it down.* It shall also be the last of the four universal monarchies *allotted to the times of the gentiles.*

The ten horns pertain to this beast; are a part of him; so the ten kingdoms, symbolized by them, according to the explanation given by the angel, must belong to the Roman Empire. So also the little horn which shall arise later among them, and which shall subdue three of those which had existed before, must symbolize a secular power, and more especially the head of this power, a most remarkably impious and daring conqueror, which shall pertain to the Roman Empire in its last state. For the power ruled over by this impious, vaunting, blasphemous boaster, must continue until the *Ancient of Days shall sit*—until destroyed by direct interposition of heaven, and the kingdom of the whole earth shall be given to the saints of the *Most High.* Therefore this little horn symbolizes the last state of the Roman Empire on earth, especially its central power and chief.

Now, we propose to show by conclusive reasons that the Apocalyptic beast, described in the passage above cited from Rev. 13th, is identical in symbolic signification with the fourth beast of Daniel 7th, and points out the same Roman Empire, and especially that state of it symbolized by the notorious little horn, Daniel, 7: 8.

That these symbols are identical, so far as pointing out the same Roman monarchy, is satisfactorily shown from the following *coincidences:*

1. Each was seen to rise out of the sea—from the people in their primary capacity; hence, their origin is the same.

2. Both shall exist in the last time, being the last secular power on earth. The beast described in Daniel shall continue until the *Ancient of Days shall sit.* Dan. 7: 9, 11. The beast of the Apocalypse shall be destroyed by the "*King of Kings and Lord of Lords.*" Rev. 19: 20.

3. Both of these beasts symbolize a universal monarchy. Dan. 7: 23—"The fourth beast shall be the fourth kingdom upon the earth, and shall devour the whole earth, and tread it down, and break it in pieces." Rev. 13: 7— "And power was given him over all kindreds, and tongues, and nations."

If then each of these symbols point out a secular monarchy, which shall be universal, and the last empire on earth, then must each symbolize the same secular monarchy; for two distinct *universal* monarchies can not exist at one and the same time.

4. Both shall come to the same end. "I beheld even till the beast was slain and his body destroyed and given to the burning flames;" Dan. 7: 11. "And the beast was taken and with him the false prophet." * * * "They both were cast into a lake of fire, burning with brimstone;" Rev. 19: 20.

5. Both of these symbols are exceeding boastful, arrogant, and blasphemous powers. "In this horn was a *mouth speaking great things.*" "And he shall speak great words against the *Most High.*" Dan. 7: 8, 25. In Rev. 13: 5, it is said: "And there was given unto him *a mouth speaking great things and blasphemies.*" The language is almost identical; the idea precisely identical.

6. They, both, symbolize a power displaying extraordinary intelligence and a spirit of daring innovation.

In Daniel 7: 8 "I beheld in this horn were eyes like the eyes of man" * * "And he shall think to change times and laws." And in Rev. 13: 16, it is said: "And he causeth all, both small and great, rich and poor, free and bond, to receive a mark in their right hand, and in their foreheads, and that no man might buy, or sell, save he that had the mark, or the name of the beast, or the number of his name." Here, in both, is pointed out the same spirit of innovation upon the established customs and laws.

7. Both these symbols point out an earthly power, which shall show an insane hostility towards Almighty God, His Saints, and against High Heaven and sacred things. In Rev. 13: 6, it is said: "And he opened his mouth in blasphemy against *God*, to blaspheme His name, and his tabernacle, and those that dwell in heaven." In Dan. 7: 25, it is said: "And he shall speak great words against the *Most High*, and shall wear out the saints of the *Most High*."

8. Both these symbols point out a power which shall make war against the saints, and shall overcome them.

In Daniel 7: 25—"He shall wear out the saints of the Most High * * * and they shall be given into his hands." Rev. 13: 7, it is said: "And it was given unto him to make war with the saints, and to overcome them." In both these passages the idea is precisely identical, and the language almost.

9. The blasphemous, persecuting, and insane triumph of each is limited to 3½ years. Of the Apocalyptic beast it said, Rev. 13: 5—"And power was given unto him to continue forty and two months," i. e. 3½ years. Of the *little horn*, Dan. 7: 25, it is said: "And they," i. e. the saints, "shall be given into his hands, until a time and times and a dividing of time," i. e. 3½ years.

Surely the identity of these two symbols is here established by mathematical certainty.

10. The political organization of the power pointed out by each symbol shall be composed of ten kingdoms.

Each beast has ten horns. These horns are, by angelic interpreters, said to represent kingdoms. Dan. 7: 24—"The *ten horns out* of this kingdom,"—the interpreter here asserts that the fourth beast represents a kingdom—"are ten kings that shall arise." Rev. 17: 7, 12—"And the angel said unto me, * * I will tell thee the mystery of the beast * * which hath the seven heads and *ten horns*. * * And the ten horns are ten kings," i. e. kingdoms, for they shall receive kingdoms. v. 12.

The identity of the subject matter symbolized by the fourth BEAST, including the ten horns, and the *notable little horn which rose* last, but all belonging to this same fourth BEAST of Daniel, 7th chapter, and the subject matter symbolized by the BEAST having seven heads and ten horns, described in Rev. 13th chapter, is conclusively shown by the coincidences above stated. Indeed, there can be no other conclusion. This is generally conceded.* There is not a parallel instance of such remarkable coincidences to be found in the Bible. It is manifest from the characteristics, from the vaulting ambition, and from the limited duration, that one and the same secular power is foretold by each of *these* remarkable symbols.

And, therefore, if the first symbolizes the Roman Empire, the second must also.

* NOTE.—The coincidence was remarked by the ancient church fathers, thus Irenæus' Lib. 5. cap. 25 and 26, p. 438. Ed. Grabe. cited by Bishop Newton.

Speaking of the "last ten kings among whom that kingdom," i. e. the Roman Empire, "shall be divided, upon whom the son of perdition shall come, saith that ten horns shall grow on the beast, and another little horn shall grow up among them, and three of the first horns shall be rooted out before him. Of whom the Apostle Paul also speaketh in his Second Epistle to the Thessalonians, calling him '*the son of perdition*' and '*that wicked one*.' So St. John, our Lord's disciple, hath in the Apocalypse still more plainly signified of the last time and of these ten kings, among whom the empire that now reigneth," i. e. the Roman, "shall be divided, explaining what the ten horns shall be which were seen by Daniel."

The foregoing might be relied upon as conclusive of our first *Proposition;* indeed, it is so. But, as there are features pertaining to the Apocalyptic *beast* that do not belong to the fourth *beast* of Daniel, 7th, it is proper to state that each of these is characteristically symbolic of some state, condition, or attribute of the subject matter typified, namely, the Roman Empire, prospective and retrospective.

These additional features are the *"seven heads," "the head wounded to death," " the ten crowns," " the names of blasphemy," " like unto a leopard," " the mouth of a lion,"* and *"the feet of a bear."*

Each of these is significant.

This complex symbol of the Apocalyptic *beast* receives a full and satisfactory explanation, with all its subordinate parts, upon the supposition that our *first proposition is true.*

It will now be shown that, independent of all that has gone before, this symbol of the BEAST, Rev. 13th, most fully illustrates and establishes the *main proposition,* i. e. that the *Roman Empire* must be *revived,* in order that the *scriptures may be fulfilled.* And,

1. There is here symbolized a universal *secular* monarchy, and the last upon the earth.

2. "Name of blasphemy"—this monarchy will prove to be the agent of satanic influence.

3. *The seven heads* symbolize seven forms of administration.

4. The ten horns of the beast symbolize the ten kingdoms which, under an imperial head, shall constitute the coming imperial confederacy; and, therefore, the *Roman Empire* under its last form.

5. The seven mountains, or hills, upon which the city of Rome—the capital, and that from which the nation was named—was built, are identified; and, therefore, the *Roman Empire* must be referred to.

EVIDENCE FROM PROPHECY. 65

6. The head of the beast, that was wounded to death, and the deadly wound healed, refers *to imperial Rome.*

7. Because the coming *monster* will establish the worship of the imperial image, after the fashion of the old *Roman Emperors.*

In presenting the proof from the *Prophecies* in support of the above propositions, it is intended that the conclusions shall be perfectly satisfactory and without a peradventure. That the evidence shall be sufficient to produce conviction in the mind of every candid and sincere believer in the authenticity and infallibility of *Divine Revelation.* The attention, therefore, of the reader is most earnestly invited to the subject, which, from its nature, requires some degree of patience and careful investigation. This is the more desirable, since there is a system and harmony in Divine Revelation which does not appear to the casual and superficial reader, and can only be apprehended by careful study and comparison of the different parts of the Bible as a whole.

CHAPTER VI.

FURTHER EVIDENCE FROM PROPHECY.

1. The apocalyptic *beast*, Rev. 13th, symbolizes a *universal secular monarchy* and the last on earth.

The reader will have observed, that in the prophecies above cited, the remarkable personage, who shall exercise the supreme authority in the state is chiefly brought to view, but not without such qualifying circumstances as connect him with the secular power or empire.

The two are inseparable, the empire can not exist without an emperor, and conversely an emperor exist without an empire, which he either represents or claims to represent or rules. Notice the following passages, as in point: "And power was given unto him, to continue forty and two months." Here it is the individual; but it is said of him, in the same context: "And it was given unto him to make war with the saints and to overcome them." This implies that he is the commander of armies. Of the little horn it is said, before cited: "He shall subdue three kings—kingdoms." Here it is the individual again, but the passage further implies that he shall head an army, as a conqueror, and subdue kingdoms, and acquire an ascendency over them, establishing an empire. And therefore, he will be the head of an empire, composed not only of three kingdoms, reduced to submit to his rule, but of ten kingdoms, over which he will become the supreme head. Dan. 7.

The Apocalyptic beast, $\theta\eta\rho\iota o\nu$ described in the passage above cited—Rev. 13 : 1—9, symbolizes a *secular power*. For a beast, i. e. a *wild beast*, must be universally regarded in the scriptures, as symbolizing a secular monarchy or kingdom. Usually an infidel, idolatrous and persecuting power. Daniel beheld in a night vision, the sea agitated by the four winds, and while rolling up its angry surges and dashing their white crested waves against the shore, there came up out of the floods four beasts of diversified appearance. The explanation that follows in the same chapter, Dan. 7, shows, that the four beasts symbolized four universal monarchies, namely, the Babylonian, the Medo-Persian, the Grecian and lastly the Roman Empire. The sea disturbed continually by currents and the force of the elements is the fit symbol of the people in their original capacity of communities, and shows that each of these monarchies symbolized by the beasts seen coming up out of the sea, agitated by a storm, fit emblem, came into existence by virtue of revolution and conquest, and not by succession or hereditary right, or according to a method prescribed in any organic law. They each rose up by virtue of the power conferred by conquest and superior strength. These are attributes of a secular power alone. So in the Apocalypse—John stood on the sands of the sea, in vision, and saw arise out of the sea, the beast under consideration. This like the four beasts above, rose up out of the sea. This therefore symbolizes a secular power, or monarchy, also the fruit of revolution and conquest.

In the explanation given, it is said, "these great beasts, which are four, are four kings, which shall arise out of the earth," i. e. the people of the earth. · "But the saints of the *Most High* shall take the kingdom and shall possess the kingdom, for ever, even for ever and ever." Dan. 7: 17, 18.

NOTE.—Θηριον.—A wild beast in opposition to domestic animals generally, and such is the force of the corresponding Hebrew word. Dan. 7.

Each of these have passed away, except the fourth, which is now in a state of abeyance, but must appear again in its last state. They were each persecuting powers, pagan and idolatrous in character. These are their inseparable attributes, and will continue to characterize the last representation until the *saints* of the *Most High* shall take the kingdom. The Babylonians persecuted the Jews, subverted the nation, and destroyed the temple. Cyrus and his successors, out of selfish motives, assisted a colony of Jews to rebuild the temple and the city of Jerusalem; but nevertheless, they permitted the surrounding nations to harass them in the work. These pagan monarchies ever regarded the Jews with a jealous and hostile eye. The Seluscidæ, especially Antiochus Epiphanes, harassed and cruelly persecuted the Jews. So the Romans, persecuted both Jews and Christians.* These four universal gentile monarchies all, ever showed hostility toward the people who acknowledged and worshiped the true God and eschewed idolatry, whether Jews or Christians. Such are the facts of history, pagan apologists to the contrary notwithstanding. These four monarchies must continue in the one capacity or another, as before stated, until the saints of the Most High shall take the kingdom,—the word kingdom is used as synonymous with universal monarchy. The kingdom of the saints of the *Most High* will not come into existence by gradual

---

*NOTE.—Some have maintained that the old Romans were tolerant toward foreign or strange religious worship, and therefore, not a persecuting people. That such was not the case, the following passage from, Cicero *de legg*, 11 c 8, s, shows. "Separatim nemo habesset deos, neve novos sed ne advenas nisi publice adscistos, privatim colunto." No one was permitted to have deities of his own choice. New and strange gods were not allowed to be worshiped unless previously approved in a public manner.

growth, but by the sudden revelation of the Lord from heaven. There is no compatability between the persecuting idolatrous reign of the gentiles and the kingdom of God on earth. The one must yield instantaneously, and give place when the "Lord of Lords and the King of Kings shall appear to assert his rightful authority." As God's chosen people, the Jews, preferred the ways of the gentiles to the ways of God. He turned the government of the earth over to the gentiles, that they might rule over them; but when He shall again take unto Himself His great power to reign, He will assert His right to the exclusion of all rivalry. God does not compromise with sin. "Thou sawest till that a stone was cut out without hands, which *smote* the *image* upon his feet, that were of iron and clay, and brake them to pieces. Then was the iron, the clay, the brass, the silver and the gold broken to pieces together, and became like the chaff of the summer threshing floors; and the wind carried them away that no place was found for them; and the stone that *smote the image*, became a great mountain and filled the whole earth." Dan. 2: 34, 35.

The destruction will be sudden. By one concussion, all the subsisting and remaining elements of these four great and universal monarchies will be dashed to pieces, reduced to nonentity and swept away from the face of the earth. The kingdom of the saints of the Most High will be ushered in suddenly, "as the lightning cometh out of the east, even unto the west, so shall also the coming of the Son of Man be"—sudden as a flash of lightning, shall all that remains of these four idolatrous, persecuting kingdoms be swept away. The Roman Empire is represented in its successive stages of existence, as a *secular power*, by the fourth beast above referred to. First the body armed with great iron teeth and nails of brass to break in pieces everything that might oppose its will. So did the Romans. A beast—a wild beast—therefore, is a symbol of a universal secular monarchy. Fierce, rapacious and cruel, fit representative of the monsters, who have trodden down the feeble nations, and domineered over them. God looks upon them as beasts. Therefore the *revived Roman Empire*, which will prove to be the culmination of atrocity in governments, is symbolized by the apocalyptic beast.

We are aware that there is a class of interpreters who maintain that the apocalyptic beast we are considering typifies the Roman Hierarchy or Papacy. This is an assumption, and results from a misunderstanding of the scriptures, and is one of the fruits of a false system, and is contradicted by the very language of the prophecy. For Rev. 17: 37, it is said: "And the angel said unto me," (John, the revelator,) "wherefore dost thou marvel? I will tell thee the mystery of the woman and the beast that carrieth her, which hath the seven heads and the ten horns." Here is the same beast we are considering, carrying an abandoned woman—universally regarded as the symbol of an apostate ecclesiastical body—in the Old Testament as well as in the New. The Papacy is nowhere referred to in the Apocalypse, except under this symbol of an harlot; and indeed nowhere in the prophecies. To make the beast that carries the woman the symbol of the Roman Hierarchy, would be to confound the two, and to make the woman and the beast that carried her one and the same animal, which would be an absurdity. And further, the ten horns of the beast are parts of him. These symbolize ten confederated kings, who shall be of *"one mind with the beast and give their power unto him;" showing most perfect accord.*

"And the ten horns which thou sawest upon the beast, these shall hate the whore and shall make her desolate and naked,

and shall eat her flesh and burn her with fire." Rev. 17: 14. The ten horns, which pertain to the beast, shall wage a war of extermination against the woman. Which shows, that if the beast should symbolize the Roman Hierarchy, and the abandoned woman also symbolize the Roman Hierarchy, as she certainly does, it would lead to the absurdity of the same power making war upon and devouring itself. Therefore, the apocalyptic beast can not symbolize the Papacy. But the confederacy symbolized by the apocalyptic beast, under consideration, consisting of the ten kingdoms, under the imperial head, shall make war upon and exterminate the Papacy. It will in fact aim to extirpate all existing forms of Theism.

So this beast can not symbolize the Papacy. Neither, therefore, can the little horn of Dan. 7th symbolize the Papacy, nor can the two-horned beast, Rev. 13: 11, symbolize the Papacy, for this beast will sustain a close relation to and act in conjunction with the first beast. Rev. 13: 1.

2. *That the apocalyptic beast above cited, Rev. 13: 1—9, symbolizes the Roman Empire, because the power pointed out will be the medium and agent of the great red dragon, and therefore of satanic influence, through which Satan will attempt to accomplish his purposes of wrath on the earth in the last times.*

In the passage cited above it is said: "And the dragon, i. e. that old serpent, the devil, gave him (the beast,) his power and his seat and great authority." Rome was from the first the habitation of the devil, his peculiar tabernacle. Satan as the prince of this world, will abdicate his seat (throne) in favor of, and will confer his power and authority upon the beast. Upon the rapture of the Church, Satan will be cast out upon the earth with his angels, and will have supreme control, all opposing influences being removed. "That which letteth (restraineth) shall be taken out of the way." 2 Thess. 2: 7. Satan, by apostolic authority, is styled "the prince of the power of the air," "the spirit that now worketh in the children of disobedience." Signifying not only that he controls the current of influences that sway the minds of evil men, and gives direction and force to the ideas and sentiments that actuate them, but that his sphere is not confined to this lower world. Of the Christian's warfare it is said: "*We wrestle not with flesh and blood*," but that the struggle is with "principalities and powers, with spiritual *wickedness in high places.*" *Principalities and powers, spiritual wickedness in high places*, are understood as referring to super-mundane influences. God, for wise purposes, has not restricted the theater of satanic action to this world alone. In the book of Job we read that God permitted Satan to appear on a certain day, before Him, among the sons of God. Where was this assembly of the sons of God? And who are these sons of God?

At the creation it is said: "*When the morning stars sang together and all the sons of God shouted for joy.*" If this be a sufficient answer, then the sons of God are in heaven, and Satan appears there also. Of this the following passages are decisive: "*And there was war in heaven. Michael and his angels fought against the dragon; and the dragon fought and his angels, and prevailed not; neither was their place found any more in heaven. And the great dragon was cast out, that old serpent, called the Devil and Satan, which deceiveth the whole world; he was cast out into the earth and his angels were cast out with him.*" Rev. 12: 7, 9.

Satan cast out upon the earth, and his sphere of action restricted, thereto dire calamities will follow. "Wo to the inhabiters of the earth, and of the sea! for the devil is come down unto you, having great wrath, because he knoweth that he hath but a short time." Verse 12. By these scriptures we learn that the earth will become the theater of satanic influence and power under circumstances which bode evil to the inhabitants thereof. But Satan must have an agent and medium, by and through which to act. He will therefore, for this purpose, confer his seat, (throne) and his power and authority upon the beast. Hence, the imperial head and every department and agency of the coming Empire, symbolized by the beast, will be thoroughly permeated by satanic influence, and will become the *medium* for the propagation of satanic wrath.

The Old Roman Empire was always from the first the instrument of Satan. Idolatry was established with the foundation of the city of Rome. Idolatrous ceremonies and rules for the regulation of the worship of the various false gods, are interwoven among the first rudiments of the State.

The worship of pagan deities was nothing less than the worship of devils. The State was dedicated to Satan in the character of Jupiter Stator and became under his control, so far as Divine Providence permitted, from the very first. Rev. 12: 3, it is said:

"*And there appeared another wonder in heaven; and behold, a great red dragon, having seven heads and ten horns, and seven crowns upon his heads. And his tail drew the third part of the stars of heaven, and did cast them to the earth.*"

Here we have the prototype of the beast with the seven heads and the ten horns. The seven crowns upon his heads indicating that the executive authority resided in each of the seven, and as the seven heads symbolize the seven forms of executive administration of the government, under which the Roman State successively existed, the great red dragon was the inspiring genius of the Roman Empire through the entire period of its history. The final form of the Roman Empire yet to come, is brought prominently into view by the ten horns. That the great red dragon typifies the invisible, inspiring genius of old imperial Rome, is further and conclusively shown by the following from Rev. 12: 1:

By the vision of the woman, clothed with the sun and the moon under her feet, being in the pains of child-birth: "And she brought forth a *man-child, who was to rule all nations with a rod of iron*; and the dragon stood before the woman which was ready to be delivered, for to devour the child as soon as it was born." Verse 4.

Now there can be no question as to whom this man-child refers. The same as referred to by the prophet Isaiah, 9: 6: "Unto us a child is born, unto us a son is given."

That the Lord Jesus therefore is the man-child referred to, there is no question.

Now what power stood ready to destroy the infant Jesus as soon as born? The Roman power, in the person of its agent Herod. Herod at this time held his crown as the direct gift of Augustus. After the battle of Actium, he visited Augustus at Rhods, and surrendered to him his crown. Augustus restored it back to him. So Herod the Great—great in enormities—was the direct agent of the Roman Emperor Augustus. Therefore the great red dragon, through Herod, the instrument of the Roman Emperor sought to destroy the young child Jesus as soon as he was born; but Divine Providence directed otherwise.

There is, therefore, no question but that the Roman Empire is pointed out by this symbol, having always been the medium and agent, through and by which Satan has afflicted the earth, and especially the worshipers of the true

God. Fit anti-type of the great red dragon. Red with the blood of saints and martyrs. Drenched with the blood of millions slaughtered in wars of conquest for the sake of dominion over the earth.

We have therefore shown that the old Roman Empire was the appropriate agent of Satan, and is consequently properly symbolized by the great red dragon; and as the dragon gave the apocalyptic beast his power and his seat, (throne) and great authority, so this beast symbolizes a power which will prove to be the agent of Satan, and therefore, this power will be the *Roman Empire* in its revival and last state on earth.

CHAPTER VII.

FURTHER EVIDENCE FROM PROPHECY.

3. *"Having seven heads."* Rev. 13: 1.

A head symbolizes the executive or supreme power in the State. The golden head of the metalic image symbolized Nebuchadnezzar king of Babylon. *" Thou art this head of gold.*

The supreme, or executive power in the State, may be exercised by one only, and often is, or by many individuals, according, as provided in the organic law of the State, either written or by custom, or by common consent. When by one only, he is styled a king or emperor, sometimes a dictator, when by more than one, the executive authority may be vested in, and exercised by consuls, decemviri or tribunes, as was the case at Rome. There were other forms, but these were the most common among the nations of antiquity.

The seven heads of the apocalyptic beast indicate that the supreme executive power in the Roman Commonwealth shall have been exercised during its historic existence, under seven different forms of government. The supreme or executive head, usually *denominates*, and otherwise, determines the *form* of government. Five forms of government had existed at Rome and passed away, and a sixth was in full power at the time this Apocalyptic vision was disclosed to the revelator on the Isle of Patmos, in the Ægean sea, A. D. 96, in the reign of the Emperor Domitian. The seventh form has not yet appeared on earth, of this there is doubt, but its duration will be brief. There will be an eighth and final. This shall partake of the characteristics of the seven above symbolized by the seven heads of the beast, blending the *peculiarities* of each of the seven, forming a distinct and *terrible power on earth*, but not presenting any original forms of government, distinct from what had already gone before, but rather resuscitating and imparting vitality to forms of ancient date.

These ideas are brought more fully into view by the following explanation given by the angel to the revelator; Rev. 17 : 7.

"*I will tell thee the mystery of the beast, which hath the seven heads and ten horns.*"

8 "The beast that thou sawest was, and is not; and shall ascend out of the bottomless pit, and go into perdition; and they that dwell on the earth shall wonder, whose names were not written in the book of life from the foundation of the world, when they behold the beast that was, and is not, and yet is.

9 "And here is the mind which hath wisdom. The seven heads are seven mountains, on which the woman sitteth.

10 "And there are seven kings; five are fallen, and one is, and the other is not yet come; and when he cometh, he must continue a short space.

11 "And the beast that was, and is not, even he is the eighth, and is of the seven, and goeth into perdition.

12 "And the ten horns which thou sawest are ten kings, which have received no kingdom as yet; but receive power as kings one hour with the beast." Rev. 17 : 8–12.

How graphic this description. *The beast that thou sawest was, and is not, and shall ascend out of the bottomless pit, and go into perdition.*" Brief, but terrible will be the career of the *revived Roman* power in its last form. A power whose history extended through more than twenty centuries, has disappeared from the earth. It has no longer any visible organization to represent it, among the nations. Yet in the contemplation of prophecy, it still subsists, though in abeyance, so far as an organized form; nevertheless, like a sleeping giant, its repose is not without signs of vitality, only temporarily suppressed. This giant will arouse himself again, to the amazement of the inhabitants of the whole world.

The seven mountains, of the *above* cited passage identify the site of the city of Rome, and therefore the power, which also derived its name therefrom, beyond controversy.

But, further of the seven heads. "*There are seven kings.*" King here is used to denote the executive head of a government.

NOTE.—"*Five are fallen and one is,* and the other is not yet come, and when he cometh, he must continue a short space." "And the beast that was, and is not, even he is the eighth, and is of the seven, (ἐκ τῶν ἑπτα) and goeth into perdition."

Five forms had passed into Roman history, when this revelation was received A. D. 96, and the seventh should when come, be of short duration. But the eighth head that shall ascend out of the bottomless pit, Rev. 9: 2, and go into perdition, symbolizes the coming revived and resuscitated Roman imperial power with its confederated kings, and especially its executive head—*That man of sin, the son of perdition.*

The introductory passage of the historian Tacitus to the Annals, is so pertinent to this place, that I can not forbear citing the whole passage. I therefore claim the reader's indulgence.

"Urbem Romam a principio reges habuere. Libertatem et consulatem L. Brutus instituit. Dictaturæ ad tempus sumebantur, neque Decemviralis potestas ultra biennium neque Tribunorum militum consulare jus diu valuit. Non Cinnæ, non Sullæ longa dominatio ; et Pompeii Crassisque potentia cito in Cæsarem, Lepidi atque Antonii arma in Augustum cessere: qui cuncta, discordiis civilibus fessa, nomine *Principis* sub imperium accepit." Lib. 1. Cap. 1.

Here are six forms of government, under which the affairs of Rome had been administered, from the founding of the city up to the time of Tacitus, which was some years subsequent to the date of the revelation given to St. John on the Isle of Patmos. Livy mainly agrees with Tacitus.

Tacitus here states:

1. "That the kings exercised supreme power over the Roman city, at the beginning.

2. "Next was the consular form of government. For, '*Lucius Brutus established liberty and the consulate.*'

3. "The dictators assumed for a time the chief management of affairs.

4. "Neither was the power of the Decemvirs of longer duration than two years.

5. "Nor did the law investing the supreme power in the Tribunes of the soldiers avail very long, in providing for the direction of public affairs.

6. "The usurpation of Cinna and of Sylla was of short duration, and the power of Pompey and Crassus quickly gave place to that of Cæsar. The arms of Lepidus and Antony were vanquished by Augustus, who received all things weary of civil strife into the empire, under himself as chief."

It would almost seem as if the spirit of inspiration had guided the pen of this pagan author.

The learned Faber professes to see another form of

governmental administration in the above cited passage from Tacitus, namely, that of Triumvirs, consisting of Pompey, Crassus and Cæsar. But a careful scrutiny of the above cited passage does not justify any such conclusion. The power of Pompey and Crassus quickly gave place to that of Cæsar, (which is a fair translation of the original,) would imply, that these three distinguished Romans were rather acting in hostility towards each other, than in concert.

There have not been wanting historians, who have sought to dignify the combination between these three powerful chiefs, with the name of Triumvirate, but they were never so recognized publicly.

The following from Ernesti, (Note on T. in loco,) seems to put the matter to rest: "Nam Cæsar, Pompieus et Crassus tantum privatim potentiæ societatem inter se inierant, neque aut publico aliquo scito accepere, aut nomine triumvirorum usi sunt." It was a private association for the promotion of their own power in the State; they were neither called to, nor did they accept any such office from the public, nor even use the name of Triumvirs.

It was nothing more than a political combination in the State for their mutual aggrandizement. And as the history of the times shows, each sought to supplant the other, and to attain to supreme power by the destruction of his rivals. So the power of Pompey and Crassus quickly yielded to the superior ability and good fortune of Cæsar.

The usurpation of Cinna and Sylla was an abuse of the consular authority by the one, and the exercise of dictatorial authority by the other, both of these forms of government are enumerated by Tacitus and Livy as having existed previously in the State.

Tacitus refers to the combination between Crassus,

Pompey and Cæsar as of short duration, and broken up by strife among its members. To dignify this combination into a distinct form of government, or to regard it as possessing any of the attributes of a government, its power in the State being that of influence alone, would imply a disregard of the facts of the times. During this combination, the affairs of the government were conducted as usual under the auspices of the Senate and Tribunes. Cæsar acted in the name and by virtue of the *authority of the Senate* and Roman people, and so did each of the others, namely, Crassus and Pompey.

The sovereignty previous to the Empire was vested in the Roman people, considered in their capacity of the three tribes, namely, the Patrician, Equestrian and the Plebian. The Tribunes represented the Roman people. This was the form of government during the period we are considering. The acts of the Roman Senate were liable to be vetoed by the Tribunes, from which veto there was no relief but by an appeal to the Comitiæ; the Comitiæ was the body of the whole people represented by their three tribes, voting as such. From the veto of the Tribunes there was no relief, but by an appeal to the Comitiæ or the sword.

This clearly appears from the proceedings which led to the *civil war*, when the friends of Pompey and the enemies of Cæsar had succeeded, by intimidation and terrorism, in carrying their measures, hostile to Cæsar, through the Senate, the Tribunes interposed their veto. The partisans of Pompey were all powerful at Rome. The confusion and excitement were great. The Tribunes, therefore, fled to the camp of Cæsar for safety. Cæsar marched directly for Rome, and the civil war commenced. Bello Civili, L. 1, S. 5—et seq.

The attempt, therefore, to magnify this combination of three, the most powerful persons at Rome, into a distinct form of government, and therefore to show that there were six before the Empire, is illusory. There was no decree of the Senate conferring civil power upon the triumvirate. No vote by the Comitiæ. It is true that Cæsar, Crassus and Pompey could carry through the Senate any measure they might desire to have adopted, but it was purely by their powerful influence.

The subsequent combinations between Antony, Augustus and Lepidus were only temporary, and led directly to the Empire. In fact the Empire commenced with the great Julius. Augustus was appointed his heir by will, and therefore was allowed to succeed to the supreme authority with little or no opposition after the battle of Actium.

If, therefore, five forms of *civil administration or heads* had existed at Rome, and passed away and given place to the sixth, that is the imperial, at the time this revelation was given to John on the Isle of Patmos, and the seventh had not yet come as we are informed, the seven heads identify, with absolute, moral certainty, the apocalyptic beast as symbolizing the Roman Empire.

But as this argument upon the *"seven heads"* is entirely independent, and therefore the more conclusive and satisfactory, we will give a brief summary of the duration of these different forms of government.

1. The kings came into power with the founding of the city of Rome, B. C. 753, and continued 245 years and until B. C. 508.

2. Immediately after the expulsion of Tarquin, the last of the old Roman kings, Brutus and Collatinus were chosen Consuls, B. C. 508. The consular government continued in all about eleven years, but the office of consul ever after remained as a military office and subordinate to the civil, until merged into the emperor.

3. Titus Lærtius was the first dictator, B. C. 497. This office, like that of the consular, continued in the State, but for the most part dormant, until merged into the imperial, B. C. 27.

4. The Decemvirate commenced B. C. 451.

On motion of Appius Claudius that ten persons be chosen out of the body of the Senate, who for one year should be invested with an authority from which there should be no appeal. By the arbitrary and libidinous conduct of Appius Claudius toward the damsel Virginia, this form of administration was cut short. The tragical death of Virginia by the hands of her own father and the indignation of the Romans against Claudius, obliterated this form of government forever.

It continued little over two years, B. C. 448.

5. The office of Tribunes as a power in the State, grew out of the terrible excitement among the people at Rome, caused by the death of Virginia, by which the Decemvirs were forced into banishment.

They first came into power about B. C. 444.

The office at the beginning was both civil and military. The military functions were subsequently laid aside, and became the chief attribute of the consular, and were under the civil power. The Tribunes, as the representatives of the Roman people, exercised the supreme civil authority in the State. They had the veto power over the acts of the Senate and participated in the deliberations of that body, but were responsible to the people alone.

The Roman Senate was a hereditary body, and therefore a constant and unchanging element in the government of the State. Under all changes and vicissitudes the Senate remained the same or nearly so. Its power at times was almost without any check, and therefore absolute.

The supreme executive authority of the government, whether that of the kings or consuls, dictators, decemvirs or tribunes, characterized and *denominated the form of government for the time*. The Roman Senate continued even under the Empire to be the most grave and dignified body on earth, renowned for its wisdom and for perpetuating the majesty of the old Roman character.

The Revelator uses the words *"seven kings"* in the passages above cited as identical with the *"seven heads"* placed at the head of this article, as more expressive and as explanatory of the idea of an executive head or department of government. Of the seven forms of administration symbolized by the seven kings, we have identified the five that had existed and passed into history, and the sixth in power A. D. 96 and many centuries after. The seventh foretold, as then, yet in the future. The eighth which shall partake of the peculiarities of the seven, will be the last and final form of government under which the Roman power shall exist.

If, therefore, six forms have been identified, six-sevenths of the prophecy has been accomplished. Skepticism will scarcely interpose a doubt, but that the remainder will be strictly accomplished. Indeed the seventh has already been accomplished in the brief but wonderful career of the great Napoleon, as thoughtful men have supposed. We wait in expectation for the eighth. Indeed there are strong reasons to believe that the inception of the eighth already appears above the horizon, if we rightly interpret the signs of the times.

4. *"And ten horns and ten crowns upon his horns."* Rev. 13: 1.

If a person should take the pains to consult a number of treatises on different branches of the common law for instance, he would find that certain fundamental principles of law are frequently brought into review, for the purpose of demonstration or illustration, as the discussion advances, even though the books may have been written at periods some centuries remote from each other.

So in revelation, certain leading thoughts or subjects of revelation are frequently brought to view. This may be verified by a very slight examination of the gospels or epistles, and it is no less the case in reference to the prophecies. Certain events, yet in the future, are referred to by the most ancient prophets, and again by others of less remote date, incidentally by our Lord, by the Apostle Paul, and finally in the apocalyptic visions of St. John. The visions of the Revelator are final and complete, given under symbolic figures, the meaning becomes intelligible and precise in the light of the prophecies that go before.

A horn, by the coincident explanation throughout the prophecies, is the symbol of a power, usually of a secular power or kingdom. Ps. 132: 17; Jer. 48: 38; Ezek. 29: 21; Dan. 7: 7, 8; 8: 3, 5; Rev. 12: 3; 13: 1, 11: Rev. 17: 3, et al.

The symbol of the ten horns occurs frequently, both in Daniel and the Apocalypse; and in each instance point out the same ten kingdoms pertaining to, and forming essential constituents of the Roman Empire, in its last state as a power on earth.

The identity in symbolic import of the "*ten horns*" on the fourth beast, Dan. 7th, and the ten horns of the apocalyptic beast, Rev. 13: 1, is evident from the identity of the fourth beast of Daniel and the apocalyptic beast, as shown in a former part of this work. And as this fourth beast has been shown to symbolize the Roman Empire, so must the ten horns point out ten kingdoms connected with that power.

The little horn, Dan. 7: 8, shall acquire an ascendency and dominion over all, forming a confederation, which shall last until the saints of the Most High shall take the kingdom.

The ten horns of the apocalyptic beast, Rev. 13: 1, have an additional symbol, very significant, namely, "*upon the horns ten crowns.*" These are explanatory and point out crowned heads. We now begin to see more clearly the character of the coming power, that it will be an *imperial confederation*. The present powers, which have grown up out of the fragments of the old Roman Empire and other commingling elements, are under the rule of crowned heads. The exceptions are merely temporary.

These consolidated under one powerful, daring and innovating, blasphemous head, and the empire symbolized by the apocalyptic beast, becomes a reality.

"And the ten horns which thou sawest are ten kings, which have received no kingdom as yet; but receive power as kings one hour with the beast. These have one mind and shall give their power and strength unto the beast. * * * For God hath put it into their hearts, to fulfill his will, and to agree and give their kingdom unto the beast, until the words of God shall be fulfilled." Rev. 17: 12, 13, 17.

Here it is explicitly stated, that there shall be ten kings or kingdoms, for the one implies the other. They existed only in the contemplation of prophecy, A. D. 96. They will come to maturity in the fullness of time.

These ten kingdoms shall give their power and strength to the antitype of the beast. This, by an agreement among themselves. A power thus constituted could be nothing less than an empire, composed of ten kingdoms, all acting in harmony, under a leader, who possessed the confidence, or was able to compel the compliance of all the subordinates.

This is the character then, which the Roman Empire, which must exist, as repeatedly shown, until the kingdom of the Most High shall come, will assume in the last days of the *times of the gentiles*. The head will be that *terrible character*, to whom Satan will give his throne and power on earth, whose coming is after the working of Satan, with all power and signs and lying wonders—a very incarnation of the evil one.

A principle may be expressed in different phraseology, by different authors, at different times, in different countries, in diverse languages, and in remote localities; but it is at once recognized as the same principle as soon as stated.

So it is respecting this most remarkable character, who shall for a short time exercise such a terrible power over the destinies of men. Whenever this character appears in the prophecies, either of the Old or New Testament, he is at once recognized. There is *but one such*. If any one doubts this, let him consult the following: Dan. 7: 25, Rev. 13: 6, 7, 2. Thess. 2: 2—7. Rev. 16: 10, 11—17: 14, also as the fruit of his doings. Dan. 12: 1, Math. 24: 21, 22. There is another character, who will sustain a subordinate relation to him, symbolized by the two-horned beast, Rev. 13: 16. These will act in concert. The latter acting by virtue of the authority conferred by the first, and in furtherance of the imperial policy, is referred to as a distinct person, in a few passages it would seem, especially in his conduct toward the Jews, out of which nation he shall arise—but will act as the chief counselor in matters of worship, at least of the first.

5. "*And here is the mind which hath wisdom.*" "*The seven heads are seven mountains on which the woman sitteth.*" Rev. 17: 9.

The first clause:—*Here is the mind which hath wisdom—*

points to something enigmatical, or hidden as to the sense, and is intended to arrest the attention and direct the mind to something implied under the figures, which does not clearly at first appear, but requires some deliberation, or perhaps research, to discover.

The seven mountains have doubtless a double symbolic signification. First, that in the purposes of Divine Providence, the city built upon the seven mountains should become the metropolis of the world and the capital of a government, which should be administered during the period of its history under seven different forms or constitutions. And second, that the seven mountains should so identify the symbol of *the woman* as to leave no doubt that the city of Rome was intended. v. 18. "And the woman which thou sawest is that great city, which reigneth over the kings of the earth." And further, as the seven heads belong to the scarlet colored beast upon which the woman was seen sitting, that that scarlet beast must symbolize no other than imperial Rome. Scarlet is the imperial color. To obtain the scarlet at Rome was to attain unto the imperial crown.

That *the seven heads*, and *the seven kings*, are identical, the latter explanatory of the former, has been shown in the former section. An additional reason is afforded by the obvious identity in import of the following passages:

"*I saw one of his heads as it were wounded to death; and his deadly wound was healed: and all the world wondered after the beast.*" Rev. 13: 3.

Again, "*The beast that thou sawest, was, and is not; and shall ascend out of the bottomless pit, and go into perdition: and they that dwell on the earth shall wonder, when they behold the beast, that was, and is not, and yet is.*" Rev. 17: 8.

These two passages can not be otherwise than coincident

in meaning. They refer to the same great historical truth, six-sevenths of which have already been accomplished. That the Roman Empire, after existing many centuries, should cease from among the powers of earth to all appearance, having no visible organization to represent it, but should yet come into the ascendency again, to the astonishment and awe of the inhabitants of the whole world.

As the head is a vital part, this wounded to death, the beast would cease to exist, but as the head denotes a form of government, only one head could be in the ascendant at one and the same time. But only one head was wounded to death by the sword.

Therefore, these passages each refer to the temporary subversion of the Roman power by the sword, which has happened; and to its revival again, in coming time, under circumstances which shall invest the event with great éclat before the world.

The passage cited at the head of this section is evidently intended, by the spirit of inspiration, to so connect all parts with, as to conclusively denominate the antitype of the beast, and the several dependent and accessory institutions, symbolized thereby. It affords a clear solution, expressed in figurative language it is true, of the import of this complicated symbol. The woman typifies the city Rome. It would be absurd to say that a literal woman sits on seven mountains. The metaphor is obvious. It is the city, that sat on her seven hills, or mountains, and ruled the world, that is intended. All follows in logical succession. The beast symbolizes a Roman power, all his subordinate parts are Roman. Even the woman symbolizes the Roman Papacy, as a woman is the symbol of an ecclesiastic body, exclusively.

6. "*I saw one of his heads as it were wounded to death; and his deadly wound was healed.*" Rev. 13: 3.

This passage has been partly considered in the preceding section. It is proposed here to look more fully into its historical fulfillment. It has already been stated that it was the sixth or imperial head that had been wounded to death. The former five existing *constitutions* of the Roman Commonwealth had been changed, or suppressed in succession, by civil revolutions in the State. But the sixth, or imperial, was stricken down by the sword, and departed only with the subversion of the State itself, as an organized power among the nations.

Some interpreters, zealous to maintain a preconceived theory, have sought to make it appear that it was the seventh head that received the deadly wound by the sword; and that this seventh head typified the first Napoleon, who was finally vanquished in the battle of Waterloo, June 18, 1815. This Napoleonic power was truly literally slain by the sword. This class therefore look for the eighth soon to arise under a Napoleon, or some such character. An imperial power formed after the pattern of the brief Napoleonic confederation. This is not improbable. But this expectation stands independent of any connection with the above stated theory as to the seventh head.

This theory that it was the seventh head that was wounded to death involves the necessity of showing that there was a continued succession of live heads to the Roman power until the time of Napoleon the First. For only one head could exist at one and the same time, and only one was wounded to death; whereas history shows that the Roman Empire ceased to exist some centuries before the time of the great Napoleon. As a secular power, it disappeared in the West with the last of the western emperors Augustulus, i. e. the little Augustus, A. D. 479. The Senate by a solemn act, disclaimed the necessity of any longer continuing the imperial succession in Italy.

In their own name, and in the name of the Roman People, they consent that the seat of universal empire shall be transferred from Rome to Constantinople. The rightful imperial head had been doubtless slain at the sacking of the city eight years before the abdication of Augustulus.

This was a weak prince; a mere tool in the hands of his unprincipled father, Orestes, by whom he had been set up for the purposes of usurpation. Orestes, the father, who was the real ruler, was put to death by Odoacier. Augustulus threw himself upon the clemency of Odoacier, his father's murderer, and was granted his life upon consideration of his resigning his official title of Emperor of the West.

The invasion and conquest of the city by the Goths and Vandals, the intestine strifes, resulting from the formation of diverse communities of barbarians in Italy, the confusion and insecurity arising from the want of a clearly defined constitution over all, gave rise to almost continual wars and revolutions. The imperial power was literally stricken down by the sword.

The eastern emperors continued for almost one thousand years longer to maintain the dignity and assert the authority of the Roman name at Constantinople. The Senate of Rome had decreed that Constantinople should be the future seat of universal Empire. And here all that remained of the imperial majesty and of the authority of the Roman Empire resided until Constantinople was stormed and captured by the Turks, May 26, A. D. 1453—2206 years after the founding of Rome by Romulus. The last of the eastern emperors, Constantine Palæologus, was slain by an unknown hand, and his body was found under a mountain of the dead. So says the historian Gibbon.

So the Roman power, as a distinct organization, was literally subverted by the force of arms, and the imperial authority stricken down by the sword both in the east and the west.

The Roman authority passed away from the earth as completely to all appearance as that of Cyrus or Alexander, or of the Seleucidæ or Ptolemies. The Roman race, though degenerate, still remained. The Roman law, language, and literature remained; and more potent than all, the renown of the Roman name. But the government had passed away. It was more than 300 years from the abdication of Augustulus to the crowning of Charlemagne, but this has no significance. It was a mere title. It conferred no authority which he did not previously have. The assumption, therefore, of title of Emperor of the Romans did not revive or resuscitate and perpetuate the existence of the Roman Empire.

The crowning of Charlemagne by the Roman Pontiff Leo, was merely a complimentary ceremony. This prince, whose dominions were north of the Alps, was on his fourth pilgrimage to Rome as a religious devotee. The kingly or imperial office can only be acquired in a peaceable way by the laws of nations, through hereditary descent, or be conferred by the suffrages of the people acting in their primary capacity. It can not be bestowed by an individual who has no authority to bestow it. The Roman Pontiff Leo had no such authority. The act of placing a glittering diadem upon the head of the distinguished visitor was a mere ceremony to elicit the applause of the populace, and seems there to have ended

Says the historian Gibbon: "On the festival of Christmas, the last in the eighth century, Charlemagne appeared in the Church of St. Peter's, and to gratify the vanity of Rome, exchanged the simple dress of his country for the habit of a patrician. After the celebration of the holy mysteries, Leo suddenly placed a precious crown on his head, and the dome resounded with the exclamation of the people: '*Long life and victory to Charles, the most pious Augustus crowned by God, the great and pacific Emperor of the Romans.*'"

From this passage it would appear as though it was understood at the time that the title of Emperor of the Romans conferred was the direct gift of God, bestowed through his vicar, the Pope. The fallacy is no less observed than the presumption of the act, offensive to all enlightened minds.

But the organization of what was styled "*the Holy Roman Empire of the German nations,*" was an event of more significance. This occurred not long after the fall of Constantinople. It was a *voluntary* and *spontaneous movement* to form a confederation among the *German princes* and *crowned heads*, primarily for mutual defense against the Turks, under the auspices of the Popes of Rome. The Emperor was elective and the confederation composed at one time of ten electors—kings and princes. The imperial crown of the Holy Roman Empire was finally vested in the House of Austria, and the Empress Maria Theresa was the last to lay claim to the dignity.

This confederation and assumption of the title of Roman seems to have some significance, for its having been the voluntary act of the nations which composed it; yet nevertheless, it was destitute for the most part of the Latin element, and composed of many nations whose territories were chiefly beyond the geographical limits of the old Empire. *Can this be the seventh head?*

The deadly wound was healed. The executive power

therefore, symbolized by this head will arise again, in all its former dignity, with additional pretension. "*And they that dwell on the earth shall wonder—when they behold the beast, that was, and is not, and yet is.*" The beast we have seen symbolizes the State, the head of the ruling power in the State, giving name to the form of government. If the head be slain, the beast dies, as a State can not exist unless under some form of administration. With the revival of the State, the head would necessarily revive also, for the State can not perform the functions of government without an executive head.

The apocalyptic beast symbolizes the Roman power, as before shown by arguments entirely independent of each other. These arguments are strengthened, indeed confirmed, by the foregoing historical summary of the downfall and final subversion of the Roman Empire, both in the west and in the east. But the beast which was, *still is*, and the antitype of which *must come into existence* again; for the head that was wounded to death by the sword did live. When, therefore, the Roman power shall come into the ascendancy, the imperial head will revive.

By the influence of a controlling mind, be he the emperor or chief counselor, rising above the complicated political situation of his time, and severing all connection with established or traditional institutions, taking in the survey of affairs, as a pure materialist, endowed with Satanic energy and sagacity, with the nations ripe for revolution, by the magic effect of a few decisive battles, the political problem of the future will be solved and the coming empire inaugurated.

7. "*Saying to them that dwell on the earth that they should make an image to the beast.*"

The worship of the imperial image was peculiar, or nearly

so, to the old Romans. Other nations bestowed posthumous honors upon heroes, regarding them as having been transferred to a place among the gods at death.

The eastern monarchs demanded servile homage by prostration, it is true, whenever a subject or any one else approached the royal presence; but the worship of a royal or imperial image, does not seem to have prevailed, at least to any great extent. Homage to the image of a living man, was peculiar to Roman demonology. This degrading offspring of gross materialism, and of servile defference to the representative of power, was confined to the Roman nations chiefly.

Homage to the imperial image followed, as a necessary sequence, that spirit of selfish ambition and lust, for exclusive power, tolerating no rival, which characterized the people in all their wars for conquest; a spirit which sought to stamp under foot all opposition and rivalry. Conscious of his supreme authority and elevation over all, the emperor through jealous and selfish vanity demanded divine honor, from his subjects, as a test of loyalty, and a recognition of his supreme dignity. And still the more to remind them of the vast distance, which separated the occupant of the throne, decorated with the diadem and clothed in purple, from the subject, to mark the elevation of the one, and the comparative degradation of the other, he demanded that honor should be paid to the imperial image, as unto a god. Such was the spirit of arrogance and intolerance, which power had engendered in this people. That the imperial image was placed among the images of the gods and worshiped, is shown by an extract from Pliny's letter to Trajan. P. L E. 96.

"*Et imagini Tuæ, quam propter hoc, jusseram cum simulacris numinum afferri, thure et vino supplicarent.*"

Pliny, the younger, who had been appointed governor of Bithynia by the Trajan wrote to this Emperor concerning the course he had pursued at the examination of those accused of being Christians.

I commanded *your image* to be brought forward with the images of the deities, that they might supplicate it with offerings of frankincense and wine. All who refused were led away to execution.

There is not a despot on earth at this time, I believe, however exacting may be the etiquette of his court, or despotic his will, that demands the idolatrous homage of personal image worship.

This imperial image worship, exacted by the old Emperors, will be revived again with the revival of the Roman Empire, and affords an additional reason in favor of the conclusion already arrived at by several independent trains of reasoning, from the scriptures cited, that the first Apocalyptic beast symbolizes the Roman *imperial power:*

11 "And I beheld another beast coming up out of the earth, and he had two horns like a lamb, and he spake as a dragon.

12 "And he exerciseth all the power of the first beast before him, and causeth the earth and them which dwell therein to worship the first beast, whose deadly wound was healed.

13 "And he doeth great wonders, so that he maketh fire come down from heaven on the earth in the sight of men.

14 "And deceiveth them that dwell on the earth by *the means* of those miracles which he had power to do in the sight of the beast; saying to them that dwell on the earth, that they should make an image to the beast, which had the wound by a sword, and did live.

15 "And he had power to give life unto the image of the beast, that the image of the beast should both speak, and cause that as many as would not worship the image of the beast should be killed." Rev. 13: 11-15.

It is true the character symbolized by the second beast, which had the two horns like a lamb and spake as a dragon, will be the active promoter of the worship of the imperial personage symbolized by the first beast, and of his image; but the second person will act in a subordinate relation to the first, and will be invested with extraordinary power, as a prime minister, or some such officer. The scriptures hitherto cited abundantly show that Satan will be the ruling spirit and inspiring agent of the times pointed to in these prophecies. The dragon, that old *serpent*, the *devil* and *Satan*, the deceiver and seducer of the first man, and the enemy and destroyer of his progeny, will take bodily possession of this prototype of the two horned beast, and will put into his mouth demoniacal utterances, and endow him with satanic wisdom, giving him power over material agencies, enabling him to work signs and wonders.

It will be seen that this image worship will be enforced upon all without exception. No one should shrink back, at the thought of the dreadful power of this most extraordinary magician, or juggler, by which he shall cause an image to speak, and to denounce and condemn to death all who will not worship the image. The Egyptian magicians, were allowed to perform miracles before Moses and Aaron. It must be remembered that these will be extraordinary times, and the world on the downward grade, to swift perdition, with Satan at the helm.

So the imperial image worship, which prevailed among the old Romans will be again revived and enforced with more rigor than of old, as it will be made a test, not

9

only of loyalty to the new regime, but of an acquiescence in the new policy, which aims to dethrone God Almighty, and to convert this lower world into a domain of Satan, where he shall rule without a rival.

CHAPTER VIII.

INCIDENTS AND ATTRIBUTES.

There are some additional incidents and attributes connected with the principal symbol presented in the above cited passage, Rev. 13: 1–9, which claim attention.

As the artist intends that every position and attitude on his canvas, as well as every figure should, be significant, so every part of the vision must be regarded as contributing to the complete sense of the whole.

1 *"I stood upon the sand of the sea."*

It has already been intimated that the "sea" symbolizes the people in their primary capacity.

Waters are explained in another place to denote *"peoples and multitudes, and nations and tongues."* The strongest expression for the people universally. As the waters of the sea are liable to be agitated by the movements of currents, and by the action of the winds, and are by these influences kept in almost perpetual commotion, so the people are almost continually agitated by some one of the many exciting topics that come under discussion, and more or less violently, according to the character of the exciting cause. Such excitements sometimes break over all restraints and lead to revolutions.

The *"sand of the sea"* constitutes the shore line. The shore line is the boundary to the waters, the restraining limits beyond which they do not pass, unless forced by some unusual or extraordinary impelling power.

The strength of the shore line depends very much upon the nature of the materials of which it is composed. If of rock, the waves may dash their fury in vain against such a barrier, but if of sand, this line would be easily carried away.

The institutions and laws of a State, as they define and limit the powers and rights of the people, may be fitly represented in the figure of the *sea shore*. While these are maintained in their integrity there is security and stability. When they become corrupt and rotten, they are no longer capable of restraining human passions and of enforcing social order.

Such will be the state of things, out of which the impending revolution, that shall revive and bring into the ascendant the Roman Empire again, will burst forth upon the world, like the upheaval of the volcanic forces from beneath the waters of the ocean, breaking over all barriers of sand.

The corrupt governments with their enfeebled institutions, laws and customs will prove mere *ropes of sand*, to restrain the revolutionary proclivities and irrepressible passions of the people when the crisis shall come. The state of public opinion is very much disturbed even at this very time in Europe, and strong repressive measures are found necessary to enforce order.

2 *"And the beast which I saw was like unto a leopard."*

The different parts of this symbol are doubtless significant and not intended merely for the purpose of embellishment, or to impart variety to the picture, as some would suggest. They must be regarded as pointing out some traits or peculiarities belonging to the power symbolized. The third beast of Daniel, 7th chapter, is represented as having the *"body of a leopard,"* and four wings of a fowl upon its back and four heads. Now it is agreed by all that the four heads symbolized the four independent monarchies into which the Macedonian kingdom of Alexander was divided after his death, and the four wings, doubtless the protection and aid furnished in his wars of conquest by the four principal officers, between whom his power was finally divided.

The Apocalyptic beast, under consideration, *was like unto a leopard*, and therefore the power symbolized by it must bear resemblance to the Macedonian Empire, which was symbolized by the third beast, Dan. 7, (the leopard is remarkable for its swiftness). But in what respect can there be a resemblance since time has wrought such wonderful changes in the conditions of the people of modern times, compared with those of ancient times? The changes in the institutions and conditions among the eastern people, have not been so sweeping as to efface all landmarks of the past; but the resemblance pointed to in the figure has reference doubtless to the composition of these two powers. The Macedonian Empire of Alexander was a confederation of the States of Greece, formed under the auspices of Philip, King of Macedon, the father of Alexander. The body of the leopard is variegated by numerous spots. It is generally understood that these spots denoted the manners and customs represented in the several States which formed the Macedonian Confederation, and were represented in the armies of Alexander. If so, and there is no reason why the spots on the body should not signify, as well as the four wings on the back, or the four heads, then we have an additional and independent reason in favor of the conclusion before arrived at, that the coming Roman power will be a confederation of States, of ten kingdoms in chief, but doubtless composed of numerous subordinate and dependent States and principalities, all under the extraordinary, willful and defiant leadership, which shall play the chief part in the last drama upon the stage of human affairs.

3 "*And feet like a bear.*"

Here is another feature found in this symbol, and doubtless points to a parallel in the Medo-Persian Empire, which is symbolized by the second beast. Dan. 7th.

The peculiarities of race are not easily effaced.

Time, like a moving avalanche, sweeps the rubbish from the surface, but there are inlaid in the rocky face of nature qualities which can not be easily wiped out. So with the types of character. Deeply interwoven with the manners, customs, laws, and more especially with the modes of thought of a people, certain characteristics endure as long as the race.

The descendants of the Medes and Persians, and Babylonians and subordinate people and tribes, shall exist to the end of time.

The old empires of the East have passed away centuries ago, but in the contemplation of prophecy, they shall exist until the God of heaven shall set up a kingdom which shall have no end. For the stone cut out without hands shall smite the gentile monarchies symbolized by the metalic image, and by its sudden concussion, break them to pieces and grind them to powder. The *iron, the brass, the clay, the silver and the gold* shall be alike broken and ground to powder, becoming as the chaff driven before the wind.

But the "*feet of the bear*" typifies something more directly descriptive of this power. The pedestals of the beast indicate that which he depends upon for support. The monarchy of Cyrus and his successors was upheld by the force of arms. All reliance was placed upon the military organization of the empire. The savage, sullen voracity of the bear fitly characterizes this eastern monarchy. The

Prophet Isaiah says of the Medes and Persians: "Their eyes shall not spare children." So we may infer that the coming Roman Empire will resemble this eastern despotism in its being a strictly military power, placing its chief dependence on the force of arms for the maintenance of its authority. Physical superiority will be the supreme logic of this arbitrary, defiant *monster*, which shall be at the head of this infamous but short lived monarchy.

4 "*And his mouth as the mouth of a lion.*"

Another proof that the germinal stock of races is perpetuated through long lines of succeeding generations, is brought to view in the following passage, Dan. 4: 13–15: "*And an holy one came down from heaven; He cried aloud, and said thus, hew down the tree, and cut off his branches, shake off his leaves, and scatter his fruit.* * * * *Nevertheless, leave the stump of his roots in the earth, even with a band of iron and brass, in the tender grass of the field.*"

This tree symbolizes the dominion of Nebuchadnezzar, King of Babylon, and its hewing down was primarily fulfilled in him, by his seven years' insanity and consequent deprivation of power for that time.

In the explanation of the dream of which this tree forms the subject, Daniel said to the king: "*And whereas they commanded to leave the stump of the tree roots; thy kingdom shall be sure unto thee.*"

Here there is nothing said about the bands of *iron and brass*.

"*The stump of his roots*" indicates the Assyrian stock firmly rooted to the soil of Mesopotamia. But the bands of iron and brass are superadded and are indicative of the Roman and Macedonian institutions, which were subsequently ingrafted by these conquerors. These symbolize, the one the indelible marks left by the conquests of Alexander the Great, and the dominion exercised for centuries by his successors; and the other, the traces left by the Roman Empire.

But *"the mouth of a lion"* is intended probably, only to indicate that there will be a resemblance in the arrogant, impious and boastful self-vaunting character of the coming head of the Roman Empire, to that of the great King of Babylon. The latter spake and said: *"Is not this great Babylon, that I have built for the house of the kingdom by the might of my power, and for the glory of my majesty?"* Assuming to himself all the glory, and something like superhuman consequence, even defiant to high heaven.

Of the apostate head of the coming power it is said, Rev. 13: 6: *"And he opened his mouth in blasphemy against God, to blaspheme his name and his tabernacle, and them that dwell in heaven."* Here is the mouth of the lion. The true Babylonian boastful arrogance, intensified by blasphemy.

5 *"And upon his heads the name of blasphemy."* Rev. 13: 1.

Frequent allusions have been made to the blasphemous character of the great apostate emperor about to come, and frequent citations from the scriptures have been given in proof, from which it is inferred that the governing principle and animating spirit of the coming power will be defiances of God and blasphemy, war upon *the saints of God* and all things sacred, aiming to establish a government, whose fundamental principle will be the denial of all things divine or spiritual, and the recognition of nothing but *positive, material force.*

The blasphemous character of this personage affords a sure mark of identification wherever referred to in the scriptures. Instance the following: Where he is designated as the little horn in Dan. 7: 25. He is represented as speaking *"great swelling words against the Most High as wearing out the saints of the Most High."* When referred to as *"that man of sin—the son of perdition,"* by the Apostle Paul, 2 Thess. 2: 3-7, *the same character* is brought to view.—*" Who opposeth and exalteth himself above all that is called God, or that is worshiped, so that he as God sitteth in the temple of God, showing himself that he is God."* (Similar is the application of this passage by Irenæus, Bishop of Lyons. See note supra.)

Such madness and impiety would seem to be incredible if it were not that we have the same spirit now in the world, and the same principles are announced from the highest seats of learning, even in this enlightened age. It is the spirit of POSITIVE and ATHEISTICAL philosophy, clothed with power, and made the fundamental doctrine of an Empire.

The motto of Voltaire and his infidel Junto was too impious to quote, but the blasphemous impiety which shall animate the ruling head of the *revived Roman Empire* during his brief career, will not only lead him to deny and execrate the Lord of Life and Glory, but will go still further and aim to take possession of the throne of the Almighty Creator and Ruler of the universe. The cardinal doctrine of the new system, which he shall seek to set up, will be, that there is nothing of the supernatural; and all belief in a purely spiritual and self-existent God, independent of nature, is delusion and must be treated as a crime against the head of the State.

The distinguished author of the spirit of the laws says: "Every form of government has its animating spirit. That virtue should be the ruling principle in a Democracy, honor in a Monarchy, but fear and obedience in a Despotism." But in that form of government which is symbolized by the Apocalyptic beast, blasphemy and defiance of

God and war upon all things *holy or venerable, will be the ruling principle*. This will reach its acme in the adoption of a system of universal proscription of all who will not acquiesce in the policy of the new regime, and receive as a token of fealty and a sign of loyalty, a mark either upon the forehead or in the right hand. "And that no man might buy or sell, *save he that had the mark, or the name of the beast, or the number of his name.*" Rev. 13: 17.

It is added: "*Here is wisdom.*" "*Let him that hath understanding count the number of the beast, for it is the number of a man, and his number is six hundred, three score and six.*" Rev. 13: 18.

The mark may imply some arbitrary character that may be adopted as a symbol or sign of a fact or principle, perhaps the initial of the name the antitype of the *beast* shall adopt. His name will be expressive of the character he shall assume. This must have relation to the remarkably impious assumption which shall constitute the chief moral attribute and characterize the coming blasphemer.

He will, as we have seen, repudiate the idea of a *self-existent, almighty, spiritual* God of the universe, and in His place magnify and deify mere force—*physical force*. "He shall speak marvelous things against the God of gods, but in his estate he shall *honor the God of forces.*" The god of fortresses as the original seems to imply. His reliance shall be placed on improved arms and ordnance, upon chemical explosives and organized physical force. These shall constitute the dynamics of war and the coercive implements of despotic government. He will assume that he as the supreme ruler and head of the State, by whose fiat the combined powers of earth are wielded, must be regarded as the representative of all authority recognized or acknowledged among men.

By a fiction of law in a monarchial government, the crown is the emblem of majesty and authority. So the coming emperor will assume that all majesty and authority, both political and religious, shall inhere in his imperial person.

He alone shall be worshiped, and his image adored. "Who opposeth and exalteth himself above all that is called God, or that is worshiped * * showing himself that he is God." Here we have the complete character of this extraordinary personage, who shall prove to be the absolute representative of the evil one in the time coming. And herein, we must look for the true solution of the mystery involved in the symbolic number 666. Of all that has been written upon this number 666, during the past sixteen centuries, there is nothing that has appeared which is quite free from objection. Irenæus, Bishop of Lyons about the close of the second century proposed an explanation, which has generally been followed by commentators, age after age, ever since. His explanation in principle is correct. He assumes that the Greek letters of the name, which shall pertain to, or characterize the antitype of the beast, when the sum of their numerical values shall be taken (the Greek letters represent numbers, as well as sounds) shall make up the total of 666.

He having his mind upon the scriptures we are considering, proposed the word $\lambda \alpha \tau \varepsilon \iota \nu o \varsigma$. This word may signify a Roman; more properly Latinus, who ruled the central parts of the Italian Peninsula when Æneas and his Trojan band arrived on the coast. Romans generally, regarding Latinus as their representative man.

This word will not make the number 666 however, unless it be spelled with an ε before the ι as above.

Herein is the objection which the learned Bengelius and

others have urged against this word, and with reason, as the word is spelled generally with ι only. Thus: λατίνος. The reader can himself verify this by consulting any *classical Greek lexicon*. Even were it not for this objection, the application is remote and without pertinence. It would favor generally, the exposition of this apocalyptic symbol given in these pages, but we shall now propose in its stead a *specific* and what seems to be a *pertinent* solution of this *mysterious number*.

The Greek verb Δυναμαί is the root from which is derived the term *dynamics*—the science of *force* or *forces energized*. Also the term *dynamite*, lately brought into use as the name of the most terribly explosive chemical compound known to the arts, recently discovered, is derived from the same.

Now since the coming emperor will claim to represent the physical and moral forces and energies of universal empire in his own person, "exalting himself above all that is called God or that is worshiped, showing himself, that he is god," he will assume to represent the embodiment of the abstract idea of *universal authority* and *unlimited power*. The dynamics of all earthly government. If therefore, we should seek to find a term expressive of such a character, we should look for it among the various forms derived from this verb Δυναμαί. And here we find it.

For, Rev. 13: 2, it is stated that the dragon gave unto him, i. e. the beast, his power, satanic energies, power over the elements δυναμίν and his seat θρόνον. His *throne* and his *power*.

Satan, the god of this world will abdicate his throne in favor of the beast, and clothe him with plenary power and authority as his vicegerent on the earth. All the forces of earth and hell will be at his command. The armies of the nations, the forces of nature, and the energies of the spirits of darkness. Such power will be invested in man only once. Hence he will represent the terrible energies, dynamics of earth and hell and the forces of nature in addition, laid under contribution.

The word that fitly describes this character is found to contain the mysterious number 666. It is $\Delta υναζια$, a verbal noun derived directly from $\Delta υναμαι$. The negative form of this word is found in the classics, the form here given seldom. This word may be latinized into Dynasian and added to the name of a man, denote the abstract idea or attribute of power, or authority energized. The *wielder of unlimited authority* or *power among the nations*, as a species of omnipotence on earth among men. For such will be the character this son of perdition will aspire to and assume. As the word $\dot{o}$ $\Sigma εβαςτος$ was added to Octavius, the first Roman Emperor, denoting *excellent, grand, august* and afterward *Augustus*, the name which he finally took, and which was retained as an appellation by the succeeding emperors, so this word Dynasian or its latin equivalent will be assumed as expressive of the unlimited power, the coming and last head of the Roman world will lay claim to it.

Considering that this extraordinary character will be the only tolerated object of worship and the representative of the supreme majesty of a universal dominion, for power was given him over all kindreds and tongues, and nations. "And all that dwell upon the earth shall worship him, whose names are not found written in the book of life."—Rev. 13: 7, 8. Add that his chief minister will cause "fire to come down from heaven on earth in the sight of men"— Rev. 13: 13—reminding the reader of the red right hand of Jupiter wielding the thunder bolt, the pertinence of the word and its application is manifest. As an illustration, it may be added that the use of the word warrants this application. The phrase Ζευς δύναται γαρ άπαντα, Jupiter is able for all things, is used by the poets to express the unlimited or irresistible power of this supreme heathen deity.

There is still another form of this word which contains the same letters, namely, Δύναςαί. The second person, singular, of the indicative mode, present tense, of the same verb Δύναμοί, and may be translated, thou art powerful, or considering the word in its connection with the supreme head of the State, indeed of universal empire, and it may be properly rendered, thou art the *invincible*, *tu es omnia potens*, considered in its active or aggressive sense. Thus:—

Δ......... 4	and	Δ......... 4
υ.........400		υ.........400
ν......... 50		ν......... 50
α......... 1		α......... 1
ς.........200		ς.........200
ί......... 10		α......... 1
α......... 1		ί......... 10
666		666

The latter form of the word will be used in direct, adulatory, personal address by courtiers and flatterers, as expressive of the same character designated by the first form.

NOTE.—But we have a strong confirmation of this as the true explanation of the number 666 in another word, or rather phrase, which is of the same import and numerically of the same value, showing a remarkable coincidence.

When Alexander, the young king of Macedon was about to lead his armies out of Greece against Asia, he visited the temple of Apollo to consult the oracle, as was the custom of his times. As he arrived at Delphi on those days in which it was deemed unlawful to give out oracles, the priestess refused to visit the temple, but Alexander, impatient of delay, and more perhaps of opposition to his will, took hold of the priestess by the arm and was leading her by force toward the temple, when she cried out: *"Thou art irresistible, my son!"* This was all the oracle the young king wanted.

The Greek word translated irresistible in the response of the priestess is $Ανίκητος$. The numerical value of its letters, considered as numerals, is just 659, wanting 7 of being 666. But the Greek word $Ζευς$, which is the name of Jupiter Olympius, has its initial $Z = 7$. Hence the phrase $Z\ Ανίκητος$. Jupiter the irresistible, will just make the number 666. The initial Z is sometimes used for the whole word, by the poets it seems.

If we consider that the coming blasphemous chief will assume to be the sole representative of undisputed and irresistible authority on earth, the above coincidences seem of striking force. It is the idea, expressed in the name, which is expressive of all visible and recognized authority in the universe. As insane as this may appear, that this blasphemous pretention will be set up, is the only hypothesis compatible with many passages of scripture, as the foregoing pages fully show. Thus:

$$\begin{aligned}
Z &\ldots\ldots 7\\
α &\ldots\ldots 1\\
ν &\ldots\ldots 50\\
ι &\ldots\ldots 10\\
κ &\ldots\ldots 20\\
η &\ldots\ldots 8\\
τ &\ldots\ldots 300\\
ο &\ldots\ldots 70\\
ς &\ldots\ldots 200\\
\hline
&666
\end{aligned}$$

It is not deemed advisable to further cite Greek phrases in confirmation of the general idea above set out. Much could be written and many examples adduced tending to further illustrate the above. The mystical word is expressive of the character and *extraordinary pretensions of the coming blasphemer.*

6 "*And power was given unto him to continue forty and two months.*" Rev. 13: 5.

This period of forty-two months, differently expressed, which amounts to just three and one-half years, occurs no less than eight different times in Daniel and the Revelations, and in each place designates the period of *triumphant* and *blasphemous denomination* of that remarkable character who shall act such an important part on the stage of human affairs in the last drama of the world's history.

So remarkable will be the part this character shall perform in the last times as the direct agent of satanic malice, that he is a prominent subject of prophecy and frequently referred to, both in the Old as well as in the New Testament. This is the more remarkable as the subjects dignified as worthy of prophetic visions, are so few.

The prophecies point to certain great cardinal events in God's providential dealings with the world. The great tide of human affairs sweeps by, noted only by the secular historian, but entirely unnoticed by the sacred writers.

A peculiar people, dedicated to the observance of the laws and to the maintenance of the institutions of Jehovah, and whatever might concern them in their internal or external relations, formed the chief burden of ancient prophecy. The Messiah who should come out from among this people and prove the benefactor of the whole world, was also foretold, and his character, offices and kingdom.

Besides, prominence is given to the character of the

great antagonist of God and all things deemed sacred and good, who in the last times shall appear as the direct agent of Satan. Who, opposing himself to all that is called God, shall place himself athwart the path of Divine Providence, claiming for himself universal homage.

This remarkable character is very significantly pointed out by the prophets.

Says Isaiah: "*Tophet was ordained of old; yea, for the king it is prepared.*" What king? The context points out none. The Assyrian, who is mentioned in the same chapter, is the type of God's enemy in the last times.

Again Isaiah, 14: 12. "*How art thou fallen from heaven, O Lucifer, son of the morning! how art thou cut down to the ground, which didst weaken the nations!*"

Again, 28: 15. "*Because ye have said we have made a covenant with death, and with hell are we at agreement.*" Who are spoken of here? Why certainly no other but the apostate Jews, who shall make a covenant with the great *antagonist* as the direct representative of hell, thinking to escape thereby the persecution which he will direct against all who shall not receive his mark.

It must be remembered that Satan acts through agencies. The Jewish (Sanhedrim) of old. The man of sin in the last times.

He is prominently brought to view, Dan. 7: 25, as one "*that shall speak great words against the Most High, and shall think to change times and laws.*"

By St. Paul, as "*that man of sin—the son of perdition, who opposeth and exalteth himself above all that is called God, or that is worshiped; so that he as God, sitteth in the temple of God, shewing himself that he is God. Remember ye not, that when I was yet with you, I told you these things?*"

This implies that this remarkable personage who should

arise before the end of the gentile dispensation, and continue until the coming of the Lord, was the subject of conversation in the intercourse of the apostle among those to whom he preached. Doubtless referring to the passages of scripture above cited, as authority or confirmation.

And as to the beast having seven heads and ten horns, Rev. 13: 1, "*unto whom was given a mouth speaking great things and blasphemies; and power was given unto him to continue forty and two months.*"

Many good men have confounded this character with that of the Jewish anti-Christ, whereas he will prove to be an entirely different personage. The anti-Christ will arise out of Judea, which will prove to be the principal theater of his acts; the great apostate and blasphemous emperor will aspire to be the secular ruler of the world. The anti-Christ will assume the office of the priesthood, and if that of prince or king, it will be subordinate to the priestly office, as in the case of John Hyrcanus and others of the Asmonæan family. He will claim to be the messiah of the old prophets, and therefore will present himself to the Jews as the long expected deliverer.

The anti-Christ is symbolized by the beast having two horns like a lamb, Rev. 13: 11, and will co-exist and co-operate with the head of the *revived Roman Empire* in the promotion of the designs of the evil one in the last days. The first Apocalyptic beast is not Jewish, he will prove to be Roman. All the symbols prove this, as has been abundantly shown.

He is designated, Dan. 9: 26, as "*the prince that shall come.*" Here he stands out, isolated and apart. Nothing in the previous context to throw any light on the seeming mystery and obscurity of the passage.

The people of the prince that shall come, shall destroy the city and the sanctuary; that is, the Romans who desolated Judea and captured the city of Jerusalem, and burned the temple under Vespasian and his son Titus, but neither of these was the *"prince that shall come."* For "*he,*" i. e. the prince that shall come, "shall confirm the covenant with many for one week: and in the midst of the week *he* shall cause the sacrifice and the oblation to cease, and for the overspreading of abomination, *he* shall make it desolate, even unto the consummation, and that determined shall be poured upon the desolate." Now, who is the prince that shall confirm the covenant with many for one week—*septenate*—if you please, and shall cause the sacrifice and oblation to cease, and shall cause the desolations of idolatry to be set up? Not Vespasian, not Titus, not any of the old Roman emperors. The Romans who captured Jerusalem and destroyed the temple, set up no abominations of idolatry in the sanctuary. Let the reader turn to Josephus' account of the capture of the city and temple, and he will see that Titus entered the sanctuary after it had been set on fire. Indeed he was compelled to burn his way into the temple proper, after the Jews themselves had set the adjacent buildings on fire. Here was no opportunity for setting up the emblems of idolatrous worship. The abomination of desolation shall stand in the *holy place*. Titus could not, did not set up any such there. He did not get possession until the sanctuary was in ruins, or nearly so, and the holy house on fire. This abomination of desolation, spoken of by Daniel the prophet, referred to by Matthew, Chapter 24: 15,* as standing in the holy place, will be fulfilled in the last times. There is not a

*NOTE.—The fulfillment of this prediction from Matt. 24: 15, has usually been sought for by expositors in the events which occurred at the siege of Jerusalem, induced thereto by an erroneous

shadow of proof that the abominations of idolatry were set up by Titus in the temple, or by any other Roman. The facts are all otherwise.

A fuller elucidation of this subject requires that the entire passage, from which the above citation is taken, be further considered.

"Seventy weeks are determined upon thy people," i. e. Daniel's people, "and upon thy holy city," i. e. the city of the Jews, "to finish the transgression, and to make an end of sins, and to make reconciliation for iniquity, and to bring in everlasting righteousness, and to seal up the vision and prophecy, and to anoint the Most Holy.

"Know therefore and understand, that from the going forth of the commandments to *restore* and *build to* Jerusalem

theory of interpretation. "The abomination of desolation here referred to was not set up by Titus in the holy place, nor by any other Roman, as yet." Let the passage be carefully scrutinized and the facts examined. It was to be for a warning to flee to the mountains, "when ye therefore shall see the abomination of desolation spoken of by Daniel the prophet stand in the holy place, (whoso readeth let him understand,) Then let them which be in Judea flee to the mountains." Now this passage can have no application to the events that occurred at the siege of Jerusalem for the simple reason that all the facts are otherwise. The Romans did not get into the holy place until the holy house was on fire, and then they were in possession of the entire lower city, which the temple had been made the citadel by the miserable wretches, who had taken possession of it, in their intestine strife and suicidal warfare; and this was at the close of the siege or nearly so, when a warning to flee to the mountains would be of no use, as the city had been cut off from all communication with the country many days previous. At this period of the siege the city was a perfect charnel house and full of dead carcasses, the temple not excepted, desecrated by the sedition Jews. We find the warning to *flee to the mountains* given in Luke 21: 20. This warning was unto the Messiah the prince shall be *seven weeks, and three-score and two weeks:* the streets shall be built again, and the wall, even in troublesome times."

"And after *three-score and two weeks* shall Messiah be cut off, but not for himself: and the people of the *prince that shall come* shall destroy the city and the sanctuary; and the end thereof shall be with a flood and unto the end of the war desolations are determined.

"And *he* shall confirm the covenant with many for *one week:* and in the midst of the *week he* shall cause the sacrifice and oblation to cease, and for the overspreading of abominations, *he* shall make it desolate, even until the consummation, and that determined shall be poured upon the desolate.

addressed to the Christians, that they might escape from the calamities of the siege. "And when ye shall see Jerusalem encompassed with armies, then know that the desolation thereof is nigh. Then let them which are in Judea, flee to the mountains." Titus surrounded the entire city with a wall of circumvallation and so disposed the legions about the work, as to guard every approach to the city, so that all egress and ingress were cut off. This is the encompassing with the armies spoken of above. And this happened many days before the end of the siege. Whereas Titus did not enter the temple until the city was in his power. For here was the last stout defence made by the Jews. The passage from Matt. 24: 15, is quite different from that of Luke 21: 20, 21, above cited, and they refer to entirely different events. The one is past, the other yet to come. Expositors have been misled by the following passage from Josephus, B. 6, C. 6, S. 1, Jewish war: "And now the Romans, upon the flight of the seditious"—i. e. the miserable, wretched Jews, who had made a citadel of the temple, "into the city"—i. e. the upper city—"and after the *burning of the holy house itself and all the buildings round about it,* brought their ensigns to the temple, and set them over against its eastern gate; and then did they offer sacrifices to them, and there did they make

This passage shows the determination of God communicated to Daniel, "*a man greatly beloved*," in reference to His people, the Jews, as to his future relation to and dealings with them for a period of *seventy weeks of years*, making in all 490 years.

The week or septenate was a well understood period among this people, and had reference to the times of tillage and rest for the land. Every seventh year was a Sabbath for the land, and thus they became accustomed to reckon time by septenates, or weeks of years.

It should be remembered that this prophecy was given during the captivity to Daniel, after earnest and protracted inquiry by prayer and supplication, doubtless moved thereto by an earnest of what was to come.

Titus *Imperator* with great acclamations of joy." Here it is stated that the holy house and all the buidings around it were burned before the Romans brought their ensigns into the temple enclosure. Here was naught but desolation already. This was a customary ceremony of the Roman armies after victory. It was meant chiefly as complimentary to Titus, by proclaiming him Imperator.

To confound the two passages above cited, the one from Luke 21 : 20, 21, and the other from Matt. 24 : 15, as predicting the same event would be a sacrifice of all precision of language in these quotations. By no possible stretch of ingenuity can they be made to refer to the same event. As stated elsewhere, the 24th chapter of Matthew does not describe the destruction of Jerusalem by Titus, except in very general terms. It speaks of the great tribulation and this is yet to come. One error leads to many. The mistaken idea, that the four Gospels are capable of being harmonized, as one continuous narrative of the acts and discourses of our Lord, has led to the confounding of the above cited passages, as referring to the same event. While the truth is, each Gospel is a distinct treatise and written with a specific object in view. Divine Revelation is complete as a whole, but each book is complete in itself for the purpose intended.

It foretells the restoration of the people to the land of Canaan and God's dealing with them, as his peculiar chosen people in their restored national capacity for the period of 490 years. Of this time 483 years have transpired. There remains yet seven years to be fulfilled.

The future restoration of the Jews to Palestine, in order that this last week of seven years may be accomplished, by Jehovah coming into relation with them in their national capacity for that period, becomes therefore a necessity. That they will be so restored is for the present taken for granted.

In confirmation we will cite the following proposition from the book of David Brown, D. D., of Aberdeen, on the "Restoration of the Jews." His authority will be readily recognized by all who are acquainted with what has been written on this subject.

The proposition is as follows:—

"That the PEOPLE and the LAND of Israel are so connected in numerous prophecies of the Old Testament, that whatever LITERALITY and perpetuity are ascribed to the one, must on all strict principles of interpretation be attributed to the other also."

Now the subject of the promise is the LAND of CANAAN *for an everlasting possession*, and this includes the literal descendants of Abraham, as the rightful and everlasting inheritors of the land. They are not in possession now. They, nevertheless, have the right of possession, and in the purpose of God will come into possession in the last times, for a period of seven years, that God may deal with them in chastisement and discipline, and then for ever and ever as the subjects of the Messiah's kingdom, after the coming of the Lord.

The seventy weeks in the passage above cited, Daniel,

9: 24-27, are distributed, as the attentive reader will observe, into three divisions.

The first division consists of *seven weeks*, i. e. *forty-nine years*; the second of *sixty-two weeks*, i. e. four hundred and thirty-four years, and the third of the remaining *one week*, i. e. seven years, making in all the *seventy weeks*, i. e. 490 years. Observe the language of the prophecy.

"Know therefore and understand, that from the going forth of the commandment to *restore* and to *build* Jerusalem until the Messiah the Prince shall be *seven weeks*, and *three-score and two weeks:*" i. e. *sixty-nine weeks* until the Messiah. "*The streets shall be built again, and the wall, even in troublous times.*"

The last sentence is a distinct and separate proposition, and is allotted to the period of *seven weeks* or *forty-nine years.*

"*And after three-score and two weeks shall Messiah be cut off, but not for himself.*"

This is an additional and distinct period, and commenced where the former ended, making *sixty-two* weeks, or *four hundred and thirty-four years*. To the attentive reader these propositions will appear as if stated with mathematical precision. For the language is capable of no other construction.

Now the seven weeks and the three-score and two weeks make just sixty-nine weeks, or four hundred and eighty-three years. There is still remaining one week or seven years of the seventy weeks yet to be accounted for.

The first division of seven weeks, or forty-nine years, commenced with the going forth of the commandment to restore and to build Jerusalem. The phrase, "*the streets shall be built again, and the wall, even in troublous times,*" limits this period.

The second division of sixty-two weeks, or four hundred and thirty-four years, commenced where the former ended, and closed with the crucifixion of our Lord. These two divisions of time are long since accomplished.

But the third and last week of seven years will commence when "*the Prince that shall come*" shall confirm a covenant for one week with the multitude, chiefly of apostate Jews, instigated thereto by the anti-Christ, who will lead astray the apostate Jews and be a prominent character after the restoration, and especially during the last seven years of the dispensation of the times of the Gentiles.

The first division of time commenced B. C. 445, when Nehemiah was at his own request, sent by Artexerxes, up to Jerusalem with a command to *restore* and *build* the wall of Jerusalem. Neh. 2d chapter.

The former decrees and mandates of Cyrus and Darius, and also of Artexerxes has reference to the building of the temple and the re-establishment of the temple services. The mandate to Nehemiah, had exclusive reference to the building of the wall and the restoration of the gates, not only of the city wall, but of the palace also. The general rebuilding and reconstruction of the wall and the city. This work was protracted through a period of forty-nine years, owing chiefly to the jealousy of the neighboring nations, and the corruptions that had crept in among the people from their strange marriages and alliances.

Taking this date 445 from 483 and there remains thirty-eight years, which would indicate that our Lord was crucified in the thirty-eighth year of his age. This would agree mainly with the statement of the historian Gieseler, who after a review of the whole subject in the light of all that had been written, especially by the more ancient of the church fathers, comes to the conclusion that our Lord's death happened between the thirty-fourth and the thirty-eighth year of his age.

But the very best authority among the ancient church fathers differ as to the date of the nativity of our Lord. Some placing it as early as the 747th year of the city of Rome, and others as late as 754 A. U. A discrepancy of seven years.

Irenæus and Turtullian fix the date of the nativity in the forty-first year of Augustus A. U. 751. The death of Herod is also assigned to this year. This date is sustained by other very ancient authority. Whereas, the commencement of our era syncronizes with A. U. 753. Thus making our Lord to have been from two to six years old at the commencement of our era. Making this correction, and according to the very best authority that has come down to us, His death happened somewhere between the thirty-second and thirty-sixth year of His age. This will agree more closely with the conclusion of the historian Gieseler, than whom there is no higher modern authority on such matters.

This is also more in harmony with the gospel of John, which makes it very probable that our Lord attended four feasts of the Passover during His ministry. Having entered upon His public mission at the age of thirty, according to Luke 3 : 23, He must have attended His fourth and last Passover, just before His crucifixion, between the thirty-third and thirty-fourth year of His age.

Thus after sixty-nine weeks or 483 years from the going forth of the commandment to restore and build Jerusalem, was the Messiah the Prince cut off, *but not for himself*, or as it should be rendered, *received nothing for himself.*

God deals directly with His people, the Jews, only in

their national capacity, as gathered in their own land and in the city of Jerusalem, though his eye is doubtless upon them in their dispersion. The seventy weeks, as divided above, do not concern any continuous period of the history of the Jews, but has reference to them, only as a nation inhabiting Jerusalem and Judea. They were restored from the Babylonian captivity, or a representative number of them, for the specific purpose that the Messiah might be presented to them, as a nation, for their reception or rejection. All was, however, foreseen and provided for. For 483 years after the restoration from Babylon, was God's providential care exercised over them as a nation, in blessings and in chastisements, in long-suffering and forbearance, until they committed the fatal crime of rejecting the Prince of Life, God's only Son, the long-expected *deliverer*,—when as a nation, God set them aside. "*Behold your house is left unto you desolate,*" said Christ unto them four days before the crucifixion. In a very few years after Jerusalem was utterly blotted out. There remains, however, yet one week of the seventy, in which God will deal with his people as a nation assembled in Jerusalem in the last days. "*For Jerusalem shall be trodden down of the Gentiles until the times of the Gentiles be fulfilled.*" Does the passage imply that it shall still be trodden down after that? Certainly the very opposite is implied.

Here we must refer to one of the most remarkable chapters in the whole history of the Divine Providence. The setting aside of the Jewish nation until the church of the Lord Jesus shall be gathered in. The suspension of God's direct dealing with his ancient, chosen people, for a limited period indefinite to man, but definite in the divine mind and his revealed purpose to come into relation with them again as a nation, for the term of seven years. Had they accepted Jesus as their Messiah when presented to them, upon the terms proclaimed by John the Baptist, of thorough reformation, and by demeaning themselves as the children of the Father in heaven should, as insisted upon in the sermon on the mount, the seventy weeks would have been accomplished in the inauguration of the Messiah's reign on earth. Had they believed as a nation, at the descent of the Holy Ghost on the day of Pentecost, Christ would have speedily returned to earth again to reign. But having rejected the Messiah, the Prince, and also the last evidence of His divine mission and character—the descent of the Holy Ghost they were set aside, until the Gentile church shall be gathered in, when the Lord shall descend to earth with His own redeemed and glorified saints, who having believed upon the testimony of a preached gospel, they shall hold the first places of honor in the kingdom, for ever and ever.

Says the Apostle Paul: "I would not have you ignorant of this mystery, that blindness in part is happened to Israel, until the fullness of the Gentiles be come in." "For, as touching the gospel they are enemies for your sakes." They will not *believe in Christ upon the testimony of preached gospel.* They will *not be saved by faith* as the Gentile believers are. They will believe when they shall look upon him whom they have pierced. The Apostle Thomas is the type of the Jews, as a people. They are beloved for the Father's sake, and for this reason they will be finally brought to repentance.

But the last week of the seventy requires further consideration. He shall confirm the covenant with the many for *one week.* Here is the wanting week found in the same context. Of the seventy, sixty-nine have been allotted to their appropriate divisions of time, pointing out specified events of which they were the limits. One week of the seventy remained, and here we find it. "*He shall confirm the covenant.*" The context shows that the pronoun *he* refers to "the *prince that shall come.*" The passage reads: "And the people of the *prince that shall come* shall destroy the city and the sanctuary." This the Romans did shortly after the Messiah had been cut off, as predicted. Hence, the Romans are "*the people of the prince that shall come.*" He has not yet come. For neither did Vespasian, or Titus, or any other Roman do what is attributed to this *prince that shall come.* If there be any doubt on this point the closest investigation is invited.

It must be borne in mind that the prophecy has reference to the Jewish people alone. *Thy people*—Daniel's people—"seventy weeks are determined upon *thy people.*" With the multitude of these, therefore, the covenant shall be confirmed for one week, i. e. the remaining week of the seventy. Titus confirmed no covenant with the multitude of the Jewish nation, nor indeed with any. The war against Jerusalem was a war of extermination. A sad fatality seemed to hang over the city and the deluded nation. There was no disposition on their part to listen to terms. The city and holy house were doomed. The city was entered by force. The Romans found in it starvation and death. The lanes and streets were strewn with dead carcasses. Homes filled with dead men, women and children. The temple in ruin and on fire. The wrath of heaven poured out upon the doomed city. No opportunity for covenants, no time to establish idolatry.

The *prince that shall come* and who shall confirm the covenant with the multitude of the Jews for one week or seven years, will do this, and is the same character as that typified by the little horn, Dan. 7: 25. The same character whom the Apostle Paul designates as that man of sin—the son of perdition. The same as that pointed out by the beast, Rev. 13: 1, who will prove to be the imperial head of the revived Roman Empire in the last days.

This conclusion is placed beyond doubt by what follows in the same context. The identification of the *prince that shall come* with the little horn, Dan. 7: 25, and the Apocalyptic beast, Rev. 13: 1, is placed beyond doubt by the period of three and a half years, with which he shall be concerned. For he shall confirm the *covenant* with the *many* for *one week*, but in the *midst of the week* he shall cause the sacrifice and oblation to cease. In the *midst* of the seven years, i. e. at the end of three and a half years. This will doubtless be a departure from the stipulations of the covenant, which shall guarantee among other things toleration to the Jewish worship at Jerusalem. For where will he cause the sacrifice and oblation to cease except at the only place where it is lawful, according to the Mosaic economy, to offer them—namely, Jerusalem. The mere fact of the offering of *sacrifice and oblation* implies that the Jews are once more in possession of Jerusalem and their ceremonial law re-established. And the causing them to *cease* implies arbitrary interposition and persecution.

The causing of the sacrifice and oblation to cease, dates the beginning of persecution, and this according to a general plan or policy, which shall apply to all the world. How long shall this continue? Doubtless during the remaining half of the seven years, that is for three and a half years. This persecution shall be directed chiefly against the *devout Jews*, for the prophecy concerns them chiefly —"thy people."

How forcibly is this set out in Dan. 12: 6–7. In answer to the question, *"How long shall it be to the end of these wonders?"* the answer is given as follows: *"And I heard the man clothed in linen, which was upon the waters of the river,* when he held up his right hand and his left hand unto heaven, and *swear* by him that liveth for ever, *that it shall be for a time, times, and an half;*—i. e. three and a half years;—*and when* HE *shall have accomplished to scatter the power of the holy people, all these things shall be finished."* Who is the HE that shall accomplish to scatter the power of the holy people? none but that *prince that shall come.* And who are the *holy people?* but the devout Jews, gathered again in the last days at Jerusalem and worshiping God according to the law of the fathers. Let the reader carefully peruse Daniel 12th, and indeed all from 9: 27, to the end.

By the solemn oath of the man clothed in linen, which was upon the waters of the river, Dan. 12: 6–7, this period of persecution and calamity is limited to three and a half years, i. e. the remaining three and a half years of the seven.

So it will be seen that the last half of the last week of the seventy affords the very *"Rosetta stone,"* for deciphering the enigmas of prophetic numbers. Here is the elucidation of the *"time, times and an half,"* or *"time, times, and the dividing* of time," or *"the forty-two months,"* or *"the* 1260 *days,"* each making just three and a half years.

The one-half of the seven years of the covenant which "the prince that shall come" shall establish with the many, that is the multitude of the Jews—being the latter half—which shall constitute the time of great *tribulation*, which shall be inaugurated by his causing the daily sacrifice to cease in the midst of the week or septenate of the covenant, and by causing the abominations of idolatry to be set up in the *holy place*, or the consecrated house of worship of the returned Jews at Jerusalem.

This *time of tribulation*, such as shall only once occur "in the history of the world, has its exact limits fixed." Its duration will be forty-two months, or three and one-half years, and this will prove to be the duration of the period of successful, *triumphant* and *blasphemous domination* of the coming man of sin—*the son of perdition.*

The restoration of the Jews to Judea and to their ancient city Jerusalem, has been alluded to as a necessity, in order that these prophecies may be fulfilled. It will now be shown that their restoration is most clearly foretold in the yet unfulfilled prophecies.

The symbolic prophecies of the Apocalypse are deemed to be more striking and conclusive than simple narration, as the truths foretold are set forth in pictures which present in one view the subject of the prophecy, with all its circumstances and the conclusions.

In Rev. 12: 1, we are presented with a view of the Jewish state, in the picture of a woman appearing in heaven, "*clothed with the sun, and the moon under her feet, and upon her head a crown of twelve stars.*" It must be borne in mind that the revelator himself had been called up into heaven and saw all things from that standpoint of observation.

"*Clothed with the sun,*" shows the plenary illumination in divine things of this favored people, to whom had been committed the oracles of God. "*The moon under her feet,*" indicating that the laws, customs and ethical system of Moses, reflecting the light of *divine revelation,* served as a guide to their feet. "*The twelve stars upon her head,*" the supreme glory and regal majesty of the Jewish state, and the perfection of the administration of its affairs under the theocracy—Jehovah being king.

"*And she brought forth a man-child,* who was to rule all nations with a *rod of iron.*" There can be no doubt as to the man-child. *"For salvation is of the Jews."* The reader will be reminded of the 2d Psalm, especially of the 9th verse, *"Thou shalt break them with a rod of iron;"* and of Isaiah, 9: 6, *"For unto us a child is born, unto us a son is given: the government shall be upon his shoulder."*

There can be no doubt but that the Lord Jesus is primarily here symbolized, but that His church is also included by the man-child, caught up unto God and to His throne. *"And* that *the woman who fled into the wilderness, where she had a place prepared of God, and that they should feed her there a thousand, two hundred and three-score days,"* i. e. three and a half years—Rev. 12: 6—symbolizes the ancient people of Jehovah and their return to the land of promise.

Why fly into the wilderness? Evidently to escape from the persecution and fury of the great red dragon. We have seen in a former part of this work that the revived Roman Empire will prove to be the medium and agent of satanic influence in the last times, and will persecute to extermination all forms of the true religion, Monotheism as well as Christianity; and hence, the Jews who shall remain attached to their ancient faith will be compelled to migrate to Palestine, where a temporary asylum of free toleration will be opened to them. This region, desolated by Mohammedan misrule and other causes, will prove to be morally and physically a desert land. Here they will find a refuge for a time from that madness and persecuting fury, which shall decree that as many as will not worship the beast, i. e. the Roman emperor and his image, shall be killed. The true Jew will not bow down to an image, neither will he tolerate idolatry in any form. Hence, the reason for the migratory movement for Palestine, however reluctant and even unwilling they might be to leave the homes of their adoption, under ordinary circumstances.

It is further disclosed in the apocalyptic vision that when the dragon saw that he was cast unto the earth, he persecuted the woman which had brought forth the man-child. The church of the Lord Jesus having been snatched up to heaven. *"And to the woman were given two wings of a great eagle,* that she might fly into the wilderness into *her place,* where she is *nourished for a time, times, and a half time,* i. e. three and a half years, *from the face of the serpent."* Rev. 12: 14. *"Her place,"* doubtless Jerusalem and the land of Canaan, which was promised to Abraham for an everlasting possession.

Under the terms of the covenant with the Roman emperor, they will expect to enjoy immunity from the persecuting scourge that shall desolate the whole earth. This covenant formed by the many, doubtless acquiesced in by the devout with reluctance, bears evidence of the handiwork of anti-Christ, and will prove a snare to the honest and sincere Jews. For in the midst of the week he shall cause the *sacrifice* and *oblation* to cease. There is no satisfactory method of explaining these scriptures, except on the hypothesis that the character termed the anti-Christ, shall act as the agent of the secular Roman power in Palestine among the Jews as their chief official, sustained by the multitude but distrusted by the devout and godly, though he will act as chief adviser of the emperor at the same time.

For the language of the Prophet Isaiah, referring to these very times, and this same covenant, seems to imply this as well as other scriptures which we can not now cite. Isaiah says: "Wherefore hear the word of the Lord, *ye scornful men,* that rule this people which is in Jerusalem. Because ye have said, We have made a *covenant with death and with hell are we at agreement;* when the overflowing scourge shall pass through, it shall not come unto us."

Now these scornful men must prove to be *the wicked Jews acting in conjunction with the anti-Christ*, who shall be the agent of the wicked emperor in Judea, either present or acting through his agents. This will prove in the end a fatal mistake. For, says the prophet, "*your covenant with death shall be disannulled, and your agreement with hell shall not stand; when the overflowing scourge shall pass through, then ye shall be trodden down by it.*" "*For I have heard from the Lord God of hosts a consumption, even determined upon the whole earth.*" This word *consumption* is used elsewhere, and has a specific meaning, indicating the total destruction of the enemies of God at an appointed time.

This covenant will prove a delusion and a snare. For at the end of three and a half years it will be disregarded by the perfidious prince that shall come, who will violate all its provisions in favor of the Jews so far as it may guarantee toleration to the pious Israelites in Jerusalem, and in the end the upholders, the aiders and abettors of the enemy of God, will be trodden down in His fury.

Though the great destroyer shall succeed to scatter the power of the holy people, yet he shall not entirely overcome them. He will doubtless succeed in disarming them, if arms shall be used in their defence, and of stripping them of all external defences, yet their integrity shall remain intact. That it is in the gracious purpose of God to shield them, even in the last extremity, we are taught in the following: The Revelator was commanded to "Rise, and measure the *temple of God, and the altar*, and them that *worship therein*. But the court which is without the temple, leave out, and measure it not; for it is *given unto the Gentiles; and the holy city shall they tread under foot forty and two months,*" i. e. three and a half years. Rev. 11: 1-2.

Those *worshiping therein* will have been set apart to the

service of the Almighty, and will be environed by His special providence—a cordon of fire. Rev. 15: 2.

This period of three and a half years points out the duration of that time of trouble, "*such as never was since there was a nation; even to that same time*, Dan. 12: 1, *and at that time thy people*—devout Jews—*shall be delivered, every one that shall be found written in the book.*"

This period of three and a half years will close up the times of the *Gentiles*. During this brief space of time the power of the evil one will have supreme control over all the earth. The church of believers in the Lord Jesus Christ will have been taken up from the earth to be with the Lord. The devout remnant of the Jews will be in Jerusalem under the special protection of God's providence until the Ancient of days shall sit, which shall end this time of *persecution*, and usher in the kingdom of God on earth. Hence, the significance of this period of three and a half years, variously expressed. Wherever it occurs it identifies this time of trouble which shall occur only once in the history of the world.

Matthew, 24: 21–22, referring to the same *time* of *trouble* as the coincidence of the language and the immediate context shows, says: " For then shall be great tribulation, such as was not since the beginning of the world to this time, no, nor ever shall be. And except those days should be shortened, there should no flesh be saved: but for the elect's sake those days shall be shortened." They are limited to three and a half years.

By the elect is meant every one that shall be found written in the book, in the passage just cited from Daniel. This shows most conclusively, if any confirmation was needed, that the 24th chapter of Matthew does not speak of the destruction of Jerusalem by Titus, except in very general terms. That great calamity is fully predicted in the 21st chapter of Luke, however.

"*And I will give power unto my two witnesses, and they shall prophecy a thousand two hundred and three-score days*— i. e. three and a half years—*clothed in sackcloth.*" Rev. 11: 3. That is, during the time of this last *great tribulation.* These two witnesses will doubtless be Elijah and Moses, the servants of God, sent on earth to encourage and support the faithful in the last calamity and trial of faith. For, nevertheless, *when the Son of man cometh, shall he find faith on the earth?*

It is plain that this tribulation will concern chiefly, if not entirely, the *devout Jews*, from the language addressed to Daniel "at that time, *thy people shall be delivered.*" The church of the Lord Jesus shall have been taken up from earth to heaven before this calamitous time shall set in. Of this we will speak hereafter.

As it appears from the scriptures just cited, that the devout Jews will be the object of persecution, in the last great calamity, a few words of explanation seem demanded to set this matter more clearly before the reader. Through this ordeal of tribulation, will they, as a nation, be brought to acknowledge the Lord, when he shall appear as their deliverer. "And so all Israel shall be saved: as it is written, There shall come out of Sion the Deliverer, and shall *turn away ungodliness from Jacob.*" Rom. 11: 26.

But historically, as we have seen hitherto, the secular power will resolve to pursue the policy of reorganizing society and all its institutions, upon the purest principles of materialistic philosophy. All of the spiritual or supernatural will be repudiated and discarded, as delusive, and hence pernicious. The acknowledgment or worship of a spiritual or supernatural being will be treated as a crime against the State. The worship of God, the Almighty *Creator* and *Conservator* of all things, will be treated as high treason, and will be suppressed by the strong arm of the law. False Christianity, the true church having been taken up from earth to heaven, will soon give way before the blandishments and rewards for apostasy held out by the new regime. But the faith of the true Jew, in the God of Abraham, Isaac and Jacob, will prove constant to the end.

A striking exemplification of the religious integrity of the Jew, and his abhorrence of idolatry is afforded by a transaction that happened in the time of the Emperor Caligula, who sent Petronius, as President of Syria, with instruction to set up the imperial image in the temple of God at Jerusalem, with instruction, if the Jews refused to allow it to be done, to compel them by force of arms. "Many ten-thousands of the Jews" says Josephus, "resorted to Petronius, as he was approaching with a great army, and besought him that he would not compel them to transgress and violate the laws of their fathers; but, said they, if thou art entirely resolved to bring this statue and erect it, do thou first kill us, and then do what thou hast resolved on."

Such is the fidelity of the true children of Abraham to the institutions and faith of the fathers.

The same sterling virtue will be wonderfully exemplified by the descendants of this people in the last times.

The short duration of this last terrible period, limited to three and a half years, should not detract in the mind of any one from the importance of the events, which shall be crowded into this short space of time, considering the present means of communicating thought and commands by recent inventions, and the facilities of transporting troops and munitions of war by steam power, over land and sea. The greatest campaign in modern warfare, perhaps in the *history* of warfare, was accomplished in a very few months.

The short duration of this period, the principal actor in this last terrible drama of the world's history, the terrible persecution, distinguished above all others, and as only once to occur, the two extraordinary witnesses, who shall appear on the scene, all go to invest this last time of trial with a prominence in the history of this world, which belongs to no other period. It will be terminated by the direct interposition of heaven.

For, "when *he* shall have accomplished to scatter the power of the holy people, all these things shall be finished." "And they shall be given into *his* hand, i. e. the holy people, until a time and times and the dividing of time. But the judgment shall sit, and they shall take away *his* dominion to consume and to destroy it unto the end. And the kingdom and dominion, and the greatness of the kingdom under the whole heaven, shall be given to the people of the saints of the Most High, whose kingdom is an everlasting kingdom, and *all dominion, shall serve and obey him.*" Dan. 7 : 25–27. The pronouns *he* and *his* in this passage can refer to no other than the prince that shall come, the little horn. Dan. 7.

The prince that shall come is a Roman. If the Romans destroyed the city of Jerusalem and the temple, he is the same as symbolized by the notable little horn, Dan. 7 : 25, as what he shall do proves, and also the three and a half years —the one-half of the seven years of the covenant show, and therefore Roman. The same as symbolized by the apocalyptic beast, Rev. 13 : 1 ; as the forty-two months equals three and a half years, renders specific. And therefore by an entirely independent train of reasoning, we arrive at the conclusion that the Roman Empire must again be revived in Europe, that the prophecies may be fulfilled.

The foregoing is but a brief summary of argument in favor of our first proposition from Daniel 9 : 27, but is sufficient to bring prominently to view the chief actor in the last terrible period of the *times of the Gentiles*, and the connection of other passages, which taken isolated are obscure, but in this connection perfectly clear and intelligible. Scores of volumes have been written upon these prophecies and all leading to confusion or unsatisfactory results. The foregoing harmonizes and makes plain many passages which were otherwise unintelligible.

CHAPTER IX.

SUMMARY.

The following summary of the matters discussed in the foregoing pages will place the subject in a more satisfactory view before the mind of the reader.

The following positions have been conclusively established, we doubt not, and to the entire satisfaction of every believer in the authority of divine revelation.

1. That the four *universal monarchies* symbolized by the great *metalic image*, described in Daniel 2d chapter, must continue from the times of Nebuchadnezzar King of Babylon, until the setting up of the universal kingdom of the God of Heaven.

2. That the four parts of the image composed of gold, silver, brass, iron and potter's clay symbolizes the four successive universal monarchies of the *times of the Gentiles;* the iron the last or Roman. The feet and toes of iron and potter's clay being the last state of this monarchy.

3. The ten toes symbolize ten nationalities, and are therefore identical in symbolic import with the ten horns of the fourth beast, Dan. 7th, which also symbolizes the Roman monarchy; and as the ten horns belong to this fourth beast, the ten kingdoms which they point out must also pertain to the Roman monarchy; and therefore, this monarchy must in the last times be represented by ten nationalities or kingdoms.

4. That the *notable little horn*, described in Dan. 7th, symbolizes a kingdom or political power, which shall spring

up during these nationalities and by superior sagacity, and by conquest acquire an ascendancy among them.

5. This notable little horn as it pertains to the fourth beast, represents one form of the Roman power; and as it attains to undisputed sway, the last and universal dominion in connection with ten confederates, which the Roman Empire shall attain to in the last days of the times of the Gentiles, i. e. of the present age.

6. That the first *apocalyptic beast*, Rev. 13 : 1, is identical as a symbol with the fourth beast, Dan. 7th, and especially with the little horn, and therefore symbolizes the same *Roman universal monarchy about to be revived.*

7. That this Roman power thus pointed out is identical with the "man of sin" foretold by St. Paul. 2 Thes. 2d chapter.—See note supra.

8. That the power symbolized by this first apocryphal beast must arise out of the present nations of Europe, which have sprung out of the ruins of the old Roman Empire.

9. That this power must continue until the God of Heaven shall set up a kingdom on earth.

10. That this power *will* prove to be no other than the old Roman Empire, *atheistic* in principle and endowed with its pristine energy and insatiable thirst for conquest and dominion.

11. That the apocalyptic beast, Rev. 13 : 1, symbolizes a *secular power* and *can not symbolize an ecclesiastical body.* This would be attributing a double meaning to a symbol and would be fatal to all precision.

12. Therefore this beast can not symbolize the Roman Hierarchy or Papacy.

13. But that the abandoned woman, Rev. 13: 7, does symbolize the Roman Hierarchy or Papacy.

14. Neither, therefore, can the "*notable little horn,*" Dan. 7: 8, symbolize the Roman Hierarchy or Papacy.

15. Neither *can* the beast having *two horns* like a lamb, Rev. 13: 11, as this beast symbolizes a character which shall act in conjunction to that of the first beast.

16. Nor can the "*man of sin,*" 2d Thes. 2d chapter, symbolize the Papacy, as the man of sin is identical with the little horn, Dan. 7th.

17. The subordinate parts of this symbol show that the Roman Empire is pointed out; because it will be animated by the spirit and sagacity of the "*old red dragon*" or Satan, as was old Rome.

18. Because the seven heads of the beast symbolize the seven forms of executive administration which shall pertain to the Roman Empire, most have already passed. See Tacitus' introduction to the Annals.

19. The head that had been wounded to death by the sword and did live, shows that imperial Rome is pointed out.

20. Imperial image worship will be a special and prominent feature in the new regime; and therefore a revival of the custom prevalent in the old Empire. See P. L. Trajan, 96.

21. The duration of the power symbolized by this beast, Rev. 13: 1, limited to forty-two months, i. e. three and a half years, so identifies this with other prophecies, that the conclusion is irresistible, that the Roman Empire in its last *revival,* but brief and inglorious career, is here pointed out.

The above statements place the argument so far as we have gone, lucidly and conclusively before the reader. Some repetition and re-statement is unavoidable from the nature of the subject discussed.

The successive stages of events which shall bring on the political changes above alluded to, are more or less fully set forth in the visions of the Apocalypse. A full understanding of these will require a review of certain parts of this wonderful book. But before entering upon this, there is another subject incidentally alluded to more than once in the preceding pages, namely, the taking up of the church of the Lord Jesus, which claims a brief consideration. This will constitute the great *moral* crisis in the world's history.

CHAPTER X.

PROPOSITION II.—THE RAPTURE OF THE CHURCH.

By the rapture of the saints, or as sometimes designated, the *taking up of the church*, is to be understood the special appearing of the Lord Jesus to his disciples, by which is understood all true believers, alone, at the end of the gospel dispensation, to call them unto himself. Those that sleep he will raise from the dead—"*incorruptible, spiritual, immortal.*" Those who are alive and remain on earth, he will change in a moment, in the twinkling of an eye, unto the same *incorruptible, spiritual and immortal* natures, and all being caught up into the clouds shall meet the Lord in the air; and so from thenceforth ever to remain with him as his glorified body.

Let it be distinctly understood that the coming of the Lord to call the true church unto Himself is not the *second advent*, but that the *second advent* points to the second *public appearing* of the Lord, with power and in great glory, accompanied by His saints who had been previously taken up from earth to heaven.

The *second advent*, which shall immediately usher in the kingdom, will occur about seven years after the coming of the Lord to call his church unto Himself. This coming of the Lord is designated—Matt. 25: 6—as the coming of the *bridegroom*.

"And at midnight there was a cry made: Behold, the bridegroom cometh; go ye out to meet him!" This shows that a profound state of indifference will be hanging over all the world at this period. Nevertheless, a certain class designated as ten virgins shall receive in advance some kind of admonition or token of His coming, communicated by the wise to the unwise, who doubtless shall not profit thereby.

The moral significance of this event is without a parallel in the history of the world. The present order of things ends with it. To the church of the living God it will signify life from the dead and the beginning of a state of enduring honor and blessedness. But to the world the death-knell of all its cherished hopes.

This event will mark the beginning of the era of moral insanity and political frenzy, of satanic power and heaven's frowns, of human madness, recklessness and barbarity, attended by God's judgments visited upon men for their sins.

While the church of the Lord Jesus remains on earth, all things will proceed in their accustomed channels; only, evil men and seducers will continue to wax worse and worse. But the ægis of a benignant Providence will cast its shadow of protection over all, falling alike upon the just and the unjust. There will continue to prevail a certain measure of tranquillity among the peoples of the earth, that the gospel may be preached as a testimony to the nations, and for the edification and comfort of those who shall believe. But when the full number of the elect shall have been called in, the gospel having been preached to all nations, the day of testimony will end; and then of the world it may be truly said, that *"Ephraim is joined to his idols, let him alone."*

Let them alone, that they may enjoy to the full the desires of their animal instincts. Let them alone, for a season at least, that they may prosecute their schemes of unholy ambition. Let them alone, that they may realize the full benefit from their boasted attainments in knowledge, and from their scientific achievements; from their wonderful improvements in the science of war and the arts of peace. They have denied the *holy one*, and renounced allegiance to heaven; therefore let them alone, that they may reap the fruit of their own ways.

The moral status of the world will be immediately changed. It will pass out of the sphere of God's providential care and government, and will pass under the auspices of satanic rule. All restraints being removed, the great adversary will reign, without any hindrance being placed upon his authority on earth. The government of the world will be in the hands of his specially appointed agents, whom he will endow with his own spirit, and will control as the agents of his will and the instruments of his malice. Calamitous times must necessarily follow. As it is written: "Woe to the inhabitants of the earth, * * for the devil has come down unto you, having great wrath, because he knoweth that he hath but a short time."

This refers to affairs on earth immediately subsequent to the reception of the church in heaven.

The coming of the Lord to call His church to Himself, will in fact be the *completion* of *the gospel mission—the consummation* of *the work* of *redemption on earth*. For the full and complete salvation of the church will not be achieved until all the *called* are not only justified but also glorified—Rom. 8: 30—and this will not be accomplished until this vile and corrupt body shall be likened unto his glorified and resurrected body, by the change from a mortal to an immortal, from a corruptible to an incorruptible, from a material to a spiritual body, at the resurrection of those who sleep, and the instantaneous and supernatural change of those who are alive and remain on earth at the coming of the Lord. His *return to call the faithful*, therefore, will *be necessary to their full and everlasting beatification.*

Christ has retired personally from the earth but temporarily. The scene of His greatest humiliation and suffering must witness His greatest triumph and exaltation. He left his disciples in the midst of a hostile world with the admonition that the world hateth you. That through trial in the kingdom and patience of Jesus they might finally enter into the rest prepared for them. But he left this soothing promise of affection and regard addressed to the heart. I will not leave you comfortless;—lo! I am with you always—though for a little while you see me not. And finally to crown with fruition their joyous hopes, He said: "*I will come again and receive you unto myself; that where I am, there ye may be also.*" Let us consider this scripture in its connection.

It will be perceived that His words are addressed pointedly to His disturbed disciples on that same memorable night in which he was betrayed, and no allusion is made as though any but themselves, (including all those who should believe in Him through their word,) would be in any wise interested in the subject of His address. What is it?

" In My *Father's house,*" placed in opposition to their then place of abode, "*are many mansions;* if it were not so, I would have told you. *I go to prepare a place for you.* And if I go and prepare a place for you, *I will come again* and *receive you unto Myself;* that *where I am, there ye may be also.*" John 14: 2–3.

By the plain, obvious acceptation of this language, the Lord Jesus promises His disciples, that having retired from earth temporarily, to prepare a place for them, He will come back to them again and *take them hence from earth into the mansions in His Father's house*, that *they may there be with Him*, with Him in the heavenly mansions. And this agrees with the petition expressed in His memorable prayer uttered this same night.

"Father, I will that they also whom Thou hast given Me *be with Me where I am;* that they may *behold My* glory *which Thou hast given* Me." "Where I am," in anticipation of being in person where He was, even then in the spirit, i. e. in the Father's house.

This can not imply the communion of the disembodied spirit at death with Christ, in the mansions of the Father, because the phrase "*they also whom Thou hast given Me,*" includes *all the elect*, the complete number of the saved; and therefore this part of His prayer can only be fulfilled when all the elect, the full complement of the redeemed are gathered home to the Father's house. This can not be accomplished until after the Lord comes to call away His saints, for at His coming there will be those who are alive and remaining on earth. Hence, the departure of the disciples, one by one called away by death, can not be the fulfillment of this scripture. They will be with Him and behold His glory after the resurrection of all those who sleep, and the change of all those who are alive and remain at the coming of the Lord.

This promise is repeated elsewhere with even more directness still, if possible; showing the complete identity of the disciples with Christ, the intimate and inseparable relation subsisting between them. "*I will not* leave *you comfortless;* I will *come to you;* because I live, *ye shall live also.*"

These passages addressed to the disciples on the eve of His departure, being the closing scenes of His ministry, can receive no other construction, if the language is allowed to have its plain and obvious import, than that His dealings with and care over them would not cease until He should return again and take them specially *unto Himself;* and that this event would not concern the world, but only the disciples themselves, as they, and they alone are addressed. He had *chosen* them out of the world, He will come again and *take* them out of the world.

His subsequent sojourn of forty days on earth after His resurrection, so far as it throws light on the subject, rather confirms the foregoing conclusion.

His communications during this period were with His disciples alone. His conferences only with them. His conversation was with none besides. There is no mention of His appearing to any other. He does not appear to have shown Himself to the world, certainly not in His real character during this period of forty days. Of His ascension, they were the only earthly witnesses, and were informed that He would *so come* again in *like manner*, as they saw Him going into heaven.

His coming again to take up the church will be the full *accomplishment of the work of redemption*, incomplete until this shall occur, because the last enemy to be overcome is death, and death and the grave shall not be completely triumphed over until the resurrection of the body.

This will be *preparatory* to the *second advent*, when the Lord shall come *with power* and *in great glory*, with His saints previously taken up, to inaugurate the kingdom.

It follows therefore, that there will be no resurrection at the *second advent*, as is generally understood and taught. The dead will not arise when Christ shall make His public entry into the world to take the kingdom. That event shall concern the living only. For the saints will have been already raised, which is the *first resurrection;* and the *second resurrection* will not take place until after the thousand years of millennial reign shall have passed. The coming of the Lord to call His saints will concern them alone, as has been stated. His *second advent* will *concern all the world besides*. It is for this promised appearing to His saints, that they are commanded to watch. This coming, the hope of the church in all ages, may occur at any moment. Of the happening of this event of such transcendent moment, the world will probably have no knowledge, except that here and there one may have mysteriously disappeared, and some excitements result for a short time; but soon all will be forgotten amid the exciting topics of the day.

A fuller examination of the scriptures having reference to this event is demanded not only by reason of its immense significance, but also, because there is much confusion and indistinctness, even contradiction in the opinions entertained in respect to the future, and especially in reference to the coming of the Lord, by those who have written upon this subject.

The only sure path to satisfactory conclusions on this, as well as other matters taught in the holy scriptures, is to exercise explicit confidence in what has been revealed, giving every passage its due weight.

The same subject may be referred to, and often is in many passages. In some more fully, in others briefly. Now for the purpose of illustration again, on account of its connection with some co-ordinate matter; in another place for the express purpose of explaining and enforcing a specific subject of divine revelation. It is obvious therefore, that all the passages having reference to any particular matter should be considered, giving to each its full weight in order to a correct understanding of the subject and its relation and application.

The coming of the Lord is frequently referred to in connection with the resurrection of the dead, but it will be observed by a careful scrutiny of all such passages, that the *sleeping saints* are invariably intended. There is no reference made, it will be found, to the resurrection of the ungodly, until after the thousand years of Christ's reign on earth with the saints, who have had part in the *first* resurrection. "But *the rest of the dead lived not again until the thousand years were finished.*" Rev. 20: 5.

The attention of the reader is invited to the vision described in Rev. 12: 1-5.

There is reason to infer that many things perfectly well understood in the time of oral instruction, while the Apostles were living, afterward were liable in a manner to become confused or confounded with other matters, and consequently to be lost sight of, because they were not recorded in distinct, didactic terms. They are incidentally referred to in the epistles of the Apostles, in connection with other topics, which form the subject of discussion and are in a manner taken for granted as truths well understood; and when their place in the great system of revealed truth is once recognized, all is clear and satisfactory. To keep alive such truths and to bring them strikingly before the world, appears to be one object of the book of Revelations. The figures of this book, when once the import of the symbols are understood, present the subject taught with most startling significance, and invest it with a freshness and reality comparable only to a painting executed by a most skillful artist—for the import of symbolic language can be determined with absolute certainty. Such is the uniformity in the use of these figures.

An illustration of this is furnished in the vision of the "little book open in the hand of the angel"—Rev. 10: 1.

This *little book open* must be considered in contrast with the book in the right hand of him that sat on the throne, written within and on the back side, *sealed with seven seals.* Rev. 5: 1. The latter contains the unrevealed things of the future, those that have not been previously disclosed; whereas the contents of the little *open book* must be regarded as embracing things about to be republished, under circumstances and in a manner calculated to render their publication most impressive and significant, and therefore of the highest moment.

The contents of the little open book comprehends matters which had been previously revealed, and were or should have been known, but had in a measure become obliterated by the departure from and corruptions of the pure revelation as first delivered by our Lord and His immediate successors. This little open book comes in as a parenthetical clause and follows the seventh trumpet, not as to continuity of sense but location only, comprehending the things recorded in chapters 12, 13 and 14 of the book of Revelations.

Among the truths herein republished, under symbolic figures, is that of the *"Rapture of the Church,"* brought to view in the figure of the *man-child* caught up unto God and to His throne.

Rev. 12: 1–5 presents to view the picture of a woman appearing in heaven, clothed with the sun, and the moon under her feet, and on her head a crown of twelve stars. We have seen elsewhere that this woman symbolized the Jewish State.

"She brought forth a man-child who was to rule all nations with a rod of iron." This man-child primarily symbolizes the Lord Jesus. See 2d Ps. and other scriptures before referred to.

But this symbol of the man-child includes the church also. Some have supposed that this woman symbolizes the Christian Church; but this can not be the case, because she is the mother of the *man-child*, respecting the symbolic signification of which there can be no question, as the language in the 2d Ps. and also Is. 9: 25, and also Rev. 19: 15 shows. Besides, *"salvation is of the Jews,"* and the mother of Jesus according to flesh was a Jewess, The man, Christ Jesus, was a Jew; from Him *sprang the church*. "Her *child was caught up* unto God and to His throne."—Rev. 12: 5. This includes *"the general assembly* and church of the first born—which are written in heaven."

This follows from the connection between the glorified humanity of the Son of God and the sanctified and glorified humanity of the redeemed. It was the child that was caught up, symbolizing the church, the body of Christ. Not but that the ascension of the resurrected body of the Lord is referred to primarily, but the full significance of the figure includes the church likewise. Because the things revealed in this book have reference to the future, "things that *must shortly come to pass.*" And the body of Christ— i. e. his humanity—is identified in the mystery of redemption with the church.

And this revelation was not given until many years after the ascension of the Lord. He was the first fruit of the resurrection from among the dead, afterwards, they that are Christ's at his coming.

But on account of the mystic connection of the church of the redeemed with the body of Christ, being *bone* of *his bone* and *flesh* of *his flesh*, in the language of the Apostle, the snatching up of the church at the end of the dispensation may identify as fulfilled, the ascension of the Lord's body and be regarded as one transaction completed and finished. So then the church therefore must be regarded as included in the symbol of the man-child. Caught up unto God and to his throne, the glorified church will participate with Christ in the government of the world.

This necessarily follows from the connection and relation subsisting between the different figures brought to view in the vision. For it is said:

"And the dragon stood before the woman which was ready to be delivered, for to devour her child as soon as it was born. And she brought forth a man-child, who was to rule all nations with a rod of iron: and her child *was caught up unto God, and to his throne.* And the *woman fled into the wilderness,* where *she had a place prepared of God.*"

The child was caught up to escape the fury of the dragon. The woman for the same cause fled into the wilderness, to the place of refuge prepared of God. These two events are presented as following each other in succession, and if not simultaneous, yet as parts of the same vision, and actuated by the same cause. If the Jewish church shall take refuge in Palestine, to escape the dire persecution of the last days, the church of the Lord Jesus will have been taken up out of the world to escape from the same great calamity, before the times of persecution shall have set in, or at least grown fierce against all who shall not bow its knee to the image of the beast. Both these events are in the future.

The church of the Lord Jesus will be caught up to heaven about the same time that the Jewish church shall take refuge in the place prepared for her protection and sustentation.

The manner in which these two events are connected in the vision, and the relation existing between them, manifestly demand this interpretation. Both are in the future, they shall occur simultaneous, or nearly so. The impelling cause in each being the same, and the end also, namely, security from a terribly persecuting adversary, who in the purpose of God, shall have free scope for his malice and fury for a short space in the last days.

It has already been intimated that the taking up *of the church* is the *event* in the *near future*, which shall mark the *beginning* of the *end of the times of the Gentiles*, and the end of tranquillity on earth. For as soon as the church is gone, calamitous times must follow. The angel having the seal of the living God cried with a loud voice to the four angels to whom it was given to hurt the earth and the sea, saying, "*Hurt not the earth, neither the sea, nor the trees, till we have sealed the servants of our God in their foreheads.* Rev. 7 : 3, until the full number of the servants of the living God are set apart to be with the Lord, for the earth will no longer be a suitable place for their abode. Then all will be changed. For as in the days of Noah, they eat, they drank, they bought, they sold, they married and were given in marriage. So shall be the state of the skeptical and deluded world when the Lord shall call his church away. As soon as Noah entered into the Ark, the flood came and destroyed them all.

Also as it was in the day that Lot fled out of Sodom— the sun rose fair upon Sodom that morning—but as soon as Lot had escaped to the mountains, God rained fire and brimstone (from God) out of heaven upon the doomed cities of the plain.

So will it be in the last times, as soon as the church of the Lord Jesus shall have been taken out of the world, the vials of God's wrath will be poured out upon the earth, given over to satanic rule. For surely the things written aforetime were written for our learning, and things past in the special providences of God are types of things to come. The lessons of Providence are few, but the examples illustrating and enforcing them are many and impressive.

Here we have then this whole truth presented in one figure, that of the "man-child" caught up unto God and to His throne.

Christ is now sitting at the right hand of glory and honor of His Father's throne, participating in the exercise of His almighty power and dominion over the universe—as He said to His disciples: "All power is given unto Me, in heaven and in earth." It is in the purpose of God the Father that the church of the redeemed shall also share with Christ in the administration of the affairs in this world.

For this purpose the dead will be raised incorruptible, and the living changed, and all caught up unto God and to His throne to be with the Lord: this will be preparatory to their descent to earth with Him, when He shall appear in triumph as "*the Lord of Lords and King of Kings.*"

A further illustration as well as confirmation is furnished by the scene in heaven described. Rev. 12: 10–12.

The grand consummation of the event, in which all heaven will manifest so lively an interest, is described in the following passage: "*Now is come salvation and strength, and the kingdom of our God, and the power of His Christ.*" Why? What grand event shall have been finally consummated? For all is yet in the future. An event in which all the heavenly intelligences seem so deeply interested and to have long anticipated. "*Now is come salvation* and *strength*, in opposition to weakness, tribulations and the trials of the saints.

And why salvation and strength? What grand moral achievement laid up in the councils of God from eternity has been accomplished, over which the heavens are called upon to rejoice? Why, "the accuser of our brethren is cast down." Cast down, whence? Why cast down of heaven where he accused the saints. He which accused them before our God day and night, has been cast down.

The redeemed from the earth by the blood of Christ, are to be understood by the words "our brethren," and that the scene described is in heaven; and therefore the redeemed are with the Lord in heaven. For it is added: "And they overcame Him by the blood of the Lamb, and by the word of their testimony." That is the devil who accused them before God. This accusation was made while they were still on the earth, but now they are with the Lord in heaven, and Satan is cast down. Therefore it is said: "Woe to the inhabitants of the earth and the sea," there will be found no place any longer in heaven for the accuser, when the glorified church shall be received and installed therein.

And by the brethren here, we must further understand the whole church of the redeemed completed. Not merely disembodied spirits of just men, absent from the body and present with the Lord before the resurrection, but the whole body of the redeemed who shall have part in the first resurrection, are to be understood as included in the phrase, *our brethren*, those of the old as well as the new dispensation. Who is speaking in heaven? Surely one who speaks with authority, and by *our brethren* is included all who shall believe. The term is used comprehensively and includes all.

The vision described in the 7th chapter of Rev. presents us the church in heaven.

Four angels are represented as standing on the four

corners of the earth, holding the four winds of the earth, signifying the elements of commotion, dissention and revolution for the time being restrained by providential agencies, which are the agents of God's purposes on earth. They were commanded "hurt not the earth, neither the sea, nor the trees, till we have *sealed* the servants of our God in their foreheads." To seal, signifies to mark, designate or set aside any thing to a particular use or for a particular purpose. Here it means the work of regenerating grace. The seal of the Holy Ghost impressed upon the conscience, is the earnest token to the believer of the final and full salvation, which includes the glorification of the body. The Revelator proceeds: "And I heard the number of them which were *sealed;* and there were *sealed* a hundred and forty and four thousand of all the tribes of the children of Israel."

This number is a complete square, multiplied by 1,000. The two factors 12x12, each denoting subordinate completeness. They are Hebrew signs. Their joint product multiplied by 1,000, comprehends fullness and exhaustive completeness. The one, the full number of God's servants, *sealed* and set apart to His service under the old dispensation, patriarchs, prophets, ancient worthies, devout men and women of old.

The other, the complete number of the redeemed of Israel, according to the election of grace, called to believe unto the justification of the soul under the dispensation of the gospel—Rom. 11:—the complete number of the redeemed of Israel.

Those are the *sealed* that are made partakers in the great salvation in Christ Jesus, through the signal mercies of God toward them. Set apart—saved beyond a peradventure.

But these are not all the redeemed. For, says the Revelator: "After this I beheld, and lo, a great multitude, which no man could number, of all nations, and kindreds, and peoples, and tongues, stood before the throne and before the Lamb, clothed with white robes and palms in their hands." This innumerable multitude includes the whole number of God's elect, *sealed* from among all nations; and therefore, with those above, the full and complete number of the redeemed. Those were sealed on earth—John 3 : 33—to believe is to be sealed with the holy seal of faith. For "he *that hath received* his *testimony, hath set to his seal* that God is true."

This host is here represented as being in heaven. But the affairs of the world will still go on, for the woe trumpets and vials of wrath are yet to come. Hence, they have been transferred from earth to heaven since they first believed. "They are before the throne of God, and serve Him day and night—i. e. unceasingly—in his temple, and He that sitteth on the throne shall dwell among them; for the Lamb which is in the midst of the throne shall feed them, and shall lead them unto living fountains of waters; and God shall wipe away all tears from their eyes." Rev. 7 : 17.

Here is the true church perfect and complete with Christ and in heaven. This is certainly before the millennium and after the days of testimony, and consequently must represent the church with Christ, being the fulfillment of His prayer: "Father, I will that they also whom Thou hast given Me be with Me where I am; that they may behold My glory which Thou hast given Me."

In the passage just cited from the book of Revelation, there are no symbols used. The language is highly figurative it is true, and the scene is described as seen in a vision. But there are no mysterious types of hidden import in the passage. It is indeed a vivid presentation of a statement of facts, shortly to come to pass, and must be so understood.

When no symbols are used, the language upon all fair principles of interpretation should be allowed its ordinary meaning. All language is more or less figurative, but the import of the figures are from long usage well understood. Because a passage is found in the Apocalypse, it should not therefore, be ruled as outside the canons of ordinary speech, which are applicable in determining the meaning of words and phrases. When language is descriptive, it should be understood as significant of the specific facts described. When narrative, of the current events set forth in the narration. And when symbols occur, they must be understood according to their ascertained meaning, as gathered from former use, or explanations given, or from the analogy of language.

Much of the difficulty encountered, and most of the errors fallen into, by those who have attempted to explain this book of Revelations, have doubtless, arisen mainly from the fact, that because this is a symbolic book, interpreters have assumed, that there must therefore, be some occult or mysterious meaning concealed under the language, which must be sought for and brought to light. And therefore, the greater the resources of the imagination, the greater will be the extravaganza and cloud of hallucinations evolved.

That the redeemed will be invested with immortal and celestial bodies while on the earth, and afterwards, transferred to heaven, is a truth taught clearly and emphatically by the Apostle Paul.

"Behold," says the Apostle, "I shew you a mystery; We shall not all sleep, but we shall all be changed," the "we" includes believers only, "In a moment, in the twinkling of an eye at the last trump; for the trumpet shall sound, and the dead shall be raised incorruptible, and we shall be changed. For this corruptible must put on incorruption, and this mortal must put on immortality." 1 Cor. 15: 51-53.

The trumpet is the signal for those who sleep to awake. The figure is taken from the custom prevalent in the sleeping camp of an army. The soldiers are awakened out of their sleep by the sound of the trumpet.

The incorruptible and immortal, resurrected from among the dead, with the living changed into the image of the heavenly, shall all be "caught up together with them in the clouds, to meet the Lord in the air: and so shall we ever be with the Lord." 1 Thess. 4: 17.

The innumerable host of the glorified, including the immortals resurrected from among the dead, and of the living changed on earth, shall all be assembled in heaven, preparatory to the grand scene, which shall mark the coming of the Lord to take the Kingdom.

11 "And I saw heaven opened, and behold a white horse; and he that sat upon him *was* called Faithful and True, and in righteousness he doth judge and make war.

12 "His eyes *were* as a flame of fire, and on his head *were* many crowns; and he had a name written, that no man knew, but he himself.

13 "And he *was* clothed with a vesture dipped in blood: and his name is called The Word of God.

14 "And the armies *which were* in heaven followed him upon white horses, clothed in fine linen, white and clean.

15 "And out of his mouth goeth a sharp sword, that with it he should smite the nations: and he shall rule them with a rod of iron: and he treadeth the winepress of the fierceness and wrath of Almighty God.

16 "And he hath on *his* vesture and on his thigh a name written, KING OF KINGS, AND LORD OF LORDS." Rev. 19: 11-16.

The *scriptures* do not *warrant* the conclusion, that there will be a *general promiscuous resurrection of the dead, of the just* and *of the unjust, at one and the same time*. This may appear to be a startling announcement to some of our readers, accustomed as they have been to look at these matters through the medium of the standards of faith and doctrine, set up by the various sects of Christendom, since the idea of a general resurrection, and a general judgment is the prevalent one. The resurrection of the saints will be a *special resurrection*, as has been shown, and will precede the period of the last *great tribulation* that shall come upon the earth. Nevertheless all will be raised, the wicked for judgment and condemnation, but the saints that they may reign with Christ on earth. The resurrected saints will rule the nations of the earth one thousand years, at least, while the rest of the dead still sleep on in their graves.

The scriptures distinctly speak of a *resurrection of life*, and a *resurrection of judgment*, i. e. for condemnation. *Two resurrections*, a resurrection of the *just* and a resurrection of the *unjust.* Of the former, that they may reign on earth over the nations with Christ; of the latter, that they may be judged and condemned, for to judge is to condemn. All who are judged must be condemned, as they must be judged according to the deeds done in the body. "*Enter not* into judgment with thy servant, O, Lord, for in thy sight shall no flesh living be justified."

These two resurrections, namely, that of the just and that of the unjust, will be at least one thousand years asunder.

"The resurrection of the saints" says one, "is a special favor of God, such as was manifested in Christ's own resurrection; because they are saved already, because they have got eternal life, because they are the delight of God, not as they are in themselves, but as they are in Christ, that they are taken up and dealt with apart by themselves, as not a part of this world's government, except in so far as they are kings of it; whereas the wicked will be raised for judgment, which is nothing but condemnation."

The passage of scripture, John 5: 24, 28, does not necessarily teach a promiscuous general resurrection of the just and of the unjust, though it has been generally so understood, and is the chief passage relied upon in support of that idea. Our Lord there speaks of the resurrection in general terms. A general resurrection, the passage plainly teaches, as to the certainty that all shall be raised, but not necessarily at the same time, as the contrary is plainly taught in other passages. The passage above referred to is as follows:— "Verily, verily, I say unto you, He that heareth my word, and believeth on him that sent me, hath everlasting life, and shall not come into condemnation;" i. e. judgment, "but is passed from death unto life." "Marvel not at this: for the hour is coming, in the which all that are in the graves shall hear his voice, and shall come forth; they that have done good, unto the resurrection of life; and they that have done evil, unto the resurrection of damnation," that is, *judgment for judgment*, and *condemnation* and *damnation* are each designated by the same word in the original.

Here we have two resurrections distinctly pointed out, a resurrection of *life*, and a *judgment resurrection*.

The phrase "the hour is coming" does not necessarily imply the same exact period in future time, but must be understood in the more general sense, as equivalent to the word age or era. The word is so used in the immediate context: "Verily, verily, I say unto you, *The hour is coming*, and now is, when the dead shall hear the voice of the Son of

God: and they that hear shall live." Here the dead implies those dead in sin, and who shall be quickened into life by the voice of the gospel message; and therefore the phrase "the hour *is coming* and now is," must refer to the gospel dispensation. This has already lasted more than eighteen hundred years. In a similar sense must the phrase "*the hour is coming*, in the which all that are in the graves shall hear His voice," be understood.

It is, therefore, conclusively shown by the above citations, that there will be a resurrection both of the *just* and the *unjust*, but the end for which they shall be raised will be quite different. The wicked will be raised for judgment —i. e. condemnation—but the righteous will be raised incorruptible, immortal, and will not come into judgment, because they have passed from death unto life; but will be raised from among the dead for quite another purpose altogether, namely, that they may reign with Christ on earth. For He said to His disciples: "Verily I say unto you, *That ye which have followed Me in the regeneration, when the Son of man shall sit in the throne of His glory, ye also shall sit upon twelve thrones, judging the twelve tribes of Israel.*"— Matt. 19: 28. How absurd to maintain that such shall be brought to judgment. St. Paul has now been in heaven eighteen hundred years with Christ, and so also the millions of the redeemed. For what purpose should such be brought to judgment? They will not be judged, because they belong to Christ, because they are identified with His resurrected—as they shall be likened unto His glorious— body; because they shall appear with Him in glory. "When Christ, who is our life, shall appear, then shall ye also appear with Him in glory." The saints, who are His mystical body identified with the Lord, shall come with Him as the redeemed, and glorified, and distinguished above all.

To judge is to exercise the function of government. This was the signification of the word among the eastern nations. The judges sat at the gates of the city and administered justice. So were the Jews governed before, and even after, the kings; for the king was a judge. The gates of the city were the marts of trade, for the intercourse of the people with those from without, and for the exchange of commodities. Therefore the judge sat at the gate to decide all questions of controversy that might arise among the people, and to publish all edicts and regulations that might be deemed necessary.

The promise therefore to sit on twelve thrones, judging the twelve tribes of Israel, implies that they shall bear rule over them, that the saints shall participate in the administration of affairs in the Messiah's kingdom, and shall have precedence over the children of Israel themselves. Not only shall they rule over them, but over all the world; for the Apostle says: "Do ye not know that the saints shall judge the world." How can these scriptures be explained on any other hypothesis than that stated, namely, that the saints of the Most High shall possess the kingdom.

A summary of what the scriptures teach upon the subject of the personal reign of the saints with Christ on earth is given in Rev. 20: 4-6: "And I saw thrones, and they sat upon them, and judgment was given unto them: and I saw the souls of them that were beheaded for the witness of Jesus, and for the word of God, and which had not worshiped the beast, neither his image, neither had received his mark upon their foreheads, or in their hands; and they lived and reigned with Christ a thousand years. But the rest of the dead lived not again until the thousand years were finished. This is the first resurrection. Blessed and holy is he that hath part in the first resurrection: on such the second death hath no power, but they shall be priests of God and of Christ, and shall reign with Him a thousand years."

By the word "*souls*" we must understand personalities, and is equivalent to living beings, ψυχας, as in Peter 3: 20: "When once the long suffering of God waited in the days of Noah, while the ark was preparing, wherein few, that is, eight *souls*, were saved by water." This is evident from the fact that those spoken of as the souls of them that were beheaded had been raised from the dead, for "they lived and reigned with Christ a thousand years. But the rest of the dead lived not again until the thousand years were finished. This is the first resurrection." Those that had participated in the first resurrection lived and reigned with Christ, and all that lived and reigned had participated in the first resurrection. But the rest of the dead lived not again until the thousand years were finished. The word "*again*" refers back to their former existence as living beings on earth, and implies that they shall be raised from the dead at the end of the thousand years. But those who shall have participated in the exalted blessing of having a part in the first resurrection, shall reign with Christ a thousand years, while the remainder of the millions, who had succumbed to the grim monster, should continue to sleep in their graves. The first resurrection must precede the thousand years' reign; and the second resurrection, which is implied in the words "first resurrection," will not take place until after the thousand years of millennial reign of the saints on earth.

This is the plain import of the above cited passage. The language is plain narrative, and to attempt to give it any other turn, is sheer trifling with sacred things, as we have seen that it is in perfect harmony with what is taught elsewhere in the epistles, especially of St. Paul.

It would be a strange contradiction to say that those who shall judge the world shall themselves be the subjects of judgment. The saints shall judge, not only men, but angels also. 1 Cor. 6: 2-3: *"Do ye not know that the saints shall judge the world?"* "Know ye not that we shall judge angels?" says the Apostle Paul to the Corinthians.

The scene of the final judgment before the great *"white throne,"* plainly points out a class, by implication at least, whose names are found written in the book of life, who will be exempt from judgment. For the books will be opened and another book shall be opened, which is the book of life; and the dead shall be judged according to the things written in *the books*, according to their works. "And the sea gave up the dead which were in it; and death and hell delivered up the dead which were in them:"—turned out their subjects for judgment—"and they were judged every man according to their works. And death and hell were cast into the lake of fire. This is the second death. And whosoever was not found written in the book of life was cast into the lake of fire." This implies that there will be a class whose names shall be found written in the book of life, and who shall be exempt from judgment, as they belonged to an entirely different order of things. Because those that shall be judged at this final judgment, shall be judged according to the things written in the BOOKS, —according to their works—and condemned, as all who shall be judged according to their works must be, and these shall belong to a class whose names are not found written in the book of life.

Here we have the second and final resurrection and the final judgment. The sea shall give up the dead, and death and Hades shall deliver up their dead for final judgment.

This can not be at the coming of the Lord as the various sects contend. For this presents quite a different state of things from that when the Son of man shall be revealed. For then, as in the days of Noah, they ate, they drank, they married wives and were given in marriage, until the day that Noah entered into the ark and the flood was upon the world; or, as in the day that Lot fled out of Sodom, clear, serene, bright shone the sun on the doomed city that morning. But here all will be terror and dismay. For "*I saw a great white throne, and Him that* sat on it, from whose face the *earth* and the *heaven fled* away; and there was found no place for them."

The final judgment of the *unjust* raised for that purpose at the end of the thousand years of the millennial reign of saints on earth, shall take place before the *great white* throne and before Him that sat on it. When the dead, both small and great, raised up from the sea and the earth yielded up by death and Hades for the express purpose, shall be judged according to their works. "*The dead, small and great,*" here referred to, are the same as "*the rest of the dead,*"—verse 5—who should live not again until the thousand years were finished, and excludes those who shall have part in the first resurrection, who shall have been raised more than a thousand years previously and for a different purpose; namely, that they might glorify God by being changed into the image of His Son, and reign with Him on the earth. From this it is evident that the saints will be raised and changed as a special favor and dealt with separate and apart from the world, because they are not of the world, but chosen out of the world.

The character of the resurrection of the saints as connected with the resurrection of the body of Christ from the grave, is pointed out by the Apostle Paul, Rom. 8: 11. He says:

"If the Spirit of Him that raised up Jesus from the dead dwell in you, He that raised up Christ from the dead shall also quicken *your* mortal bodies by His Spirit that dwelleth in you." Here is the link that connects the believer with the Lord, namely, the spirit that dwelleth in you—if ye be the Lord's—connecting the believer in an inseparable relation with the Lord now and in the resurrection. This is the end of the gracious purpose of God in the redemption of the body. To take from among men wretches, sold under sin and in extreme misery and degradation, and elevate them to glory, honor and immortality—to thrones, dominions and principalities, through the body of Christ. The regeneration of the soul, by Almighty energy, is the first step in the grand achievement which God has purposed to accomplish by His Spirit, that dwelleth in all those who shall sustain the relationship of joint heirs to His Son. "For as many *as are led* by the *spirit* of *God, they are the sons of God.*"

Regeneration is the beginning of the good work which will be perfected in that day when the Lord Jesus shall be revealed, and all so favored and so distinguished are destined to sustain the closest relation to Christ Himself. The spirit of him that raised up Christ from the dead, in dwelling in the elect of God, will link them in an inseparable union with the Lord. If they have the spirit of Christ they are his; and if his spirit dwell in them, it will raise them up to reign with him. For *He "shall change our vile body,"* if we sustain that relation, *"that it may be fashioned* like unto his glorious body, according to the working whereby he is able even to subdue all things unto himself." Phil. 3: 21.

The Apostle Paul states this relationship even more clearly and forcibly still,—Rom. 8: 29. "For whom He did foreknow, he also did predestinate to be conformed to the image of his Son, that He might be the *first born among many brethren.*" Christ the first fruits of the resurrection, then they that are Christ's at His coming.

There is not the most remote intimation in any of the numerous passages, that speak of the resurrection of the saints, that any other than the dead in Christ *will be concerned.* No mention of the resurrection of the unrighteous dead in connection with the saints, showing that the resurrection at the coming of the Lord, will be a special favor, and concern the righteous dead alone, and that those who are alive and remain on the earth, being the disciples of the Lord waiting and expecting His coming will be instantly changed from mortal to immortal.

They are called His brethren in the above cited passage. The Lord Himself so designates them. All who are conversant with the New Testament will call to mind that touching scene which happened on the morning of the resurrection, recorded John 20: 11–17. "But Mary stood without at the sepulchre weeping: and as she wept she stooped down *and looked* into the sepulchre, and seeth two angels in white, sitting, the one at the head, and the other at the feet, where the body of Jesus had lain. And they say unto her, Woman, why weepest thou? She saith unto them, Because they have taken away my Lord, and I know not where they have laid him. * * * Jesus saith unto her, Woman, why weepest thou? whom seekest thou? She, supposing him to be the gardener, saith unto him, Sir, if thou have borne him hence, tell me where thou hast laid him, and I will take him away. Jesus saith unto her, Mary. She turned herself, and saith unto him,

Rabboni: which is to say, Master. Jesus saith unto her, Touch me not, for I am not yet ascended to my Father: but go to my brethren, and say unto them, I ascend unto my Father, and your Father, and to my God, and your God." Here He calls His disciples *His brethren*, and still further declares also, that His Father is *their* Father, His God *their* God. Showing that the relation subsisting between the Lord Jesus and His disciples constituted the family of one God and one Father; and the same is true of all those who shall believe. This relationship will be completely and fully realized when the Lord shall return to call His church unto Himself. "For the Lord himself shall descend from heaven with a shout, with the voice of the archangel, and with the trump of God: and the dead in Christ shall rise first:" there is nothing said here about any other dead, "Then we which are alive and remain," but having been changed, "shall be caught up together with them in the clouds, to meet the Lord in the air: and so shall we ever be with the Lord." This relates solely to believers. 1 Thess. 4: 16, 17.

Here then is not a word said respecting the resurrection of any except the dead in Christ. They shall rise first. Then what follows? Why, "we which are alive and remain, shall be caught up in the clouds, to meet the Lord in the air." This descent of the Lord shall concern directly no one else. This is the plain statement of the passage. If any others were included, certainly it would be shown at least in some parallel passage of scripture. But it will be a vain search to attempt to find such. The voice of the archangel, and the trump of God will awake those only who sleep in Christ. This return of the Lord to awake the dead and change the living was, therefore, the cherished hope and earnest desire of the early church, while the words of the Lord Jesus and of His Apostles were yet fresh. Before they had become obscured by a cloud of false tradition, or perverted by false theories, or rendered of none effect by rationalistic exegesis.

Because it would be for them, the perfect realization of all promised blessings in Christ Jesus. The triumph over all enemies. The attainment of perfect fruition in the immediate presence of the Lord.

For this, the heart of the great Apostle of the Gentiles, yearned. "Yea doubtless," says he, "and I count all things but loss for the excellency of the knowledge of Christ Jesus my Lord." He proceeds—

"That I may know him, and the power of his resurrection, and the fellowship of his sufferings, being made conformable unto his death; if by any *means I might attain unto the resurrection of the dead.*" Phil. 3: 10–11.

Unto this he has not yet attained. Though he has been absent from the body and present with the Lord, a glorified spirit in heaven, lo, these eighteen hundred years; still the Apostle Paul has not yet apprehended that for which he was apprehended by Christ, namely, the resurrection of the body, and the perfect union with the glorified body of Christ—the head of the new creation and the supreme Lord over all.

Of this earnest desire and expectation the Apostle speaks in the immediate prospect of death. 2 Tim. 4: 6–8, he says: "The time of my departure is at hand. I have fought a good fight, I have finished my course, I have kept the faith: Henceforth there is laid up for me a *crown* of *righteousness*, which the Lord, the righteous judge, shall give me at *that day:* and not to me only, but unto all them also that love his appearing." Henceforth there is *laid up for me a crown of righteousness.* It is laid up in waiting, but not to be obtained until *that day.* What day? Why the day when the Lord Jesus shall return to raise the righteous dead; and not only for him, but for all them also that love his appearing. There will be a general participation of the resurrected and glorified saints in the psalms of victory and crowns of glory *when the Lord shall come.* We see, therefore, that his appearing is not at the death of the believer, as that day is placed in contrast with the Apostle's *departure.* His departure to be with Christ, though a blessed consummation of earth's trials, is not the Lord's appearing.

The foregoing passages lead to but one conclusion, that the coming of the Lord to raise the dead will be a special favor to be conferred on his sleeping saints alone—there is nowhere even an intimation to the contrary—and at the same time he will change the living who shall remain on the earth, waiting and expecting his coming. Taking therefore the word of God for our guide, we can nowhere find that a general resurrection of both the just and of the unjust shall take place on the same day. It is not taught. But the scriptures speak invariably of the dead in Christ, as those who shall have part in the first resurrection, and that they shall be raised from among the dead, and together with the changed living snatched up in the clouds, to meet the Lord and ever afterward to be associated with Him. This, that they be taken out of the world and shielded from the hour of temptation that shall come upon all the world, and as preparatory to their descent to earth with the Lord, when He shall come to assert his rightful authority over all as *"Lord of Lords and King of Kings."* This shall come to pass at the end of the present Gentile dispensation. For "I saw in the night visions," says Daniel, "and behold, one like the Son of man came with the clouds of heaven, and came to the Ancient of days, and they brought Him near before Him. And there was given Him dominion, and glory, and a kingdom, that all people, nations, and languages, should serve Him: his dominion is an everlasting dominion, which shall not pass away, and His kingdom, that which shall not be destroyed." Dan. 7: 13–14.

In this kingdom the saints shall participate, for in verse 18 it is said: "But the saints of the Most High shall take the kingdom, and possess the kingdom for ever, even for ever and ever."

The saints of the Most High shall reign conjointly in the kingdom with the Messiah, who is the same as the one like to the Son of man, the same as the Lord Jesus, who shall reign upon the throne of David. For the same kingdom, both in duration and in extent, shall be given to the people of the *saints* of the Most High. For it is said: "And the kingdom and dominion, and the greatness of the kingdom under the whole heaven, shall be given to the people of the *saints* of the Most High, whose kingdom is an everlasting kingdom." Dan. 7:27. By the people of the saints of the "*Most High*" must be understood those who shall constitute the innumerable army of those dwelling previously in the high or heavenly places. The saints of the *High* or *heavenly places* as the words of the original Hebrew might be rendered. These must therefore include the resurrected saints previously taken up by the Lord to heaven. The heavenly, in opposition to the Jewish saints, who shall remain on the earth until the Lord shall come. When the Lord shall come, therefore, to take the kingdom, the heavenly *saints* will come with Him.

The coming of the Lord with his *saints* to take vengeance, was among the things very early revealed to mankind, even among the antediluvians. For the Apostle Jude says, speaking of vengeance that shall fall upon the corrupters of the earth in the last times: "And Enoch also, the seventh from Adam, prophesied of these, saying, Behold, the Lord cometh with ten thousand of his saints, to execute judgment upon all, and to convince all that are ungodly among them of all their ungodly deeds which they have ungodly committed, and of all their hard speeches which ungodly sinners have spoken against him. Jude 14-15.

How fitly does the Apostle Jude describe the coming times when the ungodly, vaunting, blasphemous Roman emperor, aided and abetted by the ungodly, apostate, unbelieving Jews, under the lead of Anti-Christ, shall openly oppose himself against, and blaspheme and defy the name of God and of Christ.

The Apostle Paul also administers comfort to the brethren at Thessalonica, by assuring them that they should have rest, when *"the Lord* Jesus *shall be revealed* from heaven with his *mighty angels*, in *flaming fire* taking *vengeance on them that know not God."*

The coming of Christ to the *world in wrath* and terror will be quite a different *scene from that of his appearing to his disciples to fulfill* his promise made in love—"I will come again, and receive you unto myself, that where I am, there ye may be also." When he shall come to call his saints all the world will be lulled into tranquillity and repose. For he said: *"Behold, I come as a thief in the night;* watch therefore, for ye know not the day, nor the hour, wherein the Son of man cometh." But when he shall come *with* all his saints, to call the unbelieving nations before him, the event will be preceded by portentous signs and warnings. Signs in the sun, signs in the moon, the sea and the waves roaring, and men's hearts failing them in apprehension of the things about to come,

The coming of the Lord to call His saints from earth to heaven will be that of the return of a long expected benefactor, who had journeyed into a far country to seek a kingdom and returned to invite his faithful and chosen servants to come and participate with Him in the government. But his coming with His mighty angels to take vengeance, will strike terror and dismay into a guilty world, who will call to the rocks and mountains to fall upon them to hide them from the face of Him that sitteth upon the throne and from the Lamb, for the great day of His wrath shall have come, and who will be able to stand.

The Father is glorified by the exaltation of His Son to sit at His right hand. As the reward of His obedience God hath highly exalted Him above every name. Christ has therefore sit down at the right hand of the *majesty on high*, upon His Father's throne. But He will afterward rise up from His Father's throne and take His own throne. His kingdom is now in waiting until the glorified subjects shall be gathered in and sealed by the Holy Ghost, when the complete number of His elect shall have been called and renewed, the preparatory work will be accomplished and then Christ shall rise up from His Father's throne and descend to earth in the glory of His Father, with all His holy angels including His glorified saints. He will then come to the earth "in flaming fire taking vengeance on them that know not God, and that obey not the gospel of our Lord Jesus Christ: who shall be punished with everlasting destruction from the presence of the Lord, and from the glory of His power; When He shall come to be glorified in (that is among) His saints, and to be admired in all them that believe." 2 Thess. 1: 8, 9, 10.

For unto Him every knee shall bow and every tongue confess, that Jesus Christ is Lord to the glory of God, the

Father. Not while He sits on His Father's throne, but when He shall take His own throne. For He must reign until He hath put all enemies under His feet.

In the grand comprehensive scheme of God's moral government over the universe, results are worked out by moral influence. So Christ through the exhibition of His redeemed and glorified saints, raised from the dead, raised up to sit on thrones and reign with Himself in the kingdom, shall make such a display of almighty power and matchless grace, as will bring all the intelligence in heaven and on earth, in adoration and submission at His feet.

"*To Him that overcometh* will I grant to *sit with Me in My throne*, even as I also overcame, and am *set down* with My *Father in His throne.*" Rev. 3: 21. Christ *can not take the kingdom alone.* He must have his *saints with Him* for they are the *joint heirs* to the inheritance. For the children of God "are heirs of God, and joint heirs with Christ." Rom. 8: 17. And this scripture has direct reference to the kingdom over the earth.

In the second Psalm it is said: "Ask of Me, and I shall give *thee* the heathen for thine inheritance, and the uttermost parts of the earth for thy possession. Thou shalt break them with a rod of iron; Thou shalt dash them in pieces like a potter's vessel." Here we see what the inheritance shall be. The "man-child, that was snatched up unto God, and to His throne," was to rule all nations with a rod of iron. And the symbol of the man-child includes the church. For the saints of the *Most High* shall possess the kingdom. Also Rev. 2: 26, 27. "He that overcometh, and keepeth my works unto the end, to him will I give power over the nations: And he shall *rule them* with a *rod* of *iron;* as the vessels, of a potter shall they be broken to shivers." In these passages, the Messiah, the man-child, and "he that overcometh," are all and each to rule the nations, and in the same *manner* shall they *exercise* their *rule over them*. Positive, sure, and effectual, as with a rod of iron, breaking down and dashing to pieces all opposition, as a thing of no strength—a potter's vessel.

Whenever Christ begins to act in reference to the kingdom, he must have His saints with Him, for they are His body, they are the "joint heirs." He will, therefore, exercise no authority publicly over the world without them. For through them he will rule over the nations.

In respect to all matters yet in the future, we are to look to the strict letter of Divine Revelation as our only source of information—analogies of the past can be of little value—and in so doing it is positively essential to take the strictest heed to what is written.

A spirit of latitudinous accommodation of determining the import of one passage by interpolating a portion taken from another, or of coercing the original text into speaking something other than its plain, manifest import, in order to accommodate its meaning to that expressed in some other passage, has been the fruitful source of the present stupendous system of error which has grown up in reference to the import of what is plainly taught in the scriptures of truth as to *coming events*. If we allow our preconceived ideas to influence our conclusions, and this is the most difficult to avoid, as to what should or what should not come to pass, we assume a position independent of Divine Revelation, and supersede it by preconceived theories, while the inspired writings must be regarded as positive and ultimate authority, and our only guide in reference to the unexplored path which lies before us.

It therefore becomes our imperative duty to scrutinize carefully what has been written even to the most minute and seemingly unimportant statements, understanding that all scriptures are indited by the *spirit of inspiration*, and are therefore infallible truth, and that all truths are equally true.

That the Lord Jesus will first come to call His saints according to His promise, to take them from earth to heaven, and that this will precede the "*second advent,*" as it is called, by a period of at least seven years, the duration of the times of persecution, accords with what is most explicitly taught, and affords a satisfactory and harmonious elucidation of the scriptures which refer to the subject of the coming of the Lord, which otherwise are very confused and obscure.

The prevalent belief respecting the coming of the Lord, that it will be a phenomenon which shall burst instantaneously and simultaneously upon all the world, striking terror and amazement alike into saint and sinner, the vast concave of the heavens from pole to pole, and from the zenith to the farthest east and west, filled with the armies of the heavenly hosts, angels and archangels, principalities and powers, moving in an awfully sublime procession toward the earth that the dead will be raised simultaneously, at the blast of the archangel's trumpet, both the just and the unjust, that the judgment of the "*great white throne*" will immediately follow,—for there is to be, according to this theory, but one general resurrection and one judgment, for all must be alike judged, both saint and sinner—and that there will immediately follow a winding up of the destinies of the inhabitants of this world—the saints assigned to a state of everlasting happiness, and the sinners to one of eternal misery;—though mainly true in its parts, assigning each part its proper place, is wholly unfounded as a theory taken together as a whole. Such a theory is entirely irreconcilable with the many passages heretofore cited. It would be a thing entirely unaccountable that while so many passages of the scriptures speak of the resurrection of the saints, no allusion is made to the resurrection of the wicked in the same connection, if all are to be raised at one and the same time.

The teaching of Divine Revelation upon this subject is to the effect that the resurrection of the unrighteous dead will form no part of the dealings of God in the work of redemption, but that this will take place at the end, and for final judgment.

The attention of the candid reader is earnestly invited to the perusal of the following passages, in addition to those above cited, in further proof that the resurrection is for the special benefit of the saints. "For when they shall *rise from the dead*, they neither marry, nor are given in marriage; but are as the angels which are in heaven."—Mark 12: 25. Luke 20: 35–36 is more explicit: "But they which shall be accounted worthy to obtain that world, and the resurrection from the dead,"—*from among the dead*, implying separation as a special favor—"neither marry, nor are given in marriage: neither can they die any more: for they are equal unto the angels; and are the *children of God, being the children of the resurrection.*" Surely this passage is decisive. The *children* of *God* are the *children* of the *resurrection*. It is a special favor and privilege for them. Do the wicked come into a participation of the blessings of God's children? If not, then they have no part in *this resurrection*, as it is written: "Blessed and holy is he that hath part in the *first resurrection:* on such the second death hath no power." "Neither can they die any more." "For the rest of the dead lived not again until the thousand years were finished."

Paul preached at Athens, standing in the midst of

Mar's Hill, *Jesus* and the *resurrection*, as the two cardinal doctrines of Christianity. By Jesus came the redemption of the soul, by his resurrection, justification and the glorifaction of the body. "For we shall be also in the likeness of His resurrection." So fully impressed was the great Apostle of the Gentiles, that the resurrection was the consummation of the work of redemption, and included the sum of all the blessings—was the prize of the high calling of God—which the Father has in store for His redeemed children, that His earnest desires were drawn out toward this, the only hope; "if by any means I might attain unto the resurrection of the dead."—Phil. 3: 11. In speaking of the resurrection, he invariably associates it with the dead in Christ, none are mentioned besides. We who are alive at the coming of the Lord, shall not anticipate them that sleep. For the dead in Christ shall rise first, then we which are alive and remain shall be changed in a moment, in the twinkling of an eye; such is the Apostle's account of the Lord's coming. When the Lord shall descend with the voice of the archangel and the trump of God, the dead in Christ shall rise first. Then what next? We which are alive and remain shall be caught up together with them in the clouds, to meet the Lord in the air.

His exhortation is to comfort one another with these words. In the 15th chapter of 1st Corinthians, he spoke of the resurrection of the saints only—they which have fallen asleep in Christ,—Christ the first-fruit of them that slept: Afterward they that are Christ's at His coming.

This special favor of God toward His servants, who shall sleep as well as to those who are alive and remain on earth at the coming of the Lord, is in strict accord with the dealings of God with His servants, and is impressively illustrated by the following: "Enoch walked with God and he was not: for God took him." Elijah was caught up in a chariot of fire and did not taste death. These are types of the church. If God so favored His chosen ones of old, how much more abundantly will He manifest His love toward His own children in Christ Jesus, in the last time?

Abraham stood upon an elevation and serenely overlooked the destruction of Sodom and the cities of the plain, and saw the smoke of their ruins ascend toward heaven. Lot escaped as by fire. Abraham is a type of the church, Lot of the Jewish remnant.

So shall the church be removed from the earth to a secure elevation with Christ, when the calamities shall fall upon the nations, prepared to return with Him, when He shall sit upon the throne of His glory and with all His holy angels, desend to earth to take the kingdom. The Jewish remnant, God's earthly saints, must pass through the fires of persecution, but escape as did Lot, but the church composed of the believers in the Lord Jesus, shall be taken up to heaven and therefore preserved, as was Abraham.

CHAPTER XI.

RECAPITULATION AND SPECIFIC TERMS.

A brief recapitulation of what has been written in the foregoing pages, will serve to place the several points discussed in a clearer light. Syllogistic reasoning has not been attempted and is not intended; but it is maintained that there is no satisfactory exposition of the many passages of scripture which refer to the coming of the Lord and the resurrection of the dead, on any other hypothesis than the one maintained above, which is indeed taught in specific terms and conclusively foretold in the most significant symbol, i. e. that of the "man-child."

It has been shown:

1. That the rapture of the saints is not the *second advent*, a period of at least seven years intervening between them. For the snatching up of the man-child will be simultaneous with the flight of the woman, which will precede the seven years' covenant.

2. It will be the special appearing of the Lord to take His *saints* from earth to dwell with Him in the mansions of the Father's house, according to His promise made to them on that memorable night in which He was betrayed.

3. It will be the consummation of the gospel mission, the completion of the work of redemption in the resurrection of the body.

4. The saints who are alive and remain on the earth at the coming of the Lord will be instantly changed and caught up, together with those who have been raised from

the dead, in the clouds to meet the Lord in the air, and so thenceforth, forever to remain with Him.

5. This will be preparatory to the *second advent*, at which there will be *no resurrection* of *the dead.*

6. Wherever the coming of the Lord is connected in any passage of scripture with the resurrection of the dead, the *sleeping saints* are invariably intended.

7. This follows from the mysterious and inseparable relationship which God in His gracious purpose has caused to subsist between Christ the head. and the church which is His mystical body.

8. The symbol of the man-child—Rev. 12—caught up unto God and to His throne, and which includes the church, is conclusive of the whole subject.

9. The saints will be taken out of the world to escape the woes which shall come upon the earth in the last time.

10. As soon as the church has been taken up to heaven, Satan will be cast down thence to the earth, and will take the supreme control and direction of its affairs.

11. The account of the "sealing of the servants of our God on their foreheads,"—Rev. 7—shows that immediately after the dispensation of sealing the elect there is seen a great multitude, which no man could number, of all nations, and kindreds, and people, and tongues, which stood before the throne and before the Lamb, clothed in white robes and palms in their hands. They were sealed, that is, set apart while on earth, they are seen immediately thereafter to stand before the throne in heaven. Those only of the tribes of the children of Israel are sealed, as seen by the Revelator, but all have the seal of faith.

12. The resurrection of the saints will be a special favor of God to the chosen in Christ Jesus, because they have

got *eternal* life in Him; they will be raised up separate and apart from all the world, as Christ was raised, and that they may reign with Him.

13. The resurrected saints will reign with Christ 1,000 years, while the rest of the dead live not again until the 1,000 years have passed.

14. The resurrected saints will not be judged, but they will judge the world, and even angels.

15. There will be two resurrections, a resurrection of the just, and of the unjust, a resurrection of life and a resurrection of condemnation or judgment. These two resurrections will be at least 1,000 years asunder.

16. That the saints will be treated as a distinct class, separate and apart from all the world, and with special favor, as those whose names are found written in the book of life, is implied in the final judgment scene before the "*great white throne.*" Rev. 20: 11.

17. The Apostle Paul teaches, Rom. 8: 11, that the spirit of Him that raised up Christ from the dead dwelling in believers, so links them inseparably with Christ, that as Christ was raised from the dead, so also shall their mortal bodies be quickened by the same power that raised up Christ from the dead. The union is special and everlasting.

18. Christ the first-fruits among many brethren. Then they that are Christ's at His coming. Each in his own order.

19. Christ designates His disciples as His *brethren*, see John 20: 17, and elsewhere.

20. There is not a shadow of a warrant in the scriptures in favor of the received theory, that there will be a general promiscuous simultaneous resurrection of both the just and the unjust, followed immediately by a general judgment.

21. The coming of the Lord to take up His saints, and His coming to take vengeance on the world are two different events.

22. When the Lord shall come to take the kingdom and to execute vengeance on His adversaries, His saints will come with Him. Zech. 14: 5. Jude 14: 15.

23. Christ can not move in the affairs of the kingdom until He has His saints with Him, for they are the joint heirs.

24. When He shall come to take up His saints He will come as a thief in the night. But when He shall come to judge the nations and take the kingdom, the event will be foretokened by signs in the sun and in the moon, the sea and waves roaring, and men's hearts failing them for fear of those things coming.

25. This interpretation of the scriptures respecting the rapture of the church is necessary that the promises may be fulfilled. "To him that overcometh, will I grant to sit with Me in My throne, even as I also overcame and am set down with My Father in His throne." Rev. 3: 23.

26. The saints shall exercise the same rule on earth, as the Messiah, They "rule the nations with a rod of iron," Rev. 2: 27, 2 Ps—and as the "man-child," Rev. 12: 5, "She brought forth a man-child, who was to rule all nations with a rod of iron."

27. "Enoch and Elijah were types of the church, and as God by special interposition took them out of the world so will he deal with the church."

28. The Jews, like Lot who barely escaped the fires of Sodom, shall pass through the great tribulations that are about to come upon the world, while the church removed to a secure elevation, as was Abraham, shall look on serenely.

It has been stated in the foregoing discussion that the

coming of the *Lord* to call the true church from earth to heaven, and His coming with His saints to take the kingdom, will be two very different and distinct events, and are carefully so distinguished in the scriptures. This will appear more satisfactory to the inquiring reader when he shall be made satisfied that a separate word is used in the original Greek to designate each event, and this almost invariably.

παρουςια, which literally denotes *"to be present with"* and to come in order to be present, is uniformly, if not almost invariably employed to express the coming of the Lord to call the saints from earth to heaven.

The following are instances among many, of the use of this word in the New Testament:

The Apostle Paul says to the Corinthians: "I am glad of the *coming* of Stephanus,"—i. e. that Stephanus will be present with you—his special coming to the church at Corinth—the world taking no cognizance of the event. The word is expressive, hence, of the continued presence of the Lord with His saints. "So *shall we ever be with the Lord.*" 1 Thess. 4: 17.

It is used in 2 Cor. 10: 10, to denote the personal appearance of the Apostle Paul: "But his bodily *presence* is weak, and his speech contemptible."

In Matt. 24: 3, the coming of the Lord to be present with His disciples: "What shall be the sign of thy *coming*, and of the end of the world?"—i. e. His return to them and the completion of the age. That is the close of the times of the Gentiles.

1 Cor. 15: 23: "Christ the first-fruits; afterward they that are Christ's at his *coming.*"

In the following passage this word is used to signify the *coming* of the Lord, that He may be present to His saints;

and reciprocally, that the saints may be forever present with the Lord.

"Are not even ye in the presence of our Lord Jesus Christ at his *coming?*" 1 Thess. 2: 19.

"And saying, Where is the promise of his *coming?*" 2 Peter 3: 4.

"That, when he shall appear, we may have confidence, and not be ashamed before him at his *coming*." 1 John 2: 28.

"That we which are alive and remain unto the *coming* of the Lord shall not prevent them which are asleep." 1 Thess. 4: 15.

"And I pray God, your whole spirit, soul and body, be preserved blameless, unto the *coming* of our Lord Jesus Christ." 1 Thess. 5: 23.

"Now we beseech you, brethren, by the *coming* of our Lord Jesus Christ, and by our gathering together unto him." 2 Thess. 2: 1.

"Stablish your hearts: for the *coming* of the Lord draweth nigh." James 5: 8.

"For we have not followed cunningly devised fables, when we made known unto you the power and *coming* of our Lord Jesus Christ." 2 Peter 1: 16.

"But as the days of Noah were, so shall also the *coming* of the Son of man be." Matt. 24: 37. In this 24th chapter of Matthew, both events are spoken of. This we shall point out in the sequel.

In the foregoing passages the *coming* of the Lord shall concern the saints only, as the passages taken in their connection imply, and the word *coming*, wherever italicized above, is translated from the Greek word παρουσια.

Ἐπιφανεια, which literally means to shine upon, is the word generally used to denote the public coming of the

Lord with His saints, to take the kingdom. Though this event is sometimes otherwise expressed, as in Matt. 25: 31, 2 Thess. 1: 7, where another Greek word is used.

To *burst* upon the world with a *great light*, as the coming of the Lord in the clouds of heaven with all His saints publicly to take the kingdom. The following are examples of the use of this word:

Of the Lord's first coming to earth as Jesus the Saviour. "But is now made manifest by the *appearing* of our Saviour Jesus Christ, who hath abolished death, and hath brought life and immortality to light through the gospel." 2 Tim. 1: 10.—

"Whom the Lord shall consume with the spirit of His mouth, and shall destroy with the brightness of His *coming*." 2 Thess. 2: 8.

"I charge thee therefore, before God, and the Lord Jesus Christ, who shall judge the quick and the dead at His *appearing* and His kingdom." 2 Tim. 4: 1.

"And not only to me, but to all them also, that love His *appearing*."

"Looking for that blessed hope, and the glorious *appearing* of the great God and our Saviour Jesus Christ." Titus 2: 13.

There is manifestly two comings of the Lord spoken of in the 24th chapter of Matt. The one before, and the other after the great tribulation. (verse 27th.) "For as the lightning cometh out of the east, and shineth even unto the west; so shall also the *coming* of the Son of man be." Here the flash of lightning out of the east even unto the west, denotes the suddenness of the unexpected event. This can not refer to His second coming, which will be preceded by great signs, and by the appearing of the sign of the Son of man in heaven.

Such is the precision in the use of language in the scriptures that each word must be allowed to have its due and full force of meaning, otherwise all will be confusion and uncertainty.

The following passage speaks of the final coming, and under circumstances quite different as to the state of the world and the signs of the time. For in 29, 30th verses, it is said: "Immediately after the tribulation of those days, shall the sun be darkened, and the moon shall not give her light, and the stars shall fall from heaven, and the powers of the heavens shall be shaken: And then shall appear the sign of the Son of man in heaven:" the sign of the Son of man shall suddenly shine out upon the earth from heaven. "And then shall all the tribes of the earth mourn, and they shall see the Son of man coming in the clouds of heaven with power and great glory." The final coming of the Son of man to take possession of the kingdom. Dan. 7: 13.

But in the following passage, the appearing of the Lord to call His church is spoken of, in verses 37-41. Our Lord calls the attention of His diciples to those things which lie most nearly His heart, because they chiefly affect them.

"But as the days of Noe were, so shall also the coming of the Son of man be. For as in the days that were before the flood, they were eating and drinking, marrying and giving in marriage, until the days that Noe entered into the ark, And knew not until the flood came, and took them all away: so shall also the coming of the Son of man be. Then shall two be in the field; the one shall be taken, and the other left. Two women shall be grinding at the mill; the one shall be taken, and the other left."

Here it is stated that there shall be a separation made—a

selection—one shall be taken and the other left,— selected to be with the Lord. One shall be taken from the field, the other left—one taken from the mill, the other left at the mill.

That this is addressed directly to His disciples, and hence to all believers, is evident from the admonition in the 42d verse, "Watch therefore; for ye know not what hour your Lord doth come."

Whenever the coming of the Lord is spoken of in connection with an exhortation to His disciples to watch, or similar expressions of admonition, the personal coming to take up the saints is intended.

CHAPTER XII.

THE JUDGMENT OF THE NATIONS.

1 "Therefore, wait ye upon me, saith the LORD, until the day that I rise up to the prey: for my determination is to gather the nations, that I may assemble the kingdoms, to pour upon them mine indignation, even all my fierce anger." Zeph. 3: 8.

It has been before shown that believers will not be judged, because with them judgment is past already. They have passed from death unto life. Also that the dead, small and great, will be judged at the close of the thousand year's reign, at the sitting of the "*great white throne.*" That there will be a judgment of the *living* nations also, as such will now be shown.

One general and promiscuous judgment of both the quick and the dead, including Jew and Gentile, Christian and Heathen, saints and sinners, all arraigned before a common judgment seat, to render up an account for the deeds of this life, is the prevalent and favorite doctrine of the various sects of Christendom, and each will insist that the following passage from Matthew 25 sustains these views:

31 "When the Son of man shall come in his glory, and all the holy angels with him, then shall he sit upon the throne of his glory:

32 And before him shall be gathered all nations: and he shall separate them one from another, as a shepherd divideth *his* sheep from the goats:

33 And he shall set the sheep on his right hand, but the goats on the left.

34 Then shall the King say unto them on his right hand, Come, ye blessed of my Father, inherit the kingdom prepared for you from the foundation of the world:

35 For I was an hungered, and ye gave me meat: I was thirsty, and ye gave me drink: I was a stranger, and ye took me in:

36 Naked, and ye clothed me: I was sick, and ye visited me: I was in prison, and ye came unto me.

37 Then shall the righteous answer him, saying, Lord, when saw we thee an hungered, and fed *thee?* or thirsty, and gave *thee* drink?

38 When saw we thee a stranger, and took *thee* in? or naked, and clothed *thee?*

39 Or when saw we thee sick, or in prison, and came unto thee?

40 And the King shall answer and say unto them, Verily I say unto you, Inasmuch as ye have done *it* unto one of the least of these my brethren, ye have done *it* unto me.

41 Then shall he say also unto them on the left hand, Depart from me, ye cursed, into everlasting fire, prepared for the devil and his angels:

42 For I was an hungered, and ye gave me no meat: I was thirsty, and ye gave me no drink:

43 I was a stranger, and ye took me not in: naked, and ye clothed me not: sick, and in prison, and ye visited me not.

44 Then shall they also answer him, saying, Lord, when saw we thee an hungered, or athirst, or a stranger, or naked, or sick, or in prison, and did not minister unto thee?

45 Then shall he answer them, saying, Verily I say unto you, Inasmuch as ye did *it* not to one of the least of these, ye did *it* not to me.

46 And these shall go away into everlasting punishment: but the righteous into life eternal."

A candid and careful examination of this passage will, we trust, have the effect to more and more confirm our faith, and establish our confidence in the entire harmony of all revealed truth.

"*And before him shall be gathered all nations.*"— παντα τά ἔθνη;—Who are included? Not Jews and Gentiles promiscuously; not both the quick and the dead, but the living only; the living Gentile nations, as nations, as stated in the text.

Here, as elsewhere, we must have supreme respect to what is written, in order to rightly understand the oracles of God, and not allow their plain import to be superseded by a theory preconceived.

τα εθνη, in the New Testament Greek, means the nations outside of the Jews—the Gentile nations, and these alone.

The Jews, therefore, will not be included among the nations who shall be gathered before Him. And this accords with what we are taught elsewhere in the scriptures. For God hath separated the Jews and does not reckon them among the other nations of the earth, though they may be dispersed abroad and scattered among all nations, they are still reckoned as a separate and distinct people.

For in Deuteronomy 32: 8-9 we read: "When the Most High divided to the nations their inheritance, when he separated the sons of Adam, he set the bounds of the people according to the number of the children of Israel. For the LORD's portion *is* his people; Jacob *is* the lot of his inheritance." Here we learn that Jehovah set apart Jacob as the lot of his inheritance, and therefore not to be reckoned among the nations. For it is expressly stated in Numbers 23: 9: "The people shall dwell alone, and shall not be *reckoned among the nations.*"

God has a distinct purpose in reference to the Jews, and they will be dealt with in a manner quite otherwise than the Gentile nations.

Let it suffice, therefore, for the present, that the Jews will not be included among the *nations* that shall be gathered before *Him*. Who are the parties then that shall be arraigned? The living, not the dead. It will not be a judgment of *individuals* but of *nations*. Individuals will be reserved for the judgment of the "*great white throne*," when the dead shall be judged, "the dead, small and great, shall stand before the throne." But in the passage above cited, it is *all nations*, the living Gentile nations only as such, that shall be gathered before Him. Israel will not be among them; otherwise the scriptures above cited would be in contradiction to each other, which is impossible.

For all scriptures are in accord, when each passage is allowed its full and precise meaning.

There is another class that will not be included, those who are designated "*these My brethren.*"

The church of the living God will be exempt from judgment, as we have seen elsewhere, not only because with them judgment is already past, and they can not therefore, come into condemnation, but it is expressly stated that they too are separated from among the Gentiles.

Peter declared in the council at Jerusalem how:—"God did visit the Gentiles to take out of them a people for His name."

If Israel then be not included among the nations gathered before Him, and if the church of the living God be not included, and the class designated as *these My brethren* are certainly not included, then it can not be a general judgment that is described; and these gathered before Him, must include as stated in the text—$\tau\alpha\ \epsilon\theta\nu\eta$—the Gentile nations alone.

"And He shall set the sheep on His right hand, but the goats on the left."

Now the almost universally received interpretation of this passage is that the sheep mean God's people of every age and dispensation from the beginning to the end of time, and the goats, the wicked from first to last. But there is another party, here referred to in the address made to each of the others, who from the reference made to them appear to be placed near the king, called *these My brethren*. This party can not be included among either of the other two, who are the subjects of judgment, and therefore this can not be a general judgment, and the idea that the sheep includes the righteous of all ages and dispensations must be abandoned. The idea of a general judgment is incompatible with the scene described.

The living Gentile nations who shall be on the earth at the coming of the Lord to take the kingdom, are alone included; and it will be the final separation of the tares from the wheat, at the inauguration of the kingdom of the Messiah on earth. This will be the judgment of the quick. In Rev. 20: 11–15, we have an account of the judgment of the dead. The Apostle Paul in his second Epistle to Timothy 4th chapter, refers to both of these judgments. "I charge thee therefore before God, and the Lord Jesus, who shall judge the quick and the dead at His appearing and His kingdom." Here it is declared that the Lord will judge the living at His coming to take the kingdom, and the dead during the continuance of the kingdom, namely, at the end of the millennial reign.

The principles upon which the judgment of the nations will be conducted, will more fully appear from the following considerations, they will be judged according to their works; as in no other way could their deserts, according to their real moral proclivities be determined. Ample opportunity will be offered them for the reception, or rejection of the *gospel of the kingdom*. Their disposition will be made manifest, by their treatment of the *messengers*, who shall proclaim the everlasting gospel of the kingdom, among them, as a witness or test—"*these My brethren.*"

Many passages of scripture show that there will be a great awakening and turning to righteousness immediately after the great tribulation. The great tribulation will end with the ascension of the two witnesses. "And they ascended up to heaven in a cloud; and their enemies beheld them. And the same hour was there a great earthquake, and the tenth part of the city fell, and in the earthquake were slain of men seven thousand: and the remnant were affrighted, and gave glory to the God of heaven." Rev. 11: 12, 13.

The Prophet Zechariah (13: 9) says of the remnant who shall pass through the great tribulation: "And I will bring the third part through the fire, and will refine them as silver is refined, and will try them as gold is tried: they shall call on my name, and I will hear them: I will say, It *is* my people; and they shall say, The LORD *is* my God."

1 "And at that time shall Michael stand up, the great prince which standeth for the children of thy people: and there shall be a time of trouble, such as never was since there was a nation *even* to that same time: and at that time thy people shall be delivered, every one that shall be found written in the book.

2 "And many of them that sleep in the dust of the earth shall awake, some to everlasting life, and some to shame *and* everlasting contempt.

3 "And they that be wise, shall shine as the brightness

of the firmament; and they that turn many to righteousness, as the stars for ever and ever.

4 "But thou, O Daniel, shut up the words, and seal the book, *even* to the time of the end: many shall run to and fro, and knowledge shall be increased." Daniel 12: 1–4.

What is here predicted will happen in immediate connection with the great tribulation. This period of trial will end by a manifest interposition of the Lord Jehovah, but not by the immediate coming of the Son of Man to take the kingdom. This will be postponed for a period of seventy-five days after the end of the 1,260 days, which limits the time of *great trial.* The following passages from Dan. 12th, when carefully read, will explain all:

6 "And *one* said to the man clothed in linen, which *was* upon the waters of the river, How long *shall it be to* the end of these wonders?

7 "And I heard the man clothed in linen, which *was* upon the waters of the river, when he held up his right hand and his left hand unto heaven, and sware by him that liveth for ever, that *it shall be* for a time, times, and an half; and when he shall have accomplished to scatter the power of the holy people, all these *things* shall be finished.

8 "And I heard, but I understood not: then said I, O my Lord, what *shall be* the end of these *things?*

9 "And he said, Go thy way, Daniel; for the words *are* closed up and sealed till the time of the end.

10 "Many shall be purified, and made white, and tried; but the wicked shall do wickedly: and none of the wicked shall understand; but the wise shall understand.

11 "And from the time *that* the daily *sacrifice* shall be taken away, and the abomination that maketh desolate set up, *there shall be* a thousand two hundred and ninety days.

12 "Blessed *is* he that waiteth, and cometh to the thousand three hundred and five and thirty days.

13 "But go thou thy way till the end *be:* for thou shalt rest, and stand in thy lot at the end of the days."

"How long shall it be to the end of these wonders?"

What wonders? Doubtless the triumph of the evil over the good. "For he shall make war against the saints and overcome them." But this shall be limited to three and one-half years. For "the man clothed in linen, which was upon the waters of the river, when he held up his right hand and his left hand unto heaven, and sware by him that liveth for ever, that it shall be for a time, times, and an half; and when he shall have accomplished to scatter the power of the holy people, all these things shall be finished."

Man's extremity shall be God's opportunity. In that extremity shall Michael, the great prince, stand up for the children of Daniel's people, the elect remnant of the persecuted and now vanquished and scattered Jews. But at this crisis, Jehovah (the divine personality of our Lord) will interpose as the Ancient of Days. The enemies of the saints will be overwhelmed and destroyed. The saints will be delivered. "Thy people shall be delivered,"—i. e. Daniel's people, the faithful Jewish remnant.

It must be steadfastly borne in mind that this prophecy was given to the *Jews*, and concerns none other. That the saints spoken of in this prophecy, are Jewish saints. As soon as we lose sight of this cardinal principle we are at sea, and liable to be carried along by any wind or current.

The terror inspired by this unexpected and wonderful interposition of the Lord Jehovah in the deliverance of the saints, will cause all the hesitating to give glory to God, and silence the enemies that remain.

The two wonderful witnesses—doubtless Elijah the prophet who was promised, and Moses the servant of God—will have fully instructed the faithful people of God during their prophecy, which synchronizes with the great tribulation respecting the coming kingdom, and filled with holy ardor and zeal, the faithful will go forth among all nations, proclaiming the gospel of the coming kingdom. For "many shall run to and fro, and knowledge shall be increased."

And this is said in direct connection with the deliverance of the people from the time of trial. "At that time thy people shall be delivered." At the same time it is said: "And they that be wise, shall shine as the brightness of the firmament; and they that turn many to righteousness, as the stars for ever and ever." This is said of the last time, the time of the end—it is said of the Jewish messengers and of Jews alone—and therefore can not be regarded here as expressive of a general proposition. And further along in this connection, verse 9-10: "And he said, Go thy way, Daniel; for the words are closed up and sealed till the time of the end. Many shall be purified, and made white, and tried; but the wicked shall do wickedly: and none of the wicked shall understand; but the wise shall understand." This must be limited to the time of the end also, as the context plainly requires. Hence, there will occur a great awakening, which shall result in a separation of the *wise* from the *unwise*—those that take heed from the wicked, who shall be intent on doing wickedly and therefore shall not understand.

And that there may be time and opportunity for this reformation, and for the proclamation of the coming kingdom among all the living nations, there will be an extension of time after the time of the end of the 1,260 days, which limits the period of the great tribulation, first of thirty days. then of forty-five days, making in all seventy-five days.

Momentous events will be crowded into this brief period, it is true, but the world is preparing for it. Times do not move as of old. Thought is now communicated instantaneously to the remotest lands. Transportation over seas and lands is but the business of a few days.

God's saints will go forth from Jerusalem and proclaim the great deliverance by the direct interposition of Jehovah the Lord, and proclaim the coming kingdom among all lands in the brief space of a very few weeks, attended with such unction and proofs as must convince all who are not essentially evil. This is doubtless predicted in Matt. 24: 14, and Zechariah 14: 8: "Living waters shall go forth from Jerusalem,"—speaking of these very times.

Apocalypse, chapter 14: 6–7: "And I saw another angel fly in the midst of heaven, having the everlasting gospel to preach unto them that dwell on the earth, and to every nation, and kindred, and tongue, and people, Saying with a loud voice, Fear God, and give glory to him; (and not to the beast) for the hour of his judgment is come: and worship him that made heaven, and earth, and the sea, and the fountains of waters." This, from the language, must take place at the time of the end. For why should men be so earnestly exhorted to fear God and give glory to Him, if the beast and the false prophet were not striving to establish *materialism* by the sword? Not only this, but the hour of His judgment is *imminent*, actually come, and the process of separating the sheep from the goats commenced.

We now see the principle upon which the King will separate the sheep from the goats.

The sheep will gladly receive the heralds of the kingdom

THE JUDGMENT OF THE NATIONS.

and give them aid and comfort, for "my sheep hear my voice." But the goats will spurn the messengers of the coming kingdom of God, neglect and maltreat its heralds, and prefer to adhere to the agents of the beast and false prophet.

Hence, the King will separate the faithful and believing from the disobedient and incorrigible, and pronounce sentence according to their respective characters and deserts:—

"And he shall set the sheep on his right hand," that is, the place of friendship and honor, of favor and protection; "but the goats on the left," that is, the place of dishonor and enmity, indicative of their obstinate unbelief and stubborn resistance to the authority of the King, and of their unconquerable aversion to the principles of His government.

"Then shall the King say unto them on his right hand, Come, ye blessed of my Father, inherit the kingdom prepared for you from the foundation of the world: For I was an hungered, and ye gave me meat: I was thirsty, and ye gave me drink: I was a stranger, and ye took me in: naked, and ye clothed me: I was sick, and ye visited me: I was in prison, and ye came unto me. Then shall the righteous answer him, saying, Lord, when saw we thee an hungered, and fed *thee?* or thirsty, and gave *thee* drink? When saw we thee a stranger, and took *thee* in? or naked, and clothed *thee?* Or when saw we thee sick, or in prison, and came unto thee? And the King shall answer and say unto them, Verily I say unto you, Inasmuch as ye have done *it* unto one of the least of these my brethren, ye have done *it* unto me." Inasmuch as ye received the messengers of the kingdom, and gave them aid and comfort, ye received me also.

"Then shall he say also unto them on the left hand,

Depart from me, ye cursed, into everlasting fire, prepared for the devil and his angels: For I was an hungered, and ye gave me no meat: I was thirsty, and ye gave me no drink: I was a stranger, and ye took me not in: naked, and ye clothed me not: sick, and in prison, and ye visited me not. Then shall they also answer him, saying, Lord, when saw we thee an hungered, or athirst, or a stranger, or naked, or sick, or in prison, and did not minister unto thee? Then shall he answer them, saying, Verily I say unto you, Inasmuch as ye did *it* not to one of the least of these, ye did *it* not to me."

Here are distinctly brought to view at least four classes with whom God will deal, each separate and apart from the other. The Jews as a nation, the Gentiles as nationalities, the church of the living God, and the elect remnant of the Jews. The latter are here included among those designated "*these My brethren.*"

The Jews, as a nation, are beloved for the Father's sake; and will, most assuredly, be placed in possession of the land, promised through Abraham, Isaac and Jacob.

The Gentile nations will be judged for their slight of the wonderful mercy and condescension of God, in inviting them to become partakers in and heirs of the promise. He will dash them to pieces as a potter's vessel. On whomsoever this stone shall fall, it will grind him to powder. The church of the living God, being the joint heirs, will reign with Christ. The remnant will shine as the brightness of the firmament and as stars for ever and ever.

CHAPTER XIII.

POPULATION AND TERRITORIAL LIMITS.

In resuming the further consideration of the *revived Roman Empire*, it will be necessary to pass in review briefly, some matters already alluded to, and to consider more fully the remarkable symbol of the beast. Rev. 13: 1.

The beast seen by the Revelator rising out of the sea, as a symbol, presents to view the Roman Empire, not only in its last organized appearance on earth but the subordinate parts of this extraordinary figure symbolize this power characteristically in every stage of its existence, and under every form of administration, past and to come. It is indeed the symbol of the coming Roman Empire, revived among the nations of modern Europe, but when risen into view, it shows us comprehensively in outline, as though it had been delineated by the hand of a master artist, in well understood hieroglyphics, the character, moral and material, as God views it, of this imperious, insatiably grasping power, at all times intent upon asserting undisputed sway, satisfied with nothing short of trampling all opposition under foot.

The symbol as a whole, presents the Roman power in detail. Each subordinate part adding strength to the entire, until the argument resulting from each specification assumes a cogency and conclusiveness which are irresistible.

Indeed to a believer in the authority of Divine Revelation, allowing that the symbols of this book of Revelations are to be understood, as explained in the Old Testament prophets, the conclusion is unavoidable. There is no escaping the tremendous and startling truth here symbolized but by actually denying the authority of this book, or by attributing an entirely novel and peculiar meaning to its symbols. As before stated, the symbols of this book are not new and peculiar, but the most significant are found in the prophecies of Daniel and the writings of others of the Old Testament prophets, and their import well settled. These symbols have been explained by angelic interpreters. Nothing left in doubt. All is satisfactory, except to the skeptical and doubting.

The assumption of some modern expositors, that the beast under consideration symbolizes the Roman Hierarchy, vanishes as soon as contemplated in the light thrown on the subject of symbolic interpretation by the explanation given in the prophecy of Daniel. It is there stated by Divine authority, that a beast is the symbol of a *secular* and *universal* power, monarchy or empire, and that invariably. The import of a symbol having once been established, there is no authority for changing its meaning, the same sense must ever afterwards be assigned it. The estates of the church were too insignificant to entitle the Roman Hierarchy, in its best days, to any consideration as a secular power. Its territories were not comparable with those of the aboriginal tribes, which Æneas found inhabiting the Italian peninsula at his arrival from the ruins of Troy.

And the political power of Rome, whatever it may have been beyond the territorial limits of the States of the Church, has been chiefly exerted in reference to those matters which have grown out of the relations of Church and State. Conflict of jurisdiction, between the ecclesiastical and secular authorities, has been the fruitful source of controversy. For a century or more all such matters have been arranged in an amicable manner by a concordat or treaty, defining the rights and privileges of the Church, within the State. The extravagant claims, which the Roman Hierarchy set up, during the middle or dark ages, to supreme control over the nations of Christendom, has been greatly modified by circumstances in modern times. The reformation put a period to the claim of Papal supremacy, practically; and more recent events have proved the fallacy, as well as the folly of her high pretension, put forth during the times of Hildebrand, the Borgias, and the Medici.

Recently she has been bereft of the *Temporalities of St. Peter*, as the States of the Church were called, and her religious houses and revenues have been in some cases sequestered by the State. The Roman Catholic religion is barely tolerated in many of the States of Europe. In all, the power of the Papacy is limited to the influence which she still exerts over the religious convictions, and the conscience of her adherents.

It would be perfectly preposterous to apply to the Roman Hierarchy, the language that is ascribed to the anti-type of the beast. "Power was given him over all kindreds, and tongue, and nations. And all that dwell upon the earth shall worship him."

But the idea that the Apocalyptic beast symbolizes the Roman Hierarchy has been the favorite theory of modern commentators.

As this subject is one of importance in this connection, we will look a little further into it. It must have occurred to the reader of these pages that the *atheistic* principles and heaven-daring *assumptions* of the anti-type of the beast are strangely at variance with those of the Papal Hierarchy, which claims to teach and promote the knowledge and worship of the only true and living God, the CREATOR of the heavens and the earth.

All power or authority which this church has at any time asserted, or laid claim to in favor of her pontiff, is delegated. How can she claim to act for and in the name of God and the Lord Jesus Christ, and at the same time deny and repudiate the very existence of the God of the fathers? All that can be said in reference to the Roman papacy is, that she is an apostate, ecclesiastical organization. She is so symbolized as we have seen in Rev. 17: 1-6. That an abandoned woman is the symbol of an apostate, ecclesiastical body—see the following passages: Jeremiah 3: 6, 8, 9, 10; also 13: 27; Ezekiel 16: 3, 6, 8, 11, 12-35.

But the prophecy—Rev. 17: 1-6—seems to include more than the Papal Hierarchy, for she is there styled "THE MOTHER OF HARLOTS." Surely, then, if she be the mother of apostate churches, there must be more APOSTATES than one. Upon this subject we may derive instruction, and receive an admonition to humiliation and regret, should we look nearer home. The Apostle Paul wrote: "To all that be in Rome, *beloved of God, called to be saints.*" If this language be not applicable to the devotees of the Church of Rome to-day, as few if any will claim, where is there an organization in Christendom that can appropriate this language of the Apostle to themselves?

There is another phase of this subject which claims attention. The same class of commentators above referred to, see in the Papal Hierarchy, the anti-Christ of St. John. That the anti-type of the Apocalyptic beast will truly represent the spirit of anti-Christ which shall come, has been satisfactorily shown by what has gone before in these pages. In the FIRST EPISTLE GENERAL OF JOHN, chapter 2, verse

22, we read: *"He is anti-Christ, that denieth the Father and the Son."* This the power typified by the Apocalyptic beast *will do*. But this the Roman church has *never done*. The Papacy therefore can not be the anti-Christ.

Whatever stretch of prerogative, or abuse of authority, or perversion of the truth may be placed to her charge, she can not be indicted of unsoundness of doctrine respecting the Godhead. *A self-existent Almighty* GOD, the CREATOR and *Supreme* SOVEREIGN *of the Universe, the divine personality and incarnation of the Son, in the person of Jesus of Nazareth, as one and equal with the* FATHER, are fundamental doctrines of her creed. If the Athanasian creed which she maintains, if the decrees of councils subsequent to that of Nice, if the writings of learned doctors in divinity, which have appeared from time to time, sanctioned by the Popes, are to be received as evidence of what this church has and does maintain, then she can not be convicted of *"denying the Father and the Son."*

We think that the passage in the 2nd chapter and 18th verse of the First Epistle general of John is conclusive, that a personage styled the anti-Christ will arise in the last times, whose counsels and influence will be attended by disastrous results. He is symbolized by the two-horned beast in Rev. 13: 11. But this subject will come up again in the sequel.

Besides, this whole argument receives a strong support, indeed a conclusive confirmation, from the identity of this Apocalyptic symbol and that of the notable little horn of Daniel 7th. This identity granted, and all concede it, and the conclusion is irresistible that the secular Roman imperial power and no other is signified, for it has been shown that the notable little horn is a part of the fourth beast of Daniel, 7th chapter. This fourth beast, by universal consent, symbolizes the fourth universal monarchy—i. e. the Roman—so explained by the celestial interpreter to the Prophet himself. The notable little horn must therefore represent one phase or state of the fourth universal or Roman Monarchy. The account given by the Prophet Daniel shows that it is the last. Therefore, the beast—Rev. 13: 1—from its identity must also symbolize the same secular Roman imperial power, which shall represent the last of the four universal Gentile monarchies at the end. This subject has been more fully considered elsewhere.

This monarchy, therefore, has no visible organization at present to represent it among the nations. Yet the Roman institutions and laws have a potentiality, and actually exert an influence, greater than any power on earth, even at this time, over the destinies and domestic happiness of the nations and population of the civilized world. It, therefore, in a manner exists, and yet does not. The Roman name has been invoked at different times, and efforts have been made to arouse the slumbering giant; but he abides his time. "And they that dwell on the earth shall wonder, whose names were not written in the book of life from the foundation of the world, when they behold the *beast that was, and is not, and yet is.*" Rev. 17: 8.

The laws, rather than the various living agents who fill the political offices in the State, govern. The Roman law constitutes the civil code of almost every nation of Christendom, with slight modifications, demanded by the real or supposed circumstances of the governed, having been altered. If this be true, then it follows that the Roman laws at this time govern the principal nations of the civilized world.

The Roman power then, although she has now no visible organization to represent her among the nations, nevertheless still lives in her laws and institutions, in her literature and language, in the thoughts and sentiments which they breathe, in the heroic example of her patriots, in the wisdom of her senate, in the eloquence of her orators, in the sublimity of her poets, in the maxims of her philosophers, and even in the melancholy grandeur of her ruins.

The revived Empire will differ in many respects from the old, chiefly from a change of conditions, and the advancement made in political science, and from the influence of modern diplomacy.

It will, nevertheless, be the old Roman power, emerging from a state of partial oblivion, still maintaining its chief characteristics under its new and final organized existence.

The ancient Roman power was not a confederacy, but a consolidated imperial commonwealth, but the modern will be composed of a confederation of kingdoms, at least in its inception.

There are reasons to believe that the territorial limits of the coming power will be somewhat more widely extended than those of the old Empire, even at its zenith.

When this terrible political power shall take form as an organized confederated empire, it will exhibit in its heterogeneous parts and elements all the traits and characteristics ascribed to the various parts of the dreadful symbol of the beast seen rising up out of the sea. No element of strength, and no hue of turpitude will be wanting. The daring and adventurous head of the coming Empire will act as if impressed with the supreme conviction, that unless he can succeed in putting down, by diplomacy or by force of arms, all opposition, human and divine, and of maintaining the ascendency as the only supreme potentate to be recognized on earth, his career must be short and inglorious. And this will be the finale. For the ten kings who shall be his confederates and act in harmony, will do his behests. "These shall make war with the Lamb, and the Lamb shall overcome them: for he is Lord of lords, and King of kings." Rev. 17: 14.

In attempting to arrive at some conclusions, as to the territorial limits of the coming empire, and consequently as to the nations, who shall most likely be comprehended within its political organization, the following considerations are entitled to weight.

Peoples, rather than geographical boundaries, are to be looked to. The relation of the nations of modern Europe to the idea of a revived Roman Empire, rather than the territorial limits of the old Roman Empire.

Many good men, who hold that the Roman Empire will be revived in the last time—and of this class, there are many learned and very pious men—have been inclined to restrict the limits of the coming power, to those of the old Empire, when most widely extended; holding the Rhine and the Danube as natural boundaries toward the north and eastward in Europe, and the Euphrates toward the rising sun in Asia.

This would imply that the Roman power had made no conquests since her legions had been withdrawn from Britain, which marks the beginning of her decline; whereas the principal progress in diffusing Roman ideas throughout the European mind, has been going on ever since Rome ceased to be a power before the world, and has been making more rapid progress since the revival of learning, and the great impetus given thereby to mental activity in modern times. Her laws and literature have silently permeated; and, in a manner, achieved a conquest over the nations, while arms have ceased. It would not be wise therefore, to assume that this power, like the tides of the great ocean, must ebb and flow within certain ascertained limits. The people, and not the lands they occupy, constitute the State; and considerations of State policy are the potent influences which must determine the action of nations.

The European nations are at present banded together by common consent, which seems to imply a consciousness of a common destiny, under the lead of the great Powers. No enterprise of magnitude can be undertaken by any one power singly, unless the balance consent. This arrangement must secure unity of action, until some one power, feeling sufficiently strong, should attempt to gain the chief control over all. And this unity of action and mutual cooperation has been brought to pass by the paramount consideration, that public safety requires it, notwithstanding there exists the greatest diversity among the elements constituting these nations. The iron and miry clay truly subsisting, but not coalescing. "And whereas thou sawest iron mixed with miry clay, they shall mingle themselves with the seed of men: but they shall not cleave one to another, even as iron is not mixed with clay." Dan. 2: 43.

It should be remembered that the ancient Romans themselves, were not a homogeneous people. They did not spring from a common ancestral stock, but were the growth rather of political necessity. Æneas brought but a handful of Trojan refugees to the shores of Italy, and these were soon merged with the tribes inhabiting the central parts of the Peninsula. By conquest, and by the absorption of the adjacent tribes and territories, the State grew up from small beginnings, and when it had attained the zenith of territorial aggrandizement and political power, comprised among its population all the nationalities of the civilized world. Not all Roman citizens it is true, for this was a special privilege limited to a favored class. But there were representatives in the armies of almost all nationalities. For as the Latin element proper became degenerate through luxury and effeminacy, the legions were recruited among the remote barbarians of Gaul, and even from the tribes beyond the Rhine.

The Senate alone continued to represent and perpetuate the old Roman pedigree.

Not more diverse is the European population of this day than was that comprising the Roman Empire in the days of Augustus.

From the prophecy just cited we learn that diversity of population, even incapable of coalescence, must continue to exist to the end. We must, therefore, look out for a dominant, or controlling class or power, which shall attain to the ascendency over all. What are called the *Latin nations* of to-day seem to have degenerated, and to be sadly deficient in those sterner traits of character peculiar to the Romans. Whence then shall arise the coming controlling power? From the prophecies of Daniel we learn that it shall spring up from a small beginning. Does such a power appear upon the map of Europe, or is it still below the horizon? The answer to this question must be postponed for the present.

It would seem to be pertinent to our investigations to inquire what nation or nations of modern Europe have imbibed most of the traits, sentiments, ideas and manners of the old Romans. What people would be most likely to adopt and glory in the Roman name? What people have shown the greatest relish for, and zeal in, cultivating classical literature? Whose institutions have been the most influenced by the old models, if there be any? Modern civilization has chiefly emanated from two centers, namely, Rome and Constantinople. The Crusaders brought back to western Europe some of the rudiments of Byzantine civilization, and the arts and sciences neglected in the east flourished anew in the west. But the influence of the east was very small indeed, compared with the potent agencies which had, during ages, accumulated and been diffused abroad from the seat of the western empire.

Through a thousand channels, as through so many arteries, there flowed from this great heart of the Roman world, the rudiments of the arts and civilization, the maxims of the laws and a knowledge of the institutions, which had been bequeathed as a legacy from Imperial Rome to all nations, to whom they might have access.

The invading and conquering hordes of northern barbarians were overawed, and in turn succumbed, to the superiority of the civilization of the vanquished and after plundering and burning her cities and slaughtering her citizens, were in turn themselves subdued by the evidence of the majesty and genius of the nation, which survived in her ruins and became consequently, subservient to the fascinating influence, and the zealous cultivators of the Roman arts.

And thus by the refluent waves of the returning hordes of conquerors, Italy was literally transported to the north of the Alps, and the denizens of the forests of Gaul and Germany became the true representatives of Roman culture. Cicero and Virgil, Livy and Tacitus, diffused abroad a taste for classic elegance, and kindled afresh the extinguished *fires* of the old Roman genius, and revived a love for elegance and culture, while the research and genius of Tribonian succeeded in digesting and arranging an inimitable code of civil jurisprudence, extracted from the mass of legal lore, which had accumulated during the centuries, adapted to the wants of society in every state of advancement, from the most crude to the most refined. While the Latin element, degenerate sons of noble sires, have remained in possession of the old Roman homestead, the true heirs of the Roman name and fame have migrated to the north of the Alps, and even crossed the Rhine, if we rightly interpret the signs of the times. Nothing short of a political miracle could set the Italian States in the lead of Europe at this time. But all things are possible, if this be the purpose of Omnipotence.

If we consult the symbolic significance of the lower extremities, and especially the feet and toes of the great metalic image, we shall find reasons for inferring that the final state of the Roman power will be more widely extended than of old. Iron is the symbol of the old Roman strength and tenacity of purpose. The fourth kingdom shall be as strong as iron. But in the last times the component elements shall be changed. "And as the toes of the feet were part of iron, and part of clay, so the kingdom shall be partly strong, and partly broken." Dan. 2 : 42. Shall we conclude that the iron element, which shall still exist in the toes, must necessarily follow a Latin pedigree, or is it not rather the characteristic of a conquering people that is symbolized by iron? The miry clay with which the iron was seen to be mixed, though primarily symbolizing the barbarian element, nevertheless was intended only so as indicative of its inferiority, when compared with a civilized people. It evidently points out the weak element, for the prophet says that the kingdom, taken as a whole, shall be partly strong and partly broken. "And whereas thou sawest iron mixed with miry clay, they shall mingle themselves with the seed of men: but they shall not cleave one to another, even as iron is not mixed with clay." Verse 43.

The different nationalities of Europe have maintained in a wonderful manner their separate and distinct peoples. The Latin race has not blended with the Teutonic, and *vice versa*.

The amplitude of the feet and toes of the image, taken in connection with the foregoing considerations, lead to the conclusion that the coming Roman Empire will comprehend as the constituents, which it seems most likely shall compose it, all the continent of Europe, with the exception of the Russian Empire, which from many prophecies we are led to believe will stand outside, and for the most part in the attitude of an antagonist. Ezekiel 38: 2, 3, 14; Rev. 20: 8.

The symbolic designation for the extent of the Roman Empire in the Apocalypse, is "the *one-third part*" of the earth, considered socially and statistically rather than as to geographical boundaries. So is the old Roman Empire symbolically designated. For we have seen—Rev. 12—that this power was the agent through which the "great red dragon" exerted his malevolent influence, and sought to thwart the purposes of God in the dispensation of his schemes of beneficence toward the fallen sons of Adam. He stood in the person of Herod, an agent of Rome, "before the woman which was ready to be delivered, for to devour her child as soon as it was born."

Through the instigation of the devil—the old red dragon—the prince of life was betrayed and by wicked hands—i. e. Roman hands—taken, and crucified, and slain.

Through the Romans were the ten bloody persecutions directed against the devoted disciples of their crucified, but arisen, Lord; and through the same, many thousands were cast into the arena to be devoured by wild beasts, in the Coliseum, as the most notorious criminals were, for the amusement of the depraved populace others were burned alive, incased in garments saturated with pitch, in the gardens of Nero, as a spectacle for the gratification of the inhabitants of the metropolis of the Roman world.

Who will say that this power, which tolerated all false and pagan systems of religion, was not actuated by satanic influence, directly exerted in persecuting the true religion of Christ alone? The Roman Empire was Satan's peculiar domain.

"And there appeared another wonder in heaven; and behold, a great dragon, having seven heads and ten horns, and seven crowns upon his heads. And his tail drew the *third part of the stars of heaven*, and did cast them to the earth."—Rev. 12: 3, 4.

Here is the symbol of the animating malevolent genius of the Roman power, having under the direct control of his foul and corrupting influence the brightest intellects of the civilized world. "His tail drew the *third part of the stars of heaven.*" This influence had the supreme direction of affairs in every period. The seven heads, elsewhere shown to be the seven forms of government, under which the Roman power has, and shall appear, are here plainly shown to be powers belonging to the great red dragon. The ten horns, symbolizing the final ten confederated kingdoms, are *all his*. And the seven crowns upon his head, show that the supreme authority vests in him. Here was truly a power behind the imperial throne, directing the counsels of State.

Stars uniformly symbolize men of eminence and position, the scintillations of whose genius attract attention, or whose commanding position and wide-spread influence render conspicuous. Eminent statesmen and philosophers, and other distinguished characters, whose achievements have raised them to a position of eminence, and therefore to be looked up to as lights of the world.

The stars of heaven signify those of the visible firmament, conspicuous to beholders dwelling on the earth. The third part would imply the eminent men occupying commanding positions to the inhabitants of one-third part of the earth: and thus the Roman Empire is symbolically designated. The tail is the symbol of a false and corrupt influence. The venom of most insects, and many reptiles, resides in the tail; which is the seat therefore of their poisonous sting. By their tails they do hurt. The eminent men, therefore, of the Roman Empire, by the expression "his tail drew the third part of the stars of heaven, and cast them to the earth," are shown to have been led astray by satanic influence and corrupted by doctrines of devils. And how true to the fact? The most distinguished men were atheistic, even Cicero was so fond of philosophical speculations and drawing distinction, that it is impossible to infer from his writings what may have been his real sentiments; he is thought to have been atheist. He was most likely an Epicurean and therefore, a materialist and fatalist. Cæsar was an avowed atheist. From these we may judge as to the lesser lights.

The old Romans were men of the world, in the strictest sense; their highest ambition was to subdue and rule over it. The stars were blotted out, and cast down to the earth. First rendered subservient to satanic influence and aims, and then cast down and destroyed.

Cicero was beheaded as a felon.

Cato fell upon his own sword at Utica, in Africa—thus

ending a long and illustrious career as a Roman Senator by his own hand.

The great Pompey was stricken down as he stepped ashore on the strand of Egypt by the base hand of treachery and assassination.

And the great Julius himself, after all his conquests, his great victories and triumphs, was assaulted in the very Senate House in broad daylight, and fell beneath the repeated strokes inflicted by numerous "honorable" assassins.

So does the devil treat his own. Of the first twelve emperors, only three died a natural death.

By the third part of the stars, therefore, we must understand the distinguished men of the old Roman Empire; and, therefore, that this power embraced the one-third part of the inhabited earth. The phrase "the inhabited earth," and "the Roman world," must be limited to the known and civilized portions of the earth, in the times of the Cæsars. Many other passages in the Apocalypse give the same designation as an expression for the Roman Empire. See Rev. 8: 7-12.

From certain passages it is evident that the river Euphrates will form the eastern Asiatic boundary of the revived Roman Empire. Rev. 9: 14-16, also 16: 6-12.

The four angels which were bound in the great river Euphrates will be loosened. "These were prepared—i. e. in anticipation of being loosened—for an hour, and a day, and a month, and a year, for to slay the *third part of men*,"—i. e. to make war upon the men of the coming Roman Empire. Four angels are represented as being agents, good or bad, here doubtless bad, limited or restricted by the great river Euphrates, the evil genii or patron demons of the false systems of eastern mythology, which have so long held the countless millions of the east in the most debased superstition—Hindooism, Parseeism, Brahminism and Buddhism.

These pent-up agents of the evil one, hitherto limited to central and eastern Asia by the Euphrates, will seek to transcend this boundary and engage in the fierce religious strife which shall distract the western Empire. Perhaps the two great powers, whose armies now confront each other in no friendly attitude in central Asia, may be instrumental in stirring up and precipitating the fanatical hordes of the east upon the west.

"And the sixth angel poured out his vial upon the great river Euphrates; and the water thereof was dried up, that the way of the kings of the east might be prepared." Rev. 16: 12.

Comparing the population, approximately, of the coming Roman Empire, from the data afforded by the present populations of the nations most likely to be included, and there would be in the aggregate something less than 300,000,000. Excluding the western and southern continents, and this would not fall very short of being the one-third part of the remainder of the entire population of the earth. Absolute numerical strictness alone is not so much to be considered, but to be taken in connection with other considerations.

The population of the old Roman Empire, from data furnished in the times of the Emperor Claudius, is estimated to have been about 120,000,000. This was doubtless an approximation to the one-third part of the population of the whole earth at that time. Hence, the Roman Empire shall be limited to the one-third part, so far as its political organization shall extend; but its influence will reach the remotest limits of the civilized world, and all will yield assent to the last form of error and delusion, which shall emanate from this center of power and influence, and which shall exert such a powerful and fascinating control over the thoughts and imaginations of men. "And all that dwell upon the earth shall worship him, whose names are not written in the book of life of the Lamb slain from the foundation of the world." Rev. 13: 8.

CHAPTER XIV.

THE INCEPTION—IS IT THE GERMAN EMPIRE?

"And there are seven kings: five are fallen, and one is, and the other is not yet come; and when he cometh, he must continue a short space. And the beast that was, and is not, even he is the eighth, and is of the seven, and goeth into perdition." Rev. 17: 10, 11.

The men of this generation boast of the wonderful improvements of the age, and glory in the works of their own hands. But it must be allowed, that all this vaunted progress, which is claimed to be the crowning achievement of the world's civilization, is chiefly material progress, and is composed of the persistible—the spiritual only will endure.

It is only a continuation of that which was initiated by the immediate progeny of Cain; and which, carried forward and elaborated by the ceaseless activity of mind, through successive generations, has at length eventuated in the amazing results of human skill and energy, witnessed on every hand in this nineteenth century of the Christian era. And it is a striking proof of the wonderful forbearance and benevolence of God, in that He allows those who can find no pleasure in His ways, to delight themselves in the works of their own hands. Thus through their own choosing, they have magnified the material above the spiritual, and worshiped the *things* created, rather than the Creator. While Divine Revelation teaches us that all this elaboration and embellishment, the boast and the pride of the age, brought to pass by human genius, pertains to the domain of the God of this world, whose vicegerant is symbolized by a hideous wild beast seen rising up out of the sea. "And power was given him over all kindreds, and tongues, and nations."

In contrast with the glory of this world, which must pass away, God presents to the eye of faith a perfect celestial gem—the future home of the redeemed.

"And shewed me that great city, the holy Jerusalem, descending out of heaven from God, Having the glory of God: and her light was like unto a stone most precious, even like a jasper-stone, clear as crystal." Rev. 21: 10–11. "And I saw a new heaven and a new earth: for the first heaven and the first earth were passed away." Rev. 21: 1.

A few more chapters and the history of this dispensation must close. God will select His own agents, either directly or permissively, for the accomplishment of His decrees; and times, and seasons are of His own choosing.

The chief instrumentality among coming events, which shall precipitate the final catastrophe of this *age*, will be the *revived Roman Empire*. It therefore becomes a most interesting inquiry, which shall now claim our attention, *are there any signs of the inception of the coming power among the nations at this day?* Is there now among the nations of Europe, any political organization, which appears to embody the elements or political requisites, which shall characterize the coming Roman Empire.

The passage cited at the head of this chapter shows that the coming power will be the eighth form of administration under which the Roman Commonwealth shall be organized and administered, and the last. Of the seventh form, it is said, "when he cometh, he must continue a short space." The eighth must follow the seventh in the order of succession, and arise from the ruins of the seven. It will combine the essential characteristics of the seven, which had gone before.

Has the seventh yet appeared? We think it has, and passed away; and that the *holy Roman Empire of the German nations* was the seventh form of the Roman Commonwealth. Wise and good men look upon the brief Empire of the first Napoleon as the seventh. This is not improbable.

In favor of the German Roman Empire being the seventh, it may be said, that, such as it was, it resulted from a spontaneous movement among the German nations, actuated by a sense of threatened danger from the menacing and aggressive attitude of the Ottoman Empire. It was in form an organized imperial confederacy. It was at one time composed of ten electoral princes, chiefly independent sovereigns. The long continued duration of this organization would seem to militate against the theory above stated; but then it was for the greater part of its history only a nominal power. Its active career, as the potent political head of the Germanic body, was short.

The actual inception of the coming power, as a political phenomenon, will, it would seem, be intimately associated with the appearance upon the stage of human affairs of an extraordinary personage as its leading spirit and organizer. Preparatory steps have advanced apace already, and are still in progress; but the ambitious, the daring and unhesitating leader of the coming political movement, endowed with the prescience inspired by satanic intelligence and stimulated with the ardor of satanic malice, must appear upon the scene before the political elements shall become subservient to the *one will*, and begin to assume their allotted places in the organization of the last or eighth state of the Roman Empire.

We can not come to any certain conclusion as to what power, if any, of those at present existing on the continent shall take the lead, for it is expressly stated that this power shall spring up among ten powers previously existing and from a small beginning.

The prophecies clearly point to the ten nationalities of modern Europe as they shall appear just before the rise of the coming power.

It is not difficult at present to point out ten such States. If we shall have reference to the ten electoral princes of the German Roman Empire, it will not be difficult to show that a political power in the kingdom of Prussia has started up from among those which bids fair to attain the ascendant; or, if we shall still look to the future for the coming *arbiter* of the nations, we have at present ten independent sovereign states which fulfill every requisite, and are chiefly within the limits of the old Roman Empire. These are Italy, Spain and Portugal, France, Belgium, Holland and the German Empire, Austria, Turkey and Greece—ten. Great Britain is not on the continent, and is composed chiefly of territories to which the ancient Romans were strangers, and her possessions are scattered round the world. Should Spain and Portugal be recognized as but one power, on account of their similarity and proximity, we may include Egypt among the ten sovereign States, as she is so all but in form. And this would seem the rather to be required to preserve the balance between the East and the West.

From among the European nationalities, either as now located upon the map, or as they were antecedently or shall be subsequently, there must spring up from a small beginning a political power, which, under the lead of an extraordinary chief, shall rapidly achieve by conquest and by supreme intelligence and daring an ascendency over all the civilized world. For, says the Prophet Daniel, "I considered the horns, and behold, there came up among them another little horn, before whom there were three of the first horns plucked up by the roots: and behold, in this horn were *eyes like the eyes of man, and a mouth speaking great things.*" Dan. 7: 8. Three of the kingdoms, which shall be fully organized and recognized as separate and distinct political powers at the inception of the power symbolized by this little horn, shall be subverted by conquest. By conquest there shall be formed the nucleus of an Empire, but when the Empire shall be fully formed there will still be ten confederate kingdoms. For Rev. 17: 12–13: "And the ten horns which thou sawest are ten kings, which have received no kingdom as yet; but receive power as kings one hour with the beast. These have one mind, and shall give their power and strength unto the beast."

A survey of the map of Europe as at present, must convince every one who has given but even slight attention to passing events, that, should any great revolution arise on the continent at the present time, the *German Empire* must either take the lead or be disintegrated and wholly subverted, and its elements arranged under new organizations. Success is the life of this imperial confederation. But on a first view there seems to be objections to considering Prussia, the center of this confederation, as the power symbolized by the little horn of Daniel's fourth beast, unless we shall take into consideration the entire history of the rise of this State from a very small beginning to its present position, and also the animating spirit which was inspired by Frederick II. Would not this necessitate the appropriation of more time to be occupied in the development of this power than we are authorized by the words of the prophet to allow? That the claims of Prussia to this distinction are not wholly without foundation, the following considerations will show.

The rise of this Prussian State has been rapid and extraordinary. The kings of Prussia trace their origin to Count Thassilo of Zollern, one of the generals of Charlemagne. In 1411, a Count or Prince of Zollern, or Hohenzollern, was invested by the Emperor Sigismund with the Province of Bradenburg. This same prince obtained the rank of an elector in 1417.

The province of Frederick, first king who placed the crown on his own head, at Königsburg, June 18th, 1701, contained a population of less than 1,500,000. When Frederick II, called the Great, ascended the throne in 1740, his disjointed dominions did not contain 2,500,000 inhabitants, all told. From such small beginnings has this power sprung up, and chiefly within the past century; and owes its present commanding position to the genius and energy of one man, or more correctly perhaps to the spirit infused by his example, namely, Frederick the Great. This monarch united in his character almost every extreme. He was destitute of all religious convictions; in his address he was courtly; in his habits, frugal and self-denying. In youth given to excesses. As a sovereign, he had little regard for treaties and compacts with his neighbors. As a general for the lives and comfort of his own soldiers. That he was a great general, has by universal consent been adjudged. But this was among his chief merits. It required twenty years of industry to rebuild and restore the wastes and desolations of the seven years war. Such was the monarch, who laid the foundation of the Prussian power; and here we have the *beau ideal* of a Prussian king. Should another such arise it is easy to foresee, that this German

Empire would strike for undisputed supremacy and control on the continent of Europe, and that a restoration of the Roman Empire in more than name would follow, is manifestly foreshadowed by the past.

If there be, therefore, any evidence above the political horizon, of the inception of the last and disastrous political experiment on earth, we see more evidence of the fact in this Prussian Monarchy than of any that has yet appeared. To her geographical position, there are seeming objections, but then we have seen that in her infancy she was a part of the German Roman Empire, and that the true Roman spirit passed with the Imperial crown, even in the middle ages, to the countries washed by the Danube and the Rhine. This German Roman Empire of the past may occupy an important place in the programme of Divine Providence, if the seventh form of the Roman Commonwealth, then we see the eighth and final.

Germany and especially Prussia, stands pre-eminent for her unrivaled system of public instruction, and for her renowned universities. These celebrated seats of learning, have proved literally orbs of light, in the literary firmament, to the nations. Nothing in oriental or antiquarian research has escaped the vigilance and industry of their savants. There is nothing in modern science or criticism, which has not passed the severest ordeal of rescension, at their hands. The conclusion arrived at by the German universities in reference to the problems of physical science and metaphysics, have been accepted as oracular by the civilized world. Eager students from every clime have resorted to these fountains of thought, that they might drink in the latest and most approved phase of learning and philosophy. Can these be considered *the eyes*, that "were eyes like the eyes of man?"

It is a significant fact that these great schools of philosophy and criticism have paved the way for a new departure in theology and sacred exegesis, which has already in a measure brought about a revolution in Biblical interpretation, unfavorable to the ultimate authority of the sacred oracles; and which bids fair to end in the total elimination of all that is supernatural, and therefore vital, from theology. It has been too much the ambition of these seminaries of learned research to enunciate startling dogmas; many of the learned doctors, who have held positions of high professional influence, have not hesitated in their dogmatic disquisitions to speak of the Lord Jesus Christ as a mere man, and to treat the doctrines of the Christian religion not as ultimate authority, but that they must be tried and finally determined by human reason. Have we here the mouth speaking great things and blasphemies? I have no doubt but we have here the rudiments of the coming blasphemous departure, which shall be attended with dire woes, for the short space allotted to this last form of organized wickedness on the earth.

There are rife in Germany and the immediate adjoining States at this time the elements of revolution. Pent up within the body politic are the internal forces of religious, and social, and skeptical fanaticism, which must prove too strong for the bands of society. Here slumber the germs of those ideas which the "man of sin" shall fulminate and seek to use as ready-shaped instrumentalities in working out the final destiny and catastrophe of the age. Here is atheism in its manifold enunciations, such as Pantheism, Rationalism, Neology and Transcendental Philosophy, Socialism and Liberalism. Their heresies in their manifold forms have pervaded the whole mass of society, from the highest to the lowest, in the one form or the other. This has begotten a strong dislike for the things of the past, dissatisfaction with the present, and an almost uncontrollable impatience to embark upon a new era of experiment. Such is the present state of feeling among the masses of the people on the continent at this day, or the signs of the times teach no lesson.

But should it be asked if Prussia be the head of the revived Roman Empire, symbolized by the little horn in Daniel 7th, where are the three subverted kingdoms symbolized by the three horns which were plucked up by the roots? If the inquiry be insisted on for the present, we answer: We find these in the three following kingdoms, which have been absorbed by the German Empire; but time may prove that not these, but other vanquished States are intended by the prophet. There is the kingdom of Saxony, which, for a century or more, took rank among the second rate kingdoms of Europe. This State, through the agency of Prussian arms and diplomacy, has ceased to be an independent sovereignty, but has been swallowed up by the German Empire. And there is also the kingdom of Bavaria, equal to Prussia one hundred years ago. This has met with a similar fate with the kingdom of Saxony, and if we inquire for a third, we shall find that the late kingdom of Hanover has followed in the wake of the two former—been absorbed into the German Empire.

Besides, it may be asserted, without fear of successful contradiction, that the Germans are characteristically the modern Romans. More Roman than the Latin races themselves.

The old Romans were simple in their manners and tenacious of their customs which, consequently, underwent few changes. Their houses were built on the same general plan in every age of the commonwealth. Their clothing consisted chiefly of the same garments from first to last. The toga and the tunic were the principal and indispensable articles of wearing apparel of all classes and at all times. So also with the true German. He is slow to adopt new customs, or to admit of innovations upon the established usages of the past.

The Romans, though clannish in their habits, were stern in exacting exact justice from man to man. Love of country, coupled with a hearty dislike for foreigners, and with great contempt of danger, with a passion also for wars of conquest, that they may assert their superiority over their neighbors, were the ruling characteristics of the ancient Romans. In these respects the Germans resemble them more than any modern nation. Especially do the Germans emulate the old Romans in their ardor for military pursuits.

The Prussian, or the German, Empire has astonished the civilized world within the past few years, with their military achievements, and have introduced a new era in modern warfare. For strength of will and pertinacity of purpose, for thoroughness of organization in civil, in educational, as well as in military matters, and in a hearty disdain for all foreign powers, the Prussians have no equals. The German army has shown itself to be absolutely invincible of late.

Says an eye-witness of the military operations of the late war between Germany and France, "No more awful instrument of destruction than the German army has ever done its destined work. It is the physical force of a nation brought together and directed against the foe, after such training and discipline, and with such ready concurrence of every man in the army, that it acts as a single man would act under the volition of his heart and brain. The result is seen at large in the advance from the Rhine to the

Saar, from the Saar to the Moselle, from the Moselle to the Meuse."—*Cor. L. Times.* It may be studied in detail on every battle field of the war.

Such energy and precision in marching, such absolute certainty in attaining the results aimed to be accomplished, has never been equaled in the most successful campaigns of either ancient or modern warfare. Every student of history must concede this. Who will venture to assert then that this superiority will not be turned to the purpose of conquest and national aggrandizement? The reigning monarch of this empire, as well as his chief advisers are all old men, and must soon yield their places to others. What demon may inflame the passions of the incoming imperial regimé, it is not difficult in the light of the past history of this power to conjecture?

Frederick the Second found a large and well disciplined army when he ascended the Prussian throne, left him by his father. He was not long in finding employment for it. The horrors of the seven-years' war ensued. Prussia was launched upon a career of conquest, which has been only temporarily intermitted since his time.

There are embarrassments in the way of the hypothesis that the present German Empire is the inception of the coming Roman Empire, but these are incidental in their nature, and may be only apparent. The symbol of the little horn in Daniel 7th seems to point out rather a single individual as the head of a power which sprang up from a small beginning, as the chief of the coming power—"that man of sin—the son of perdition"—whose rise will be sudden, and career brief. But it will not do to press this idea too far, for he must be the chief over an imperial confederation of ten kingdoms. Prussia commenced her career of conquest and aggrandizement during the past century. The

German Empire is only of to-day. The history of the whole, including Prussia, it must be allowed, is brief, compared with the lives of other nations.

This hypothesis furthermore requires that we should regard the government as a whole, including the council of State, rather than a single individual. This finds confirmation from Rev. 13: 11-12: "And I beheld another beast coming up out of the earth, and he had two horns like a lamb, and he spake as a dragon. And he exerciseth all the power of the first beast before him." Here is symbolized a chief counselor and powerful minister of State, civil and ecclesiastical. He will have the chief direction of affairs, and especially in promoting the new innovations upon the established customs and religion.

A horn in the prophecies of Daniel seems to symbolize primarily the individual leader, or royal personage rather, but it necessarily includes the realm or monarchy ruled also. See Daniel 8: 3. "Two horns, one higher than the other,"—Cyrus and Astyages, the former a Persian and the latter a Mede, so explained afterward, but Persia and Media are necessarily included. Also 8: 5: "The he-goat had a notable horn between his eyes," symbolizing Alexander, King of Macedon. Again, 8: 8: "There came up four notable ones (horns) toward the four winds of heaven." Here the territorial dominions of the four principal generals of Alexander, who parted his conquests at his death among themselves, are evidently intended; for in Dan. 8: 9 it is said: "And out of one of them—i. e. of the four notable horns—came forth a little horn, which waxed exceeding great" This little horn doubtless symbolized primarily Antiochus Epiphanes, the head of the Syrian monarchy, and the persecutor of the Jews. So in each instance a political power, including the State, is intended.

So this branch of the subject is not quite free from difficulty; but they do not affect the general conclusions, nor the certainty that the events pointed out in the prophecies we are considering will come to pass in their allotted time.

The House of Savoy has suddenly mounted the throne of a united Italy. If it be the will of God, one of the Swiss cantons may attain to the ascendant among the nations of the earth.

The present position and past history of France, being a nation of ancient regimé, certainly excludes this power. But great political changes may supervene, as calamitous times, attended by revolutions most radical and widely extended, must precede and usher in the *eighth* and last form of the Roman Empire.

Great Britain, and Russia on the continent of Europe, will stand at bay; but their people will, more or less, sympathize with the grand movement of the nations. The western continent will be powerfully affected, sympathetically, as her populations have sprung from among all the nations of the old world.

The appointed agents, in any event, will be forthcoming to accomplish the purposes of Divine Providence. For as the volcano spews out upon the surface of the earth the gems of gold and precious ores which lie deeply buried beneath the superincumbent strata of rubbish, so must the convulsions of society force to the surface those who shall be endowed with the capacity to guide the storm of human passions.

A distinguished British statesman, in an address delivered not many years ago, said: "A dreadful war is about to commence on the continent which will to all appearance terminate in the undisputed supremacy of one power." What such power will be, he adds "as yet lies buried in the womb of time." Had he as closely studied and compared with the signs of the times the sacred oracles, as he had doubtless observed the aspect of the political horizon, he would not have been at loss on this point.

Here we must leave this branch of our subject. Time only can resolve every doubt. The cardinal facts we have. The whole is in the keeping of Him whose secrets are His own.

CHAPTER XV.

HISTORICAL CAREER AND END.

"The beast that thou sawest, was, and is not; and shall ascend out of the bottomless pit, and go into perdition." Rev. 17: 8.

We are discussing a real subject, not mere creations of the fancy, or imaginary theories. However skeptics may scoff at, and false teachers prevaricate, in respect to the truths of Divine Revelation, we hold these to be the most absolute and unerring certainties.

The *historical career* of the Roman Empire, when once fully organized, will be disastrous, and its duration brief. Its end will be hastened by the signal interposition of heaven, in judgments upon the ungodly and blasphemous agents of Satan, who shall direct the councils of State. We are authorized by prophecy to conclude that the entire period of its rule, as the supreme arbiter of the nations, will not much exceed seven years. From the beginning of the organization of the empire until its final overthrow, we are not authorized to assign a longer period than about nine years. To assign the reasons for this, would require more space than can be allotted here.

The brief historical career of this government will be characterized by an *insane frenzy for religious persecution*—by the *migration of the Jews to Palestine*—and by an *attempt*, *which will* mainly succeed, to *root out of the minds of men all* traces of *religious* belief. The idea will gain the ascendant that spiritual religion has proved to be the bane of society, that the worship of a supreme, spiritual God is a *pernicious delusion* to which all the evils of the past can be mainly traced. It will be urged that religion is the offspring of priest-craft, and all the enormities that have grown out of spiritual despotism have sprung from the same source; namely, moral degradation and slavery, poverty and want.

It will be held that the chief and crowning attribute of man, consists in his *intellectual superiority* over the beasts of the field; that this is his normal and rational status. That he is a moral and worshiping being; and that he possesses a moral and religious nature, is a pernicious delusion. Whatever is pernicious to the individual, must prove damaging to the State; as the State is composed of individuals in the aggregate. The worship, therefore, of an invisible Almighty Being is a pernicious delusion, and before society can be remodeled upon a rational and harmonious system all belief in, and worship of, the one invisible God must be treated as a crime. Nor is this a new idea, for in Pliny's letter to Trajan, from which an extract was before quoted, we find the following: "Interim in iis, qui ad me tanquam Christiani deferrebantur, hunc sum secutus modum. Interrogavi ipsos, an essent Christiani: confitentes iterum ac tertio interrogavi, supplicium minatus; perseverantes duci jussi."

"I have followed this practice," he says, "in reference to those accused of being Christians. I first interrogated them individually as to whether they were Christians. If they confessed that they were, I questioned them a second and third time, threatening them with punishment. Those that still remained obstinate in their profession, I ordered to be led out and executed." A return to the Roman Empire will be a revival also of the practice that prevailed under Roman rule. For it was the custom of this power, while it patronized idolatry, and the worship of the imperial image, to put to death for their faith the worshipers of the true and living God. So will the revived empire do.

Here is the whole theory. A reign of terror will ensue. A system of cruel espionage will be set on foot. Tests of acquiescence in the new regimé, and of loyalty to the powers that be, will be demanded of every soul. Says one:

"That this age shall end in a terrible apostacy, and that man of sin—the son of perdition shall be revealed, is clearly taught in 2 Thess. 2: 7-8."

For the first time in the history of man, evil, pure and unqualified, will become organized and attain without any check the supreme control over the earth. Infidelity has boasted long of the fitness of its principles to regenerate and reorganize society upon a model constitution, compatible with the greatest freedom to the individual, and at the same time of the fullest intellectual and physical development and the highest degree of happiness to the human race. It will now be given an opportunity to demonstrate its vaunted superiority.

It is an attribute of the divine government over the universe to allow to all the most ample opportunity to show their true character, that the evil may be condemned by the works of their own hands. And such an opportunity will be granted to the emissaries of the evil one, under the short, but disastrous, rule of the man of sin. We have seen that all hindrance to evil will be removed when the church of the Lord Jesus shall be taken away. God's special Providence will be withdrawn and Satan allowed full scope to accomplish all his malicious purposes. Formal systems of religion and hirelings in priestly garments will become pliant agents in his hands. So it was in the French revolution, so it will be again.

Unity of councils, and oneness of aim, will characterize

the daring spirit of innovation which shall assail all established institutions. A haughty disdain for all opinions, past or present, not in harmony with the policy which shall rule in the ascendant for the time. The marvelous utterances of the chief of State, his daring innovations and blasphemous proclamations, will be received with applause, almost universal.

Such will be the outburst of applause and enthusiasm for the ruling potentate, that the kings of the earth will, by common consent, confer upon him supreme, dictatorial authority. "These have one mind, and shall give their power and strength unto the beast." Rev. 17: 13. So it appears that the coming empire will assume the form of a consolidated, despotic imperial confederacy. "For God hath put in their hearts to fulfill his will, and to agree, and give their kingdom unto the beast, until the words of God shall be fulfilled." Rev. 17: 17.

From the Revelations of St. John we learn that the inception of the Roman power will be attended with special judgments, which shall lead on *step by step to the final catastrophe.*

3 "And another angel came and stood at the altar, having a golden censer; and there was given unto him much incense, that he should offer *it* with the prayers of all saints upon the golden altar which was before the throne.

4 "And the smoke of the incense, *which came* with the prayers of the saints, ascended up before God out of the angel's hand.

5 "And the angel took the censer, and filled it with fire of the altar, and cast *it* into the earth: and there were voices, and thunderings, and lightnings, and an earthquake.

6 "And the seven angels which had the seven trumpets prepared themselves to sound,

7 "The first angel sounded, and there followed hail and fire mingled with blood, and they were cast upon the earth: and the third part of trees was burnt up, and all green grass was burnt up.

8 "And the second angel sounded, and as it were a great mountain burning with fire was cast into the sea: and the third part of the sea became blood;

9 "And the third part of the creatures which were in the sea, and had life, died; and the third part of the ships were destroyed.

10 "And the third angel sounded, and there fell a great star from heaven, burning as it were a lamp, and it fell upon the third part of the rivers, and upon the fountains of waters;

11 "And the name of the star is called Wormwood: and the third part of the waters became wormwood; and many men died of the waters, because they were made bitter.

12 "And the fourth angel sounded, and the third part of the sun was smitten, and the third part of the moon, and the third part of the stars; so as the third part of them was darkened, and the day shone not for a third part of it, and the night likewise.

13 "And I beheld, and heard an angel flying through the midst of heaven, saying with a loud voice, Woe, woe, woe, to the inhabiters of the earth, by reason of the other voices of the trumpet of the three angels, which are yet to sound!" Rev. 8: 3–13.

Moses constructed the tabernacle in the wilderness after the "pattern shown him on the mount—the patterns of things in the heavens." One article of sacred furniture was the golden censer, in which the high priest burnt incense before the mercy seat, when he entered the Holy of Holies once a year to make intercession, while the whole congregation stood without, offering up their prayers to Jehovah, their King. But the earthly service has given place to a better economy. Christ, our Great High Priest, has entered into the heavenly place by virtue of the merits of His own blood, offered once for all, as a final and perfect propitiation for the sins of believers, and is offering the incense of the gracious perfumes of His own spotless perfection.

Who can offer this incense in heaven but Christ Himself—the angel of the *everlasting covenant?* Hence, the angel with the golden censer is none other than Christ Himself. "The smoke of the incense, which came with the prayers of the saints, ascended up before God out of the angel's hand."

This is the figure of the services in the heavenly sanctuary while the saints shall remain on earth, and have need that their prayers be presented acceptable through the mediation of their Great High Priest, the Lord of life and glory. But this mediation shall cease. "For the angel took the golden censer"—which had been accessory to the offering of much incense before the mercy seat, as a token of the perfect satisfaction made by the final sin-offering, and as a symbol of the gracious perfumes of Christ's perfect righteousness and spotless purity, the delight of the Father, an emblem also of peace and good will toward earth—"and filled it with fire of the altar," indicative of God's judgments, "and cast it into the earth." As the fire upon the altar of sacrifice consumed the sin-offerings, which were interposed in a figure between man and his sins, so shall the fire of God's judgment destroy the subjects of sin, if unrepentant and unredeemed. Surely when the golden censer filled with fire shall be cast into the earth, the saints will no longer be there.

The judgments foretold in the above cited passage will not be visited upon the nations, until after the *rapture of the church*.

The earth, during the brief period which shall limit the duration of the Roman Empire, shall be scourged by the judgments of heaven. The phrase "*the third part*," limits the calamities to this power.

The effect of these judgments upon the temper of the ungodly multitude, will be most radical and demoralizing. They will stir up all the native depravity of the heart, beget a distrust of Divine Providence, and arouse an open hostility toward high heaven—the manifest source of the scourge visited upon them for their sins. These judgments will affect the air, the seasons, the soil, most likely the temperature and the productions of the earth, including vegetable and animal life.

"*Hail and fire mingled with blood.*"—

"Hail denotes an assailing calamity from without," most likely storms and tornadoes, attended by great destruction of property resulting in distress; and with floods of water inundating the lands, followed by pestilential disease destructive to life. This is implied in the phrase "*fire mingled with blood*," which indicates judgments of God, resulting in the destruction of human life.

The spiritual and moral effects of these plagues will be most appalling. "The third part of trees were burnt up," indicating that men of eminence shall become totally demoralized and recklessly abandoned. "And all green grass was burnt up,"—that the moral blight and desolation shall be universal. The moral and spiritual sentiments of the people shall become in a manner obliterated, withered, parched and burnt out by the fierceness of the fires of the evil passions, stirred up by these plagues.

The first trumpet will be the prelude to the second, as the demoralizing effects of the plagues foretold under the first trumpet will prepare the way for the grand insurrectory movement, symbolized by the great mountain burning with fire. The plagues foretold under the first trumpet, will be attended with great calamities and distress; producing despondency and desperation, which will stir up the slumbering passions of the masses and urge them forward blindly and recklessly, to plunge into the vortex of revolution in the desperate hope of finding alleviation from a change of government and institutions. This will prepare the way for the advent of the man of sin, symbolized by the star falling from heaven under the third trumpet.

"The second angel sounded, and as it were a great mountain burning with fire was cast into the sea." By a "burning mountain," a volcano is manifestly to be understood, such as Vesuvius or Ætna. The volcanic fires of these mountains are inactive sometimes for a century or more, and then burst out again with new violence, demonstrating what tremendous forces lie slumbering in these grand mountain crucibles of nature's laboratory. The terrific violence and awful grandeur of a volcanic eruption, has been witnessed lately in one of the Sandwich Islands in the Pacific Ocean. Mauna Loa, whose summit rises to an elevation of 14,000 feet above the sea, poured out a deluge of fire, which descended in a liquid river of molten heat, three miles wide and twenty miles in length, to the ocean.

In the first century of the Christian era, the memorable eruption of Mount Vesuvius, at which the elder Pliny, the *naturalist*, was suffocated, overwhelmed the cities of Herculaneum and Pompeii, and buried them out of sight beneath a deluge of lava and ashes; and these cities remained for

HISTORICAL CAREER AND END. 241

centuries lost, in all but the name. The pen of inspiration employs such an illustration to describe the eruption of the fires of the human passions, when once stirred up and fanned into flame by a gust of frenzy and madness, provoked by grievances, too intolerable to be longer borne. The reckless fury of an insurrectory mob has been often witnessed. The worst instincts of a very bad class of people are aroused and excited to deeds of violence. Demoniacal passions rule the mass of infuriated men and women. Destruction and murder mark their progress. No work of art, however costly, or ornamental, or highly prized for its antiquity, escapes the brutal violence of the maddened multitude. Such was the case in the times of the French revolution. Such was the conduct of the commune of Paris, during the late German and French war. We have seen that a wide spread insurrectory movement, among the great mass of the European populations, "the sea," will be the immediate cause, which shall lead to the revival of the Roman Empire. This revolution will be attended by widespread destruction of life and property, and by the paralysis of all departments of industry, and the destruction of trade and commerce;—"and the third part of the ships were destroyed."

When the people who shall dwell within the limits of the Roman Empire, the one-third part shall have become completely disorganized and demoralized by revolution and intestine disorder, exhausted and famished by disease and want, desperate and reckless from their hapless condition, and consequently desirous for a change—the apostate symbolized by the great star that "fell from heaven, burning as it were a lamp," under the third trumpet, will make his advent upon the scene, and inaugurate the agitation, which shall lead on to the last and disastrous political experiment, the revival of the old Roman Empire,—the apocalyptic trumpets will sound the alarm, and one woe will follow another in quick succession. Like a flaming meteor shall he fall from the firmament, and his light go out forever. His mission will be to introduce strife and bitterness. He will corrupt the "rivers and fountains of water," symbolic of moral and spiritual instruction. Here schools and universities are intended, and instructors and teachers, who shall occupy the places of authority, and therefore be the channels of communication to the body of the people; and therefore, when they shall be corrupted by the doctrine of devils, which this apostate will disseminate, the great body of the people will likewise be led astray. For it is said of these very times, "God shall send them strong delusions, that they should believe a lie," and fall under condemnation because they shall prefer error to the truth, "have pleasure in unrighteousness." Strife and bitterness will be the immediate result, fierce and acrimonious debate, with the triumph of the doctrines of the evil one. Men will die a moral death from their effect.

Under the fourth trumpet it is said; "and the third part of the sun was smitten, and the third part of the moon, and the third part of the stars." The sun symbolizes Divine Revelation, thus the source of all moral and spiritual light will be smitten, and superseded by the false theories which shall acquire the ascendancy over the deluded and depraved inhabitants of the Roman Empire—"the one-third part." Worse than the dark ages will be again renewed. Complete dereliction of morals must ensue, Christian ethics will be wiped out. The moon, which reflects the light of the sun, and therefore symbolizes the social and domestic institutions will be smitten, and confusion, uncertainty and moral depravity will ensue. A sad picture of moral desolation is here presented. The way will thus be fully prepared for the reign of Satan through his vicegerent, the antitype of the beast. But other woes shall quickly follow. The things foretold under the fifth trumpet refer to the Jews. This will appear from internal evidence as conclusive, as that "the one-third part" in the above passage limits the events there predicted to the Roman Empire.

There is reason to believe that in the openings of Providence, colonies of Jews will be formed in the no distant future in Palestine.

A resident missionary writing from Beyrout, April, 1879, speaks of a project "to form a company, and buy up the old lands of Gilead and Mount Ephraim, and to colonize them with Jews. He also speaks of a new city springing up at Jerusalem, between the Jaffa and Bethlehem roads. There are still other schemes looking to the colonization of the waste lands of Syria."

The first symptoms of the coming political revolution, will be manifested in a growing hostility toward all classes of Theists—Christians and Jews. This intolerant spirit will induce many of the Jews to join their brethren in Palestine.

We have seen that the Jews are, of all people, the most tenacious of their religion, and the customs, and the traditions, handed down from their fathers. What is left of formal Christianity will quickly disappear before the blandishments of the deceiver, or the storm of persecution which he will stir up. Not so with the children of Abraham, they will prefer to seek an asylum for liberty of conscience and worship, in the deserts of Syria, rather than bow the knee to the image of the beast. For four thousand years they have maintained their separate status, as a distinct people in the world amidst persecution the most cruel, and hardship the most extreme, in many instances exiles from the land of their fathers. The attempt of the coming power to establish homogeneity in religion, as well as other things, by the inauguration of pure atheism, will be strenuously resisted by the Jews. The result will be, their immigration in a body, to Palestine.

The migration of the children of Israel from all the countries of western Europe, and it may be from those still more remote, will be a marked event in the beginning of the new era. It will call forth much discussion and produce much excitement.

Their departure will be in haste, as from the land of Egypt of old. "The woman *fled* into the wilderness, where she hath a place prepared of God." Their migration will be attended with dangers, and the urgency great. Two protecting powers will come to their assistance. "And to the woman were given two wings of a great eagle, that she might fly into the wilderness. And the serpent cast out of his mouth water as a flood, after the woman, that he might cause her to be carried away of the flood. And the earth helped the woman; and the earth opened her mouth, and swallowed up the flood which the dragon cast out of his mouth." Rev. 12: 14-16.

Here is direct intervention in aid of their migration. A wing is the symbol of protection, an eagle of an imperial power. What two protecting powers, springing from the same body, will there be likely to intervene? Will they be Great Britain and the United States? both sprung from the same indomitable Anglo-Saxon race, whose ships of war and commerce spread their white wings on every sea. Most likely. Floods here symbolize armed multitudes, stirred up and impelled forward by the sentiments which shall emanate from the mouth of the devil, who is the father of lies from the beginning. "But the earth shall help the woman."

By armed intervention of friendly powers, and by the pestilence that walketh in darkness, and by the destruction that wasteth at noon-day, shall the pursuing hosts fall by the way. As the armies of Pharaoh were swallowed up by the waters of the Red Sea, which literally opened its mouth to engulf them, so the earth shall swallow up the persecuting hordes of the son of perdition.

The Jews colonized in Palestine will enjoy repose for a season only. For in the meantime trouble at home shall arise in the new commonwealth, and especially in their chief city, Jerusalem. The new heresies of the West will have traveled to the East. Emissaries will spring up everywhere.

An exceedingly gifted and powerful rabbi, who will have obtained great power and influence over the multitude at Jerusalem, will apostatize. This wonderfully gifted man, and equally distinguished for his selfish ambition, who shall probably rise to the chief ecclesiastical and civil office in the State, will, in the meantime, turn out to be an apostate from the ancient faith. This character will prove to be the anti-Christ of St. John.—"*Ye have heard that anti-Christ shall come.*" (We can not give the reasons in full for this conclusion here.) The things foretold under the fifth trumpet most clearly point out this personage. The beast with two horns like a lamb—Rev. 13: 11—refers to such a character who shall exercise ecclesiastical as well as civil functions, but counterfeiting the Lord's Christ Himself—"two horns like a lamb."

The great eastern apostate is symbolized by the star seen falling from heaven in Rev. 9: 1-12:

1 "And the fifth angel sounded, and I saw a star fall from heaven unto the earth: and to him was given the key of the bottomless pit.

2 "And he opened the bottomless pit; and there arose a smoke out of the pit, as the smoke of a great furnace; and the sun and the air were darkened by reason of the smoke of the pit.

3 "And there came out of the smoke locusts upon the earth: and unto them was given power, as the scorpions of the earth have power.

4 "And it was commanded them that they should not hurt the grass of the earth, neither any green thing, neither any tree; but only those men which have not the seal of God in their foreheads.

5 "And to them it was given that they should not kill them, but that they should be tormented five months: and their torment *was* as the torment of a scorpion, when he striketh a man.

6 "And in those days shall men seek death, and shall not find it; and shall desire to die, and death shall flee from them.

7 "And the shapes of the locusts *were* like unto horses prepared unto battle; and on their heads *were* as it were crowns like gold, and their faces *were* as the faces of men.

8 "And they had hair as the hair of women, and their teeth were as *the teeth* of lions.

9 "And they had breastplates, as it were breastplates of iron; and the sound of their wings *was* as the sound of chariots of many horses running to battle.

10 "And they had tails like unto scorpions, and there were stings in their tails: and their power *was* to hurt men five months.

11 "And they had a king over them, *which is* the angel

of the bottomless pit, whose name in the Hebrew tongue *is* Abaddon, but in the Greek tongue hath *his* name Apollyon.

12 "One woe is past; *and*, behold, there come two woes more hereafter."

This prophecy has reference to agitations which shall lead to a great apostacy, and, consequently, to a schism among the Jews. That the prophecy refers primarily to this people, is evident from the following facts found in the passage itself. As the former cited passage from Rev. 8th chapter was, by its symbolic reference to the "*one-third part*," limited to the Roman Empire, so this passage from Rev. 9th is, by its own internal evidence, shown to apply to the Jews.

And first, the "star fell from heaven unto the earth." The Greek word here rendered earth, primarily means the land, and by way of eminence, the land of Palestine, and where not otherwise qualified, or the sense of the passage where the word is used, clearly demands a more general application, it has this sense generally in the book of Revelation, though translated by the word earth. When more is intended, some additional limiting word is used, as "the earth and the sea," or, "the earth and the world." So this word is to be limited in its meaning to the land of the holy prophets and of the sacred writings.

And second, in verse 4th we have these words: "but only those men which have not the seal of God in their foreheads." This implies that there will be some who shall have a special immunity, because they shall have the seal of God in their foreheads. But who were sealed in their foreheads? We read of none in the book of Revelations but those that belonged to the tribes of the children of Israel. This shows, therefore, conclusively, that the Jews will be concerned.

Again, in the third place, in verse 11th it is said: "they had a king over them, which is the angel of the bottomless pit, whose name in the Hebrew tongue is Abaddon, but in the Greek tongue hath his name Apollyon." This Hebrew designation identifies the prophecy. The Greek name shows that the east will be affected by the agencies set at work by the angel of the bottomless pit.

Palestine and the eastern countries adjacent will be visited by this moral pestilence. "The star fell upon the land," in opposition to the sea.

That the star symbolizes an individual here, as elsewhere, of distinction, is shown by the language: "And to him," i. e. the star or person symbolized by the star, "was given the key of the bottomless pit." He will be a person. Hell, from beneath, will be stirred up. All its pent-up fumes of malice and rage will be belched forth. All the appliances of satanic ingenuity, for the delusion and destruction of men, will be set in motion, in this final assault against God's ancient people.

"And he opened the bottomless pit; and there arose a smoke out of the pit, as the smoke of a great furnace." The moral atmosphere will become polluted, as by a moral pestilence, blinding and nauseating to the moral sensibilities, drawing a vail over the heart, shutting out the light of Divine Revelation from the understanding and conscience, and so introducing doubt into all things, human and divine.

The power and utility of symbolic representations are fully shown in this and the preceding chapter. As no power of language could so fully and expressively set forth the terrible ravages, which the emissaries of error and delusion will accomplish, as seen in verses 3–11.

"Locusts," indicative of the multitudes of the agencies

of falsehoods and delusions both as to doctrines and miracles, peculiar to the times. The ravages of this insect are chiefly confined to the orient, another proof that these woes will be limited to the east.

They are commanded to "not hurt the grass of the earth, neither any green thing, neither any tree; but only those men who have not the *seal of God* in their foreheads." There are no such exemptions, where the plagues are directed against the western portion of the Empire, see chapter 8th, as there were none left there, who had the *seal of the living God*.

By the "trees" we are to understand the devout Israelites, men of eminence, who have the knowledge and fear of the only *true and living God;* and by "*any green thing,*" any soul, man or woman, who should fear God and reverence His name. The church of the Lord Jesus having been taken up before these plagues shall come upon the earth, there shall not be throughout all nominal Christendom, a true worshiper of the living God remaining outside the Hebrew Commonwealth, all will have become the willing and subservient subjects of the devil, and have given in their adherence to his vicegerent, symbolized by the beast.

By seeking to interpret Moses and the Prophets, so as to harmonize with the materialism of the west, a Jewish rabbi symbolized by the star will come into great favor with the western despot—becoming even the chief minister to the imperial chief of State. Rev. 13: 11, 12. These two characters, designated as "*the beast and the false prophet,*" will frequently appear in our examination of the remaining parts of the book of Revelations. The first is doubtless symbolized by the star, Rev. 8: 10, and the second by the star. Rev. 9: 1. This is manifest from the internal evidence already pointed out.

"To them it was given," in command, "that they should not kill them, but that they should be tormented five months." A painful suspense is induced in the minds of men by the discussion of new ideas. Men are not at once slain morally by them, but are in great doubt and troubled; and this indecision shall continue five months, when these discussions shall end.

The formidable character of the agencies of Satan is strikingly pointed out by the imagery: "And the shapes of the locusts were like unto horses prepared unto battle." A horse is the symbol of an organized political power, generally of an *imperial power*. Horses prepared for battle here indicate a menace or threat of armed intervention by the ten kings which shall subsequently take place.

"On their heads were as it were crowns like gold." But not gold, a mere counterfeit. Assuming to be the messengers of truth, they are false deceivers. Professing to be the prophets and teachers of the sacred oracles of the children of Israel, they will prove to be the emissaries of atheism in disguise. The promoters of a false theology, the setters up of a false god.

"And their faces were as the faces of men." There should be no astonishment at this. For the countenance of man, which, as the mirror of knowledge and true holiness, should reflect the image of God, has been so transformed by sin that it has become the reflector of all manner of dissimulation.

"And they had hair as the hair of women." Female influence and blandishments will be employed as auxiliaries in the work of deceiving and destroying susceptible victims, as is usual in the propagation of falsehood.

"And their teeth were as the teeth of lions." No limit to their voracity.

"Breast-plates, as it were breast plates of iron." They will have an assurance that nothing can daunt.

"And the sound of their wings was as the sound of chariots of many horses running to battle." The din and confusion will be immense. All the weak and undecided will be swept along by the insanity and madness of the excitement.

"They had tails like unto scorpions, and there were stings in their tails." Indicates that their manner of propagating their falsehoods will be most obtrusive and offensive. Their doctrine, most foul and surcharged with venom, producing moral insensibility and final death. This propagandism will be limited to five months.

"They had a king over them." The arch deceiver.

We will now turn our attention to the persecution that will be directed against what shall remain of formal Christianity, within the limits of the Roman Empire.

As an evidence of the renunciation of all belief in spiritual, or supernatural religion, and as a test of loyalty to the new regimé and its imperial head, homage to the emperor and his image will be required of all, without distinction of person or nationality, or religious antecedents.

Homage paid to the imperial image will not necessarily imply a belief that the emperor is a god, but only that there is no power or authority above his on the earth. He is the representative of power in the State, and this *is the highest* attribute. But as the mass of ignorant and superstitious men demand some object of worship, be it an heathen idol, a consecrated shrine and madonna, or a crucifix, or a sacred relic, the imperial image will be offered as a substitute for all.

This will be a device set on foot by the anti-Christ, it seems.

"And he exerciseth all the power of the first beast before him, and causeth the earth and them which dwell therein to worship the first beast, whose deadly wound was healed. And he doeth great wonders, so that he maketh fire come down from heaven on the earth in the sight of men, and deceiveth them that dwell on the earth by the means of those miracles which he had power to do in the sight of the beast; saying to them that dwell on the earth, that they should make an image to the beast, which had the wound by a sword, and did live. And he had power to give life unto the image of the beast, that the image of the beast should both speak, and cause that as many as would not worship the image of the beast should be killed. And he causeth all, both small and great, rich and poor, free and bond, to receive a mark in their right hand, or in their foreheads; and that no man might buy or sell, save he that had the mark, or the name of the beast, or the number of his name." Rev. 13: 12–17.

It is amazing what devilish strategy will be resorted to in order to deceive and destroy the deluded. Will these things be accomplished by the aid of physical science, or will they be the work of invisible demons?

The Papacy, and other kindred forms of the Christian religion, will still strive to maintain their visible existence. Their immense cathedrals, and other religious edifices, their ample endowments for religious orders of different names, and for schools and seminaries, for convents and asylums, and the swarms of ecclesiastics required to supervise these, constitute the cohesive elements of one of the most perfect, as well as the strongest organizations ever devised by the ingenuity of man. The parts of this huge ecclesiastical fabric will long cling together from the mere force of habit, and the instinct of self-preservation. But the Papacy, with all other formal religious institutions, is doomed. Rev. 17: 15-18.

15 "And he saith unto me, The waters which thou sawest, where the whore sitteth, are peoples, and multitudes, and nations, and tongues.

16 "And the ten horns which thou sawest upon the beast, these shall hate the whore, and shall make her desolate and naked, and shall eat her flesh, and burn her with fire.

17 "For God hath put in their hearts to fulfill his will, and to agree, and to give their kingdom unto the beast, until the words of God shall be fulfilled.

18 " And the woman which thou sawest is that great city, which reigneth over the kings of the earth."

That the whore is the apostate Romish Church or Papacy, has been fully shown in another place. But there are other apostate ecclesiastical bodies here brought to view. For the Revelator informs us. Rev. 17: 3-6.

3 "So he carried me away in the spirit into the wilderness; and I saw a woman sit upon a scarlet-coloured beast, full of names of blasphemy, having seven heads and ten horns.

4 "And the woman was arrayed in purple and scarlet-colour, and decked with gold and precious stones and pearls, having a golden cup in her hand full of abominations and filthiness of her fornication:

5 "And upon her forehead was a name written, MYSTERY, BABYLON THE GREAT, THE MOTHER OF HARLOTS AND ABOMINATIONS OF THE EARTH.

6 "And I saw the woman drunken with the blood of the saints, and with the blood of the martyrs of Jesus: and when I saw her, I wondered with great admiration."

The *mother of harlots*, implies that there are daughters also. The fury of this persecution will include all.

"They shall hate the whore." At the inception of the coming Roman Empire, the Roman Catholic Church will be, as at present, the State religion of many of the countries embraced, for the seven heads and ten horns of the scarlet-colored beast point to the imperial Roman power in its last form. The ten kings will be, upon the complete consolidation of the imperial confederation, in perfect accord with the imperial dictator, who shall exalt himself above all that is called God, or that is worshiped.

So "these shall hate the whore, and shall make her desolate and naked, and shall eat her flesh and burn her with fire." They will seize her religious edifices and turn them to secular uses. They will confiscate her endowments, and seize upon her revenues and appropriate them to the use of the State, and pursue her officers, and teachers, and devotees generally, with the fire and sword of persecution, even to extermination, for God will put it in their hearts so to do.

And so shall great Babylon come in remembrance before God, and the news shall go forth to the ends of the earth. Babylon the Great is fallen. There is no such rejoicing described in the Revelations, says one, as that over the fall of Babylon.

Thus shall pass away suddenly and forever this great clerical fabric, which grew up from simple elements, step by step, through successive centuries, and spreading out, has extended over the fairest portion of the civilized world, the most perfect piece of workmanship ever devised by human skill, to gratify ambition and lust of power, and to turn away the light of divine truth from the understanding and conscience of men.

There will remain throughout the whole circle of the domain, now denominated Christendom, but one sentiment, and all shall offer incense before the imperial image as to a household god.

But in the remote east it will not be so. The prophecies point, as we have seen, to trouble in this quarter. The emissaries of the anti-Christ, in their zeal, will visit the countries around and beyond the Euphrates. These emissaries will stir up a religious war. There will ensue an invasion like an inundating flood from that quarter.

The four angels, bound in the river Euphrates, which were prepared for an hour, and a day, and a month, and a year, for to slay the third part of men, will be let loose.

"The third part" means the men of the Roman Empire. This invasion will be composed of an innumerable army of the devotees of the four principal systems of false religion, found along and beyond the Euphrates. The four angels namely, Brahminism, Parseeism, Hindooism, Buddhism. Their hosts will be almost countless, British counsels and arms, and British gold will be seen to aid and direct the movement. The imagery indicates that modern implements of warfare will be employed, and the destruction of life great. Arguments and diplomacy will not be wanting and the result will be a compromise it would seem, each party remaining essentially as before, only there will be at least a treaty, recognizing the pretensions of the western Emperor; for his recognition in some form will be universal. See Rev. 9: 15-21.

There will also be formed a covenant or treaty, with the Jewish Commonwealth in Palestine. "He shall confirm the covenant with many, the mass of the nation, for one week, that is seven years." Dan. 9: 27.

There will be two parties, among these people in Jerusalem, one party termed, Rev. 12: 17,—"the remnant of the woman's seed." "And the dragon was wroth with the woman, and went to make war with the remnant of her seed, which kept the commandments of God, and have the testimony of Jesus." "For the testimony of Jesus is the spirit of prophecy." Rev. 19: 10.

This remnant of true Israelites will retain their traditional constancy of attachment to the laws and customs of their ancestors, and their zeal for the worship of the only *one true and living God the Creator of heaven and the earth.* These, therefore, will repudiate the new interpretations of the law and the prophets, which would strip Jehovah of His independent, self-existent, purely spiritual attributes, and identify Him with a law or force in nature of His own creation. This would be the logical result of the doctrines of the anti-Christ.

On the other hand, the great mass of the nation will enter with zeal into the councils and plans of the great innovating Rabbi Armillus.* This great apostate, commissioned by the *angel of the bottomless pit*, will so work upon the imaginations of the people, by his skill in magic and satanic jugglery, performing such signs and wonders in the sight of men, that he will succeed in deceiving and leading astray all who are not in the secrets of the Almighty. His followers will constitute the larger class. These are described by the Prophet Isaiah 28: 14, 15, "as scornful men;" "Ye scornful men, that rule this people which is in Jerusalem. Because ye have said, We have made a covenant with death, and with hell are we at agreement." These think to escape when the overwhelming scourge shall pass over the land, by entering into a covenant with the ruling power. They will make a covert of lies.

"When the overflowing scourge shall pass through, it shall not come upon us," say these scornful men.

*NOTE.—Jewish tradition of the anti-Christ.

"Wherefore hear the word of the LORD, ye scornful men?" * * * "Your covenant with death shall be disannulled, and your agreement with hell shall not stand; when the overflowing scourge shall pass through, then ye shall be trodden down by it." Verse 18.

The terms of the covenant are not given. But we may infer that there was some stipulation, respecting toleration of religious worship for the term of seven years as a politic measure, inserted at the instance of the Apostate Armillus, thinking to bring over, or banish in time, all not of his party. However, this shall prove, it is manifest, from the prophecy of Daniel, that he will suffer the religious ceremonies to be publicly celebrated only one-half of the stipulated time. For in Dan. 9: 27, we read: "And in the midst of the week—i. e. of the seven years of the covenant—he shall cause the sacrifice and the oblation to cease, and for the overspreading of abominations, he shall make it desolate, even until the consummation, and that determined shall be poured upon the desolate." Until God shall intervene in judgments at the end.

This abomination of desolation, intruded or enforced idolatrous image worship, shall continue three years and a half.

This shall mark the period of the *great tribulation.* That there will be two classes, the devout remnant and the "scornful men," is clearly pointed out in the following passage from Rev. 11: 1–2: "And there was given me a reed like unto a rod:" says the Revelator, "and the angel stood, saying, Rise, and measure the temple of God, and the altar, and them that worship therein."—The scornful men will not worship.—"But the court which is without the temple, leave out, and measure it not; for it is given unto the Gentiles: and the holy city shall they tread under foot forty and two months."—i. e. three and a half years, the same time the remnant shall be shielded by the special Providence of God.

God will take strict account of the temple, and the altar, and them that worship therein. They will be under His holy keeping; but the scornful men will be in league with the Gentiles.

Among the extraordinary occurrences of this time of trial for the faithful, will be the appearing upon the scene of two remarkable witnesses, confronting the emissaries of the evil one with signs and miracles. They are termed "*my two witnesses,*" signifying their ancient and approved character and standing.

They shall remind the faithful that all these things that are transpiring round them and so sorely afflicting them, had been long since foretold by ancient seers and recorded in the holy scriptures by the prophets and apostles of the Lord himself. From the powers ascribed to these two witnesses, the characters of Moses and Elijah appear. They both appeared upon the mount of transfiguration. Elijah was taken up to heaven in a chariot of fire, and Moses disappeared from among the people, and his sepulchre was not found. "There arose not a prophet since in Israel like unto Moses, whom the Lord knew face to face." "Behold, I will send you Elijah, the Prophet, before the coming of the great and dreadful day of the Lord."

"I will give power unto my two witnesses, and they shall prophesy a thousand two hundred and threescore days, clothed in sackcloth."—i. e. three and a half years. "And if any man will hurt them, fire proceedeth out of their mouth, and devoureth their enemies: and if any man will hurt them, he must in this manner be killed." "And when they shall have finished their testimony, the beast that ascendeth out of the bottomless pit shall make war against them, and shall overcome them, and kill them. And their dead bodies shall lie in the street of the great city, which spiritually is called Sodom and Egypt, where also our Lord was crucified. And they of the people, and kindreds, and tongues, and nations," [showing that all nations will be represented in the armies of the enemies of God before the city,] "shall see their dead bodies three days and an half, and shall not suffer their dead bodies to be put in graves. And they that dwell upon the earth," [being informed daily by telegraph as to what is occurring at the common center of interest to all the world, i. e. Jerusalem,] "shall rejoice over them, and make merry, and shall send gifts one to another;"—mutual congratulations—"because these two prophets tormented them that dwelt on the earth. And after three days and an half the Spirit of life from God entered into them, and they stood upon their feet; and great fear fell upon them which saw them. And they heard a great voice from heaven, saying unto them, Come up hither. And they ascended up to heaven in a cloud; and their enemies beheld them. And the same hour was there a great earthquake, and the tenth part of the city fell, and in the earthquake were slain of men seven thousand: and the remnant were affrighted, and gave glory to the God of heaven." Rev. 11: 3, 5, 7–13.

Here is the temporary triumph of "*that man of sin—* the son of perdition" over the saints, for "*it was given unto him to make war with the saints and overcome them.*" But the triumph shall be of brief duration. Here shall be direct interposition from heaven, and this will be the end of the great tribulation and the beginning of the end of the power of the beast and the false prophet.

Of this terrible persecution our Lord spake Matt. 24:21-22:

"For then shall be great tribulation, such as was not since the beginning of the world to this time, no, nor ever shall be. And except those days should be shortened, there should no flesh be saved: but for the elect's sake those days shall be shortened."—The elect of Israel.

Away back in the depths of antiquity a voice is heard echoing through the night of ages past, *"How long shall it be to the end of these wonders?"* And another voice from the same source is heard giving back an answer in solemn asseveration, by a man clothed in linen, who stood upon the waters of the river, "That it shall be for a time, times, and an half;"—i. e. three and a half years—"and when he shall have accomplished to scatter the power of the holy people, all these things shall be finished." Dan. 12: 7.

What things? The things pertaining to the sufferings of God's elect remnant, who will not bow the knee to Baal or any other image.

The Prophet Zechariah 14: 1-4 says: "Behold, the day of the LORD cometh, and thy spoil shall be divided in the midst of thee. For I will gather all nations against Jerusalem to battle; and the city shall be taken; * * * and half of the city shall go forth into captivity, and the residue of the people shall not be cut off from the city. Then shall the LORD go forth, and fight against those nations, as when he fought in the day of battle. And his feet shall stand in that day upon the mount of Olives, which is before Jerusalem on the east."

Here will be direct interposition, by the Lord Jehovah, as promised of old, in natural phenomena; such as upheavals and disruptions of the mountains on the east of the city, by earthquakes, and by fire, by pestilence, and by the sword, will the armies assembled before Jerusalem and in and about the city, be overthrown and destroyed. Alarm and dismay will seize the enemy near and remote. The saints will be delivered, every one found written in the book. The *Ancient* of days *will appear* in a cloud, and by Urim and Thummim, and by the glory of the Lord in the sanctuary restored.

But the end is not yet. This is the beginning of the end. The end will be reached in seventy-five days more. But the Ancient of days shall sit and the judgment of the nations commence.

"I beheld," says the Prophet Daniel, "till the thrones were cast down," [more correctly were arranged] "and the Ancient of days did sit, whose garment was white as snow, and the hair of his head like the pure wool: his throne was like the fiery flame, and his wheels as burning fire. A fiery stream issued and came forth from before him: thousand thousands ministered unto him, and ten thousand times ten thousand stood before him: the judgment was set, and the books were opened. * * * I beheld even till the beast was slain, and his body destroyed, and given to the burning flame." Dan. 7: 9–11.

Here it appears that the beast will not be slain immediately at the sitting of the Ancient of days. "I beheld even till the beast was slain," implying the intervention of some time before that occurrence. This intervention of time before the final destruction of the enemies of God is a happy illustration of the ways of God toward man. "Because sentence against an evil work is not executed speedily, therefore the heart of the sons of men is fully set in them to do evil." Ecc. 8: 11.

There will be first a period of thirty days of a revival of the knowledge and fear of God, then of indecision and declension for forty-five days more, when the destruction of the wicked will be overwhelming and final. "The beast will be slain, and his body given to the burning flame."

This will be the time of the harvest—Matt. 13: 30—and of separation. "And in the time of harvest I will say to the reapers, Gather ye together first the tares, and bind them in bundles to burn them: but gather the wheat into my barn."—Also Matt. 24: 31. And in Rev. 14: 6 we read: "And I saw another angel fly in the midst of heaven, having the everlasting gospel to preach unto them that dwell on the earth, and to every nation, and kindred, and tongue, and people." As was the proclamation of the Prophet Jonah to the Ninevites, "yet forty days and Nineveh shall be overthrown," so shall the proclamation of the everlasting gospel of the kingdom be limited to forty days.

The *"Ancient of days"* is no other than the God of Abraham, and of Isaac, and of Jacob, the Jehovah of the burning bush. *"I am that I am."* He abdicated the throne of this lower world and turned over the government to Nebuchadnezzar, the first monarch of the *times of the Gentiles*. He will now come to assume His rightful control over the whole world as of old,—God of all the earth.

Jehovah incarnate is the Lord Jesus Christ, the Logos of Saint John's gospel and the Redeemer of the world; and, therefore, their power and authority is one. But the man Christ Jesus with the heavenly saints—His church which will have been taken up to heaven—will not appear for a period of, we think clearly, seventy-five days after the Ancient of days. "I saw in the night visions, and behold, one like the Son of man came with the clouds of heaven, and came to the Ancient of days, and they brought him near before him. And there was given him dominion, and glory, and a kingdom, that all people, nations, and languages, should serve him: his dominion is an everlasting dominion." Dan. 7: 13-14.

The Lord will return in the clouds of heaven. He ascended up and a cloud received him out of sight. He will so come in like manner.—Matt. 24: 30.—He will come to the Ancient of days. This implies that the Ancient of days, or Jehovah, shall have come to earth before, and shall be in His Holy Temple at Jerusalem, as in the days of old. "And the Lord, whom ye seek, shall suddenly come to his temple." Mal. 3: 1. This is Jehovah —Jesus.

We infer from the scriptures that extraordinary phenomena, indicative of divine wrath upon the armies of the despotic emperor and his apostate lieutenant, the anti-Christ, by which they shall be destroyed and dispersed, as also manifest interpositions in favor of the faithful, will signalize the end of the great tribulation. The news of these wonders will be telegraphed to the ends of the earth. Great terror will seize the enemies of God everywhere. Many will fear God and give Him the glory; but the wicked will hesitate, and do wickedly still.

Here will be poured out the seven vials—Rev. 16:—during the last forty-five days chiefly. Here step by step you see, reader, the handwriting on the wall—read and be amazed. We will give one citation only:

"And the fifth angel poured out his vial upon the seat of the beast; and his kingdom was full of darkness; and they gnawed their tongues for pain, and blasphemed the God of heaven." Verses 10, 11.

But a terrible reaction will shortly set in, which shall go on to the end; and men will become seven fold more desperate and defiant of God than ever before.

The arch enemy never slumbers, he knows that he hath

but a short time. Hence, he will dispatch abroad for the last and final struggle, the agents of a fatal delusion.

"And I saw three unclean spirits like frogs come out of the mouth of the dragon, and out of the mouth of the beast, and out of the mouth of the false prophet. For they are the spirits of devils, working miracles, which go forth unto the kings of the earth, and of the whole world, to gather them to the battle of that great day of God Almighty. And he gathered them together into a place called in the Hebrew tongue Armageddon." Rev. 16: 13, 14, 16.

These agencies, "the spirits of devils working miracles," will be sent forth by the arch enemy to counteract the truths of the everlasting gospel, and to check its further progress, calm the fears of those disturbed by recent events, by falsehoods and deceptions, to reassure the halting, by means of signs and miracles wrought by devils.

"Then if any man shall say unto you, Lo, here is Christ, or there; believe it not. For there shall arise false Christs, and false prophets, and shall shew great signs and wonders; insomuch that, if it were possible, they shall deceive the very elect. Behold, I have told you before." Matthew 24: 23–25. God's protection will be around about them as a cordon of fire.

"And I saw as it were a sea of glass mingled with fire: and them that had gotten the victory over the beast, and over his image, and over his mark, and over the number of his name, stand on the sea of glass, having the harps of God." Rev. 15: 2.

These emissaries symbolized by the unclean spirits, will succeed in stirring up the evil passions in a wonderful manner. The father of lies will supply them with misrepresentations. False miracles; and signs, will enable them to deceive. They will work up the evil passions of cupidity and revenge, of malice and hate, of love of power and conquest, among all nations to the remotest east; for the river Euphrates will have been dried up to make way for the kings of the east. There will be a second eruption from the orient. The nations from beyond the Euphrates, and the valley of the Ganges, will pour out their hosts; this time in sympathy with the west. They will be gathered together before Jerusalem, to the battle of that great day of God Almighty. The topography of the land will have been changed at the coming of the Ancient of days. There will be an extensive plain to the north-east and south-east of the city. Here will be the valley of decision. These hosts will be led on by the Imperial dictator himself. His object will be the dethronement of the Ancient of days, the Almighty Himself. The son of man with the armies of heaven will now appear on the scene, "*The King of Kings, and Lord of Lords.*"

Stimulated by his late partial success over the two witnesses, and by pride, ambition, and lust of power, the son of perdition will press on to ruin. As the angry waves of the sea, lashed into fury by the storm, will the surging ranks of all nations rage at his heels. All must be put to the issue in one foul stroke of battle.

Let the pen of the inspired writer describe the rest.

"And I saw heaven opened, and behold, a white horse; and he that sat upon him *was* called Faithful and True, and in righteousness he doth judge and make war. His eyes *were* as a flame of fire, and on his head *were* many crowns; and he had a name written, that no man knew, but he himself. And he *was* clothed with a vesture dipped in blood: and his name is called the Word of God. And the armies *which were* in heaven followed him upon white horses, clothed in fine linen, white and clean. And out of his mouth goeth a sharp sword, that with it he should smite the nations: and he shall rule them with a rod of iron: and he treadeth the wine-press of the fierceness and wrath of Almighty God. And he hath on *his* vesture and on his thigh a name written, KING OF KINGS, AND LORD OF LORDS. And I saw an angel standing in the sun; and he cried with a loud voice, saying to all the fowls that fly in the midst of heaven, Come, and gather yourselves together unto the supper of the great God; that ye may eat the flesh of kings, and the flesh of captains, and the flesh of mighty men, and the flesh of horses, and of them that sit on them, and the flesh of all *men*, *both* free and bond, both small and great. And I saw the beast, and the kings of the earth, and their armies, gathered together to make war against him that sat on the horse, and against his army. And the beast was taken, and with him the false prophet that wrought miracles before him, with which he deceived them that had received the mark of the beast, and them that worshiped his image. These both were cast alive into a lake of fire burning with brimstone. And the remnant were slain with the sword of him that sat upon the horse, which *sword* proceeded out of his mouth: and all the fowls were filled with their flesh." Rev. 19: 11–21.

THE END.

BS
647

Deacidified using the Bookkeeper process
Neutralizing agent: Magnesium Oxide
Treatment Date: May 2005

PreservationTechnologies
A WORLD LEADER IN PAPER PRESERVATION
111 Thomson Park Drive
Cranberry Township, PA 16066
(724) 779-2111

LIBRARY OF CONGRESS

0 014 241 540 9

www.ingramcontent.com/pod-product-compliance
Lightning Source LLC
Chambersburg PA
CBHW031947230426
43672CB00010B/2075